MODERNISM AND MAGIC

Edinburgh Critical Studies in Modernist Culture
Series Editors: Tim Armstrong and Rebecca Beasley

Forthcoming Series Volumes:

Modernism and Magic: Experiments with Spiritualism, Theosophy and the Occult, Leigh Wilson

Sonic Modernity: Representing Sound in Literature, Culture and the Arts, Sam Halliday

Modernism and the Frankfurt School, Tyrus Miller

Late Modernism, Laura Salisbury

Modernism, Space and the City, Andrew Thacker

Modernism and the Idea of Everyday Life, Leena Kore-Schroder

MODERNISM AND MAGIC
Experiments with Spiritualism,
Theosophy and the Occult

Leigh Wilson

EDINBURGH
University Press

*For my parents, with love,
and in loving memory of Helen Litt*

© Leigh Wilson, 2013, 2015

Edinburgh University Press Ltd
The Tun – Holyrood Road
12 (2f) Jackson's Entry
Edinburgh EH8 8PJ

www.euppublishing.com

First published in hardback by Edinburgh University Press 2013

This paperback edition 2015

Typeset in Sabon and Gill Sans
by Servis Filmsetting Ltd, Stockport, Cheshire, and
printed and bound in Great Britain by
CPI Group (UK) Ltd, Croydon CR0 4YY

A CIP record for this book is available from the British Library

ISBN 978 0 7486 2769 1 (hardback)
ISBN 978 0 7486 2770 7 (paperback)
ISBN 978 0 7486 3165 0 (webready PDF)
ISBN 978 0 7486 7233 2 (epub)

The right of Leigh Wilson
to be identified as author of this work
has been asserted in accordance with the
Copyright, Designs and Patents Act 1988,
and the Copyright and Related Rights
Regulations 2003 (SI No. 2498).

CONTENTS

Series Editors' Preface — vi
Acknowledgements — vii

Introduction — 1

1 'But the facts of life persist': Magic, Experiment and the Problem of Representing the World Otherwise — 22

2 'And what has all this to do with experimental writing?': Words and Ghosts — 44

3 A 'subtle metamorphosis': Sound, Mimesis and Transformation — 75

4 'Here is where the magic is': Telepathy and Experiment in Film — 103

5 'Disney against the metaphysicals': Eisenstein, Pound, Ectoplasm and the Politics of Animation — 135

Bibliography — 168
Index — 184

SERIES EDITORS' PREFACE

This series of monographs on selected topics in modernism is designed to reflect and extend the range of new work in modernist studies. The studies in the series aim for a breadth of scope and for an expanded sense of the canon of modernism, rather than focusing on individual authors. Literary texts will be considered in terms of contexts including recent cultural histories (modernism and magic; sonic modernity; media studies) and topics of theoretical interest (the everyday; postmodernism; the Frankfurt School); but the series will also re-consider more familiar routes into modernism (modernism and gender; sexuality; politics). The works published will be attentive to the various cultural, intellectual and historical contexts of British, American and European modernisms, and to inter-disciplinary possibilities within modernism, including performance and the visual and plastic arts.

ACKNOWLEDGEMENTS

I am extremely grateful to Becky Beasely and Tim Armstrong for giving me the opportunity to write this book, for their patient support during its writing, and for their useful comments and suggestions. The book would have taken even longer to complete without the generous funding of research leave by the Department of English, Linguistics and Cultural Studies at the University of Westminster. I am very grateful for this, and more generally for the friendship and support provided by members of the department. In particular, my thanks go to Alex Warwick for her long and most valued friendship. Alex, David Cunningham, Michael Nath and Anne Witchard all read portions of this book, and gave generous comments and advice. Along with them, I would like to thank other colleagues in the department and elsewhere for friendship and support during the long gestation of the ideas that make up the book, in particular Simon Avery, Monica Germanà, Mary Grover, Tatiana Kontou, Roger Luckhurst, Sas Mays, Kaye Mitchell, Laura Salisbury, Justin Sausman, Marquard Smith, Louise Sylvester, Andrew Teverson, Pam Thurschwell. Thanks too to all at Edinburgh University Press, especially Jenny Daly, James Dale and Rebecca Mackenzie.

Thanks also to my family and friends outside the academy for their sterling attempts at being interested ('What, you're *still* working on the same book?'). Special thanks go to my parents, Bob and Averil Wilson, for their love and support; and thanks and much love to Toby Litt, Henry Wilson-Litt and George Wilson-Litt, who are magic.

Figure 5.1 from Sergei M. Eisenstein (1986), *Eisenstein on Disney*, edited by Jay Leyda, translated by Alan Upchurch, introduced by Naum Kleiman, is reproduced with kind permission of Seagull Press.

Extracts from 'The Love Song of J. Alfred Prufrock' and *Four Quartets* by T. S. Eliot reproduced by permission of Faber and Faber Ltd.

Excerpts by Ezra Pound, from *The Cantos of Ezra Pound*, copyright ©1934, 1937, 1940, 1948, 1950, 1956, 1959, 1962, 1963, 1965, 1966, 1968, 1970, and 1971 by Ezra Pound. Reprinted by permission of New Directions Publishing Corp and Faber and Faber Ltd.

Extract from 'Spring and All' by William Carlos Williams from *Imaginations*

(1970), edited and with an introduction by Webster Schott, is reprinted by kind permission of New Directions Publishing Corp. (USA and Cananda) and Carcanet Press (UK and Commonwealth).

INTRODUCTION

This book argues that the aesthetic experiments of the first half of the twentieth century that we call modernism drew on the discourses of the occult dominant during the period – in particular on spiritualism and theosophy – because in them it saw the possibilities for a reconceptualisation of the mimetic. While these discourses have been much investigated in critical works of the last few decades, what neither recent scholars nor many practitioners, or indeed critics, at the time have admitted is the extent to which they have magic at their heart. Yet these occult discourses provided possibilities for experiment for writers, filmmakers and artists because in them resided a productive magic; productive because it was a magic that fundamentally understood that the mimetic is able to produce, not just an inert copy, but an animated copy powerful enough to enact change in the original.

That the period encompassing the end of the nineteenth century and the beginning of the twentieth century experienced an occult revival is now well established. There have been numerous cultural histories of this over the last thirty years or so, establishing occult beliefs, magical thinking or belief in the survival of the individual beyond death as central to the construction of modernity during this time (Oppenheim 1985; Owen 1989; Thurschwell 2001; Luckhurst 2002; Owen 2004; Warner 2006). Rather than embarrassing aberrations, in these works such beliefs are claimed as central to the production of what was considered modern. These cultural histories have been accompanied by works attempting to establish the importance of these discourses for modernist artistic practice. In these it has been demonstrated that such discourses inform the work of some of the central modernists, such as Ezra Pound and W. B. Yeats, and dominate the work of some of the more marginal modernists, such as H. D. and Mary Butts. This work has often, and for good reasons, focused on establishing the centrality of the occult against modernist studies' previous embarrassed near silence, rather than trying to establish why the occult and associated beliefs and practices were so attractive. Timothy Materer, in his *Modernist Alchemy* (1995), for example, does not really discuss why or how the discourses of the occult inform as *modernist* the work of the poets he considers. He asserts early on that 'the ancient connection between poetry and religious ritual suggests a natural link between poetry and occultism' (Materer 1995: xiv), and establishes well that which all poetic practice shares with the occult. Materer's analysis of the thematic engagements with the occult in the poetry he looks at is exemplary, but he does not really deal with its form at all. He rightly challenges those critics who downplay the occult interests of poets such as W. B. Yeats by reading them as 'artistic effect' or 'aesthetic experience' (p. 26), but this necessary work of revision stops short of asking what it is that the occult shares with the aesthetic, and so does not consider the possibility that Yeats's attraction might not be merely aesthetic, but fundamentally about a reimagining of the aesthetic.

Materer accounts for the marginalisation of the occult in modernist studies as the result of the critic's desire that the writers and artists they work on be as 'learned and respectable as they are' (p. 26). In his groundbreaking study of Ezra Pound's relation to the occult tradition, Leon Surette also challenges the tendency of some scholars to read modernists as being as wedded to 'scepticism and relativism' as they are (Surette 1993: 161). However, Surette's work, while asserting modernist engagement with the occult tradition, retains the status of 'learned and respectable' for both himself and the poets he considers by distancing himself from those places where magic returned in contemporary occult practice: 'My interest is neither in the subgenre of horror literature nor in the shady world of "phenomena," but in the relation between occult speculation and mainstream aesthetic theory' (p. 6). Indeed, he goes further: 'Certainly, it is not my contention that such supernatural phenomena or beings are important to the history of modernism' (p. 11). Surette works hard to exclude magic from his definition of the occult, and to argue that it is what is left after this exclusion that has an importance for modernism (p. 36). In the work both of Materer and of Surette, then, the precise shape of, and reasons for, the coming together of contemporary occult phenomenon and modernist formal experiment are left unexplored. Before considering in more detail the implications of recent scholarly work on modernism and the occult, I want first to revisit the dominant occult discourses of the early twentieth century in order to show that it is magic that lies at the heart of their practices and constitutes for experimental artists the attraction to them.

Spiritualism, Theosophy and the Occult as Magic

My focus in this book, then, is the use in modernist experiment of the contemporary occult, in particular of those occult discourses, such as spiritualism and theosophy, which saw themselves as modern. It is the case that the insistence of these discourses on their status as modern has obscured the extent to which they are deeply entwined with the magical, and therefore the extent to which they represented for experimental artists a chance to remake the mimetic through magic without disavowing the modern. The taxonomic difficulties that this insistence produces, in apologists, in their turn of the century critics, and in more recent critics and cultural historians, can be seen in Leon Surette's attempt to distinguish his sense of the occult as an intellectual tradition from spiritualism and the magical in general:

> There is also, it must be admitted, a branch of the occult more interested in magic and communication with spirits or gods than in metaphysics or history. W.B. Yeats's participation in séances, spirit manipulations, evocations, and the like is unusual for the occult artist. However, a much more extreme case is Yeats's London contemporary, Aleister Crowley ... a notorious magician of the day ... Such activities are quite unlike the ritual practices of religions. They are not forms of worship but are more like athletic contests or spectacular shows. Typically, the object is to induce a ghost or divinity to inform the theurgist on some topic ... The theurgic practices of occultists such as Crowley, Lévi, and Joséphin Péladin were quite distinct in provenance from spiritualist séances, even though the latter were very common throughout Europe and North America during the late nineteenth and early twentieth century ... Spiritualism, however, communicates exclusively with deceased humans and with neither gods nor demons. Nor is the séance truly theurgic, for it does not produce magical events – except, of course, for the apparitions and voices. (Surette 1993: 23–4)

Here, the magical practices of Yeats are unlike the usual relation between modernist artists and the occult even though, as Surette is forced to admit, the occult is always implicated in the production of magical phenomena; the practices of Crowley, while like those of Yeats, are unlike spiritualist séances, although Yeats was a regular séance-goer, and although the central point of the séance was to produce precisely cognates of the magical phenomena produced by Crowley. As Surette's difficulties show, the relationship between the dominant discourses of the occult in the late nineteenth and early twentieth centuries – spiritualism, theosophy, occult ritual and interest in the occult tradition – and all kinds of magical practice was strained. On one side, the tricks of entertainment magic were a dangerous mirror image of the phenomena of spiritualism, theosophy and magical ritual, suggesting that intelligences other than the discarnate could produce such marvels, and numerous individual stage magicians, and the Magic Circle itself, investigated mediums and were often involved in their exposure as frauds (During 2002). On the other side, 'real' magic, increasingly linked to the 'primitive' through contemporary anthropology and to the bohemian revivals of the occult tradition in groups such as the Order of the Golden Dawn, threatened the strong desire for respectability in the institutions of both spiritualism and theosophy. They knew that their critics focused on precisely those elements that would most link their beliefs and practices to the primitive, the ignorant and the pathological (see, for example, Owen 1989, in particular Chapter 6).

It is for this reason that the relation between their practices and the experiment of the modernists relates rather differently to the question of primitivism. The claiming of a modern status wedded to the progressive values of a developing liberal democracy distanced the practices of spiritualism and theosophy from similar practices among those peoples named 'primitive' by contemporary anthropology. However, at the same time, that such practices are so clearly magical and related, as I show in the following chapters, to contemporary readings of 'primitive' magic, yet are at the same time located within modernity, attests to the extent that magic is a discourse of the material world rather than necessarily related to the metaphysical or transcendent. While primitivism, following Barkan and Bush's important work, is indeed 'an Occidental construction, a set of representations whose "reality" is purely Western' (Barkan and Bush 1995: 2), its coordinates must change when the 'primitive' behaviour identified by such primitivism is within the realm of the modern. It is my contention that the magical practices of the contemporary occult were attractive to artists trying to remake an idea of mimesis precisely because of their modern status. For the artists I write about, this magic was clearly about the matter and form of the world rather than a straightforward desire to either return to the 'simplicities' of non-European culture or to link such cultures to a recoverable human essence.

Indeed, rather than straightforwardly romanticising the 'other', both spiritualism and theosophy variously attracted involvement from those who either wished to make stronger their claims to authority and respectability or those whose claims, through class position and education, were unimpeachable. The northern spiritualists of the upper working classes, the Cambridge academics of the Society for Psychical Research (SPR) and the theosophists of the colonial periphery implicitly depended upon the conservative values of spiritualism and theosophy even when their aims were often heterodox. The fundamental messages of spiritualism and theosophy were deeply unchallenging to the status quo. Life after death was pretty much the same as life before it; it was the consolation gained by the bereaved from contact with the dead that put an end, in the words of Theodor Adorno and Max Horkheimer, to mourning's potential as a 'wound in civilization . . . showing that it has still not been possible to compel men to indulge solely in purposeful behaviour' (Adorno and Horkheimer 1997: 215). Rather than mourning resisting the aims of capitalism, the consolations of spiritualism in particular enabled its believers to shore up the claims of bourgeois individuality.

Theosophy was founded by Madame Helena Blavatsky in 1875, after her dalliance with more orthodox forms of spiritualism, and it soon became an influential and widely disseminated occult system of belief, taken up by many intellectuals and artists in Europe, the US and India. While in India, Madame Blavatsky was investigated by the British Society for Psychical Research in 1884–5, and the subsequent report claimed she was a fraud, albeit 'one of the most accomplished and interesting impostors in history' (Gurney et al. 1885: 201). However, this did not stop theosophy from being immensely appealing to artists and intellectuals in Europe and the US, and indeed, Blavatsky's return to Europe to escape the subsequent scandal fuelled this appeal. In 1884, she set up a Theosophical Society in Germany, and theosophy went on to influence numerous artists in central Europe, including the artist Wassily Kandinsky and the composer Alexander Scriabin. W. B. Yeats set up his Hermetic Society in Dublin in 1886 after reading Blavatsky, and in 1887 he joined her Theosophical Lodge in London (for an account of the history of theosophy, see Washington 1995).

Like many of its offshoots, such as Rudolf Steiner's anthroposophy, theosophy preached notions of the resolution of conflict through brotherly love and an idealist conception of the place and mechanics of change (on the extent to which the ideas of the Russian mystic G. I. Gurdjieff throw into relief the conformism of most theosophy, see Washington 1995: 170). Indeed, for Blavatsky, what distinguishes theosophy from magic is the extent to which the theosophist practises his or her powers within 'the loftiest moral ideal', strives 'to realize his unity with the whole of humanity' and works 'with the whole of humanity' (Blavatsky 1893: 18).

Spiritualism and theosophy then, on the whole, resisted the transgressive associations of magic. Where they went instead, of course, is to science. Spiritualism, and psychical research in particular, attracted some of the most important names in nineteenth- and twentieth-century science. As an example of this deep imbrication, the Italian materialisation medium Eusapia Palladino was investigated by an astonishing roll call of the great of European science, among them Cesare Lombroso, Charles Richet, Pierre and Marie Curie, Camille Flammarion and Henri Bergson. Of course, not all of these scientists were spiritualists, and many remained sceptical of spiritualist claims, but they did take the claims seriously enough to investigate them, and they did very often suggest that 'supernormal', if not spiritualist, explanations were more likely than fraud. That some scientists were attracted to spiritualist beliefs, and that many others took them seriously enough to investigate them, lent to spiritualism a respectability that distanced it from any associations with magic.

Madame Blavatsky called the movement she founded a synthesis between religion and science, and worked hard to distinguish it from magical ritual – power without responsibility according to her (Blavatsky 1893: 18) – and spiritualism. While she insisted that modern science was wrong to ignore 'the occult side of Nature' (Blavatsky 1888: vii), she claimed the methods of contemporary science in establishing her authority. Theosophical beliefs consist of a complex synthesis of existing beliefs, from Neoplatonism to evolution, and a rigid and incredibly detailed schema which links the macrocosmic to the microcosmic and the historical event to the eternal via symbols and a strict numerology. Theosophists insisted that their beliefs did not constitute a religion, but were 'Divine Knowledge or Science', and that neither was their aim to found a religion, but to reconcile all existing 'religions, sects, and nations under a common system of ethics, based on eternal verities' (Blavatsky 1893: 1, 3). Theosophy asserted its links to science rather than religion, then, and Blavatsky's works are large and complex systems for reading and interpreting the world. For Blavatsky, her work is not about mystical or religious revelation but about the methodical gathering of the results of empirical observation:

> These truths [which the work intends to convey] are in no sense put forward as a *revelation*; nor does the author claim the position of a revealer of mystic lore, now made public for the first time in the world's history. For what is contained in this work is to be found scattered throughout thousands of volumes embodying the scriptures of the great Asiatic and early European religions, hidden under glyph and symbol, and hitherto left unnoticed because of this veil. What is now attempted is to gather the oldest tenets together and to make of them one harmonious and unbroken whole. The sole advantage which the writer has over her predecessors, is that she need not resort to personal speculations and theories. For this work is a partial statement of what she herself has been taught by more advanced students, supplemented, in a few details only, by the results of her own study and observation. (Blavatsky 1888: vi–viii; emphasis in original)

Theosophy is distanced from both the dangers of 'black magic' and the passivity of spiritualist mediumship because it represents the 'true sciences' (Blavatsky 1893: 16). While Blavatsky does acknowledge that theosophy includes some of the magical practices of the occult because these are fundamentally about a particular conception of material nature, it is magic tempered by the rational bases of orthodox science:

> For the Occultist practises *scientific* Theosophy, based on accurate knowledge of Nature's secret workings; but a Theosophist, practising the powers called abnormal, *minus* the light of Occultism, will simply tend towards a dangerous form of mediumship, because, although holding to Theosophy and its highest conceivable code of ethics, he practises it in the dark, on sincere but blind faith. Anyone, Theosophist or Spiritualist, who attempts to cultivate one of the branches of occult science . . . without the knowledge of the philosophic *rationale* of those powers, is like a rudderless boat launched on a stormy sea. (p. 19; emphasis in original)

However, while the beliefs of spiritualism and theosophy strove toward respectability via an invocation of science, the *material* practices and phenomena of both, as admitted by Blavatsky, returned magic to the modern. Indeed, the movement toward science, while it attempted to disavow the embarrassment of magic, can be seen as in fact part of the return to it. The complex relations among science, religion and magic during the period have been elegantly set out by Randall Styers in his *Making Magic: Religion, Magic and Science in the Modern World* (2004). What is at stake in the relations among them, according to Styers, is the status in modernity of the material of nature. The widespread revival of interest in magical beliefs and practices from the middle of the nineteenth century on coincided with a huge interest in magical practices in the social sciences as they constituted themselves as academic disciplines. For Styers, magic functioned in these, sometimes explicitly but often implicitly, as a way of addressing debates far closer to home than 'primitive' ritual and belief. As he argues at the beginning of his book:

> Perhaps the most significant subtext that will emerge from these theories is the scholarly effort to conjure – or conjure away – what it means to be modern. Debates over magic provide an extraordinarily rich ground for exploring the nature of modernity, its values, and its limits. (Styers 2004: 4)

In particular, the focus on magic and the desire to separate it from the modern made possible the privileged status of that crucial institution of modernity, science. While different theorists proposed sometimes opposing views of magic's relation to social order (p. 192), the dominant position of the theoretical writings Styers considers is to see magic as dangerous in order to shore up and naturalise capitalist modernity. Making magic anathema to contemporary 'civilization' works to justify not just the systems of anthropology, as in E. B. Tylor and James Frazer, but also the instrumental rationality necessary to carry out capitalism's domination of the natural world. Much of that which could resist this is relegated to the increasingly interior, privatised world of religion, and that which remains is stigmatised as magic, as having no place within modernity:

> [T]hese theories of magic prescribe a notion of modern rationality that, through the workings of science and capital, is ceded unbridled control over the material world. Magic is deployed as the stigmatized mediator between these modes of religion and scientific rationality, reinforcing their separation. Deviant desires and behavior that resist this channeling of social power, that seek to intermingle the spiritual and material realms or to enlist other forms of nonrationalized or surreptitious power, are condemned as magical and irrationally primitive. (p. 212)

Magic and science present competing visions of the natural world and humanity's relation to it, but they are on the same side when compared to religion. Both magic and science concern themselves with the matter of the world rather than the transcendental. It is for this reason that occult phenomena in both spiritualism and theosophy which challenge a conventional view of the natural world, while attempting to ground this within the discourses of science, move dangerously close to magic.

That an occult desperate for respectability should wish to deny its status as magical is understandable when magic per se was seen fundamentally as error. As Marcello Truzzi has argued, this idea of error is central to any definition of the occult:

> A common denominator for most (if not all) perspectives labeled occult (by anyone) is that they have in some way concerned themselves with things anomalous to our generally-accepted cultural storehouse of 'truths'. That is, we are here dealing with claims that contradict common-sense or institutionalized (scientific or religious) knowledge. This contradiction of accepted beliefs is the very thing which makes the occult somehow strange, mysterious and inexplicable. It is the very character of the occult that it deals with dissonant or contradicting knowledge claims. (Truzzi 1974: 245)

As I will argue in Chapter 1, the double sense of magic as an understanding of the material world and magic as error is precisely what made it so productive as a way for aesthetic experiment to change the relationship between art and the world, and in so doing to attempt to change that world.

Contemporary occult practice, then, was magical. In particular, the séance – the crucial site for most occult practice during the period – demonstrates most of the principles of magic as categorised by contemporary anthropology. Numerous cultural histories of the séance have appeared over the last two decades or so, linking it to, for example, scientific method, or artistic experiment, or to the politics of gender, class and ethnicity/national identity (see

Owen 1989; Viswanathan 1998, 2000; Connor 1999, 2000; Sword 2002). It has been seen as laboratory and testing ground of experimental psychology and as imbricated with various technologies. Simon During has demonstrated the links between the séance and 'secular magic' in the nineteenth century, seeing this relation as crucial to the particular place of secular magic in modernity (During 2002). However, very few studies have considered the séance as depending on the beliefs and practices of 'real' magic. As I have suggested, during the second half of the nineteenth century and the first half of the twentieth, both apologists for and opponents of spiritualist practice downplayed the séance as magic. Apologists wanted the séance to be seen as scientific, as rational, as evidence for the truth of spiritualist beliefs and claims; opponents wanted to undermine the power of the séance by presenting it as banal, seedy and vulgar. More recently, interest in spiritualism and psychical research has in large part come out of a reconsideration of the history of science, and a remaking of the relation between the sciences and the pseudosciences. While this does have the effect of challenging the distance between science and its putative 'other' – the irrational, the mystical, the occult, and so on – it also necessarily focuses on the fact that those involved saw themselves as 'doing science' rather than 'doing magic'. The Society for Psychical Research has always made much of the scientists among its members and leaders, and so too have those cultural historians who have brought the Society back to the centre of the history of the period. Pericles Lewis has argued that critiques of religion from the social sciences in the early twentieth century are problematic because they replaced the transcendental cause of the phenomena they observed with another 'unseen process for which religion has served as a substitute or a sort of rationalization'. As these replacement forces are also 'transcendent in the sense of not being empirically verifiable', they risk re-establishing the transcendent at the heart of their systems of rational critique (Lewis 2010: 45). It is possible to see the explanations of spiritualist practice and the methods of psychical research suggested by more recent critics in the same way. Gender, sexuality, class, colonialism and so on are substituted for ghosts as the forces behind the séance. However, the magical principles on which the practices and beliefs of spiritualism in the end rely precisely undo the idea of transcendence. A central task of the social sciences in the early twentieth century was to distinguish between magic and religion, and the most powerful distinctions described religion as a withdrawal of force and power from the material world, and a relocation of it in the privacy of the individual. While the beliefs embedded in the séance can certainly be seen as part of this, its *practice* was magical. The dead were returned through a series of ritualised practices which implicitly used language as a creative and not just a descriptive medium; which established telepathy as the least improbable causation for the phenomenon; and which produced material phenomena that both shattered contemporary materialist beliefs and at the same time turned the more speculative notions of the new physics into a kind of magic. The relations among magic, religion and science during the period were mobile, as Styers' work has shown, and the attempt to fix boundaries tells us most about the investments and anxieties of those doing the fixing. As his work also shows, it was always practices designated as magical that were most problematic, most dangerous and most disavowed. This was as true within the practices and institutions of spiritualism and theosophy as elsewhere, but it was precisely the problematic presence of the magical within discourses which strove to be modern that made the phenomena at the heart of them so attractive to experimental artists.

Modernist Experiment, the Contemporary Occult and Mimesis

If the practices of contemporary discourses of the occult were based on magic, this changes the way the relation between them and the practices of experimental artists can be read. As I have suggested, in the last thirty years or so interest in the occult and its relation to modernism has exploded, encouraged of course, to a large extent, by the work of Surette and Materer, and some of this work has focused on those aspects left out of their accounts. Recently, Stephen Ross has suggested that this interest is due, not to poetry's intrinsic link with the occult, nor to a solely conceptual link between an occult tradition and experimental poetics, but to questions of form. He links this to an anxiety at the heart of contemporary modernist studies, that is, the question of what modernism is (Ross 2009: 33). In particular, the obsession with issues of reanimation and ghostly return, with the uncanny, in recent modernist studies, he sees as a symptom of our inability to locate and articulate the significance of aesthetic value in our contemporary critical project. It is, says Ross, now 'accepted knowledge' that modernists concerned themselves with '[a]ttending séances, toying with telepathy, extra-sensory perception, metempsychosis, clairvoyance, dematerialization, and so on' (p. 35). More than this, though, he goes on to suggest that the beginnings of an interest in the relation between modernism and the occult – just before the beginning of what he calls 'the new modernist studies' associated with the founding of the Modernist Studies Association – in the work of Materer and Surette, and in that of James Longenbach, Daniel Cottom and Demetres Tryphonopoulos, can be seen as not just an illumination of the uncanny in modernist work but as itself 'rooted in the uncanny' (p. 35). In particular, Ross focuses on one of the discipline's most uncanny returns – the compulsive return of the idea of a singular modernism, despite many efforts, not least in the 'new modernist studies' itself, to challenge this and to insist on plurality, on *modernisms* (pp. 40ff.). This repeated return of singularity Ross locates in the centrality of aesthetic value – in the works themselves, in the beginning of academic interest in them in New Criticism, and in contemporary scholars' initial attraction to them:

> [L]ong before we enter into the debates about the production of literary value, cultural capital, various ideologies of modernism, we learn that modernist art and literature is great, that *Ulysses* is the greatest novel ever written, that *The Waste Land* is the greatest poem, that the incantations YeatsPoundEliot and ConradWoolfFaulkner carry with them magical properties and that their knowing invocation elevates us too. (pp. 41–2)

Indeed, scholarly challenges to the singularity of modernism, rather than showing once and for all the unhelpfulness of the term and jettisoning it, take 'modernism' far and wide, making it 'into a truly transhistorical and global term', but crucially leaving the existence of the category unscathed (p. 42). In conclusion, Ross claims that both the persistence of the category and the continued debates over its limits and meanings reveals the fact that:

> modernism persists as a phantom, a symptom whose particular content is vastly less important than the form it takes and the effects it produces. It derives its consistency from the subjects who sustain it, from our very attentiveness, just as being itself derives its consistency from the consciousness(es) observing it. (p. 51)

Ross's analysis usefully suggests reasons for the rise of critical interest in the relation between modernism and the occult and uses an occult vocabulary itself to describe our own assumptions and practices as modernist scholars, locating at the heart of both the question of aesthetic value. It was, of course, such questions of value which primarily motivated those writers and artists we now call modernist in their experiment. Ross persuasively argues that the strangeness of the occult describes the relation between these writers and artists and us; I want to argue that it is more complex even than this. The incantatory effects on us of 'YeatsPoundWoolf', or 'KandinskyPicassoMatisse' or even 'TzaraHausmannSchwitters' are as powerful as Ross suggests, but in part because such magical invocations were woven into aesthetic experiment from the beginning. In our engagement, despite ourselves, with the lexicon and practices of magic – Ross describes contemporary critics of modernism as those who 'conjure' with the term (p. 51) – our repetition is not just structural but because we share with the objects of our study a broad historical location. Ross's article suggests that much of the uncanny trouble of modernist studies comes from the mismatch between the elitist and exclusionary aims of both modernists and their first critical champions, the New Critics, and our contemporary will to ethical and political responsibility, our desire 'to be open to the other in general and to modernism's other in particular' (p. 40). It is certainly the case that aspects of the New Critical version of aesthetic experiment sit uncomfortably with attempts at inclusion and pluralism, but this leaves out of account the extent to which experimental work of the first half of the twentieth century itself is an attempt (even if sometimes a failed one) to expand possibilities, an attempt to represent the possibility that the world could be other than it is. What this book argues is that aesthetic experimentation in modernity, the attempt, that is, to challenge representational practices in order to remake the world, can only work conceptually if it uses, relies on and has at its heart an idea of magic. That this underlies experiment per se can be see even in, perhaps particularly in, those artists who are horrified by the disreputabilities of the occult. Virginia Woolf's class position and her anxious defence of her intellectual superiority against the lack of its conventional markers make disgust her only possible reaction to most occult beliefs and phenomena. Her diaries are full of this disgust, couched in obvious class terms. A novelist of her acquaintance, who is 'what the self-taught working man thinks genius should be', has 'dabbled in mysticism, & had made tables walz & heard phantom raps & believed it all' (Woolf 1979: 113, 114). Nevertheless, Woolf's attempts to articulate what happens during artistic creation hover around the transformations of magic. Lily Briscoe, at the end of *To the Lighthouse* (1927), is famously 'haunted' by Mrs Ramsay, but her ability to complete her painting is dependent, in the end, not on the insubstantiality of haunting and the extent to which it can be read as psychological, as the projection of the interior life on to the world, but on the ability of the work of art to reproduce the material reality of the thing, in all its mystery and miraculousness. The return of Mrs Ramsay does not point to the beyond – whether she returned to haunt at all is left ambiguous – but brings Lily back to the material substance of things:

> Some wave of white went over the window pane. The air must have stirred some flounce in the room . . .
> 'Mrs Ramsay! Mrs Ramsay!' she cried . . . And then, quietly, as if she refrained, that too became part of ordinary experience, was on a level with the chair, with the table. Mrs Ramsay . . . sat there quite simply, in the chair, flicked her needles to and fro, knitted her reddish-brown stocking, cast her shadow in the step. There she sat. (Woolf 1977: 186)

Finally, as the lighthouse is reached and Lily completes her painting, both are celebrated and perhaps produced by Mr Carmichael's ritualistic behaviour – he stands by her, looking like 'an old pagan God' – and by the telepathic communion between them (p. 191).

As is clear from the above, of vital importance in my argument for this crucial role of magic is a particular reading of the way the experimental work that we call modernism engages with ideas of mimesis. It is my argument that modernists engaged with contemporary occult practices because they offered the chance to rethink the meaning of mimesis, and that a consideration of this can reconfigure the relation between modernism and mimesis. It is this relation that the most comprehensive investigation of occult practice and modernist form so far – Helen Sword's *Ghostwriting Modernism* (2002) – takes on. Sword, in contrast to Timothy Materer, does attempt to ask why modernist practice as such should have an attraction to occult discourse, in her case the practices of spiritualism. This is the great strength of her book, that she takes seriously the relation between spiritualism and modernist form, that she argues that 'we can regard the spiritualist pursuits of modernist writers and intellectuals as central rather than aberrational elements of their modernist aesthetics' (Sword 2002: 57). In substantiating this claim, however, she constructs modernist works as straightforwardly mimetic copies of modernity's lacks – reproducing the deadening effects of fragmentation and loss – rather than seeing experimental work as a will to create. Here, mimesis merely repeats the world rather than using that repetition to remake it. Sword's subject is the relation between the figure of the medium and mediumistic practices, and writing. Her focus is, as she says, on 'the forms of mediumship most closely allied with writing and the forms of writing most closely allied with mediumship' (p. 9). While her subject is a modernist practice that is most clearly distinguished from other kinds of representation through its formal experimentation, she acknowledges that the particular occult practices she focuses on are anything but experimental:

> otherworldly narratives from the modernist era, although largely devoid of formal experimentation and ironic self-consciousness, engage with many of the dominant tropes of literary modernism – linguistic playfulness, decenterings of consciousness, fracturings of conventional gender roles – and betray a characteristically modernist obsession with all things textual: reading, writing, literature, authorship, publication, libraries, and even the discourses and methodologies of literary criticism. (p. 11)

Her focus, then, is the crisis in language. For her, modernist language is one that is fundamentally fragmented, as she argues is the case for even the most credulous of modernists, for Yeats (p. 109) and for H. D. (p. 128). The paradoxical, fragmented, marginalised séance room, and more particularly the figure of the medium, and the messages she relayed from the dead, are such a crucial model for modernist writers, Sword argues, because they figure, they make legible, the loss of faith in the ability of language to communicate fully and without loss. The difference is that, while mediums have no idea that what they are doing is revealing the materiality of language, and all that implies, modernist writers know full well what is at stake.

Throughout her book, and most particularly in her epilogue, Sword carries out a trenchant critique of those post-structuralist critics who appropriate the language and tropes of spiritualism without concerning themselves, in the way a literary historian must, with spiritualism as such. She notes the extent to which the lexicon of ghosts, haunting and mediums has deluged contemporary scholarship of all varieties: 'Thus terms such as "possession," "dictation," "spectral," "apparitional," and "medium" pepper the writings even of contemporary critics who show little interest in spiritualism as a historical phenomenon' (p. 165). For Sword, metaphors are not enough; Jacques Derrida's 'breezy interweaving' of discourses through the glue of spectrality threatens to empty out the very concepts on which he is relying (p. 163). She is critical of those critics who are not interested in belief in these ideas, in modernist writers' 'real-life fascination with the historical phenomenon of popular spiritualism', but only in them as metaphor (p. 55). Strangely, given her attack, Sword acknowledges that she too sees modernist uses of spiritualism as metaphorical. She argues that 'spiritualism acquired a sometimes surprising metaphorical currency among early-twentieth-century intellectuals, including many who eschewed its claims and mocked its vulgarity' (p. 78). So here belief is not the issue, but only the extent to which spiritualist tropes can articulate aspects of modernity, precisely their use for post-structuralists. For Sword, while the metaphors of Derrida empty out the historical specificity of spiritualism, the metaphors of modernists are responsible for precisely their rich and valued aesthetic successes.

This problem with metaphor is telling, and is linked to my argument that Sword's description of modernist experiment is problematic. It is not that belief and metaphor are opposites; the use of occult discourses is not *just* metaphorical, but that it engages with metaphor is a clue that magic is at the heart of this relation. For the forces of instrumental reason that so powerfully contribute to the shaping of modernity, metaphor is merely metaphor. Magic, on the other hand, takes metaphor seriously by literalising it in order to create and transform. Metaphor is a kind of repetition with a difference. In magic, something is like something else in a way that is not inert repetition, but rather it is in repetition precisely that power resides. Magic, as understood during the period, and as embedded in the familiar discourses of the occult, returns to mimesis its power to transform. As Christopher Bracken has argued, Aristotle posits two kinds of mimesis, one which is indeed an inert copy, it 'imitates what already is', but another which 'projects an image of what is not yet, modelling a form for what cannot give form to itself. One copies things; another finishes' (Bracken 2007: 18). Following Philippe Lacoue-Labarthe, Bracken calls the first of these a restricted mimesis and the second a general mimesis: 'Restricted mimesis stands for reality; general mimesis takes part in the realization of a still unfinished reality' (p. 18). In Bracken's argument, the combination of these two forms of mimesis remakes the relation between 'the order of nature' and the 'order of representation' in the work of some of the central thinkers of the early twentieth century in their creation of what he calls 'savage philosophy'. It is my argument that the magic of the contemporary occult enables the return of this second form of mimesis to artistic practice and experiment during the period.

INTRODUCTION

Magic concerns itself with the material world and is crucially about actions; the magical act works through harnessing the vital materiality of world. This lies at the heart of James Frazer's famous Law of Similarity and Law of Contact or Contagion, the two laws which constitute his theory of sympathetic magic as set out in *The Golden Bough* (1890–1915). While Frazer uses these laws as the basis of his conceptual system of magic, what the practice associated with the laws demonstrates is the power of matter and its reproduction. Frazer suggests an alternative name for his first law may be mimetic magic (Frazer 1996: 13), but this, and the focus on conceptual system, obscures the extent to which all magical practice engages in mimesis, in a reproduction of the specificities of the material world. Magical practice as implicitly made clear by Frazer, but not acknowledged by him, assumes that the same powers are present in the material objects once in contact with a person (a lock of hair, nail clippings) as they are in obvious copies of the person – the doll, for example. The repetition of the materiality of the world *is* mimesis, but a mimesis which, scandalously for scholar after scholar from E. B. Tylor onwards, mistakes representation for the real thing, the ideal for the real (see, for example, Tylor 1920: 115).

That magic is about mimesis is usefully explored in Michael Taussig's *Mimesis and Alterity: A Particular History of the Senses* (1993). Taussig reconsiders the relations among anthropology, magic and mimesis by arguing that mimesis does act out the imitative that is so central to James Frazer's explanation of magic, but that, contra Frazer, this act is not utilitarian but symbolic. In the mimetic act the power of the original is transferred to the copy and, more than this, the copy becomes more powerful than the original, powerful enough to reverse the transformatory magic and in turn transform the original: 'For this is where we must begin: with the magical power of replication, the image affecting what it is an image of, wherein the representation shares in or takes power from the represented' (Taussig 1993: 2). Appearance, in this reading of mimesis, is never 'mere', does not exist just as a cover for the real underneath. Appearance has 'density and substance' (p. 176), it is the thing, not just the thing's cover. Appearance, or reappearance, is precisely the point, and '[t]he fetish power of imagery in shrines and magic is merely a heightened and prolonged instance of this tangibility of appearance' (p. 176). For Taussig, this rethinking of mimesis and its relation to language is fundamental to reimagining colonial relations. The magical mimesis that is so often 'found' by anthropology in non-modern cultures is in fact a response to the relation between the modern and non-modern, so that mimesis and alterity are not opposites but necessary elements of the same process. This relation is therefore fundamental to the actions and conceptions not just of the colonised but of the colonisers themselves. Taussig ends with an idea of 'mimetic excess', 'mimetic self-awareness, mimesis turned in on itself' (p. 252), which has the potential to create 'reflexive awareness as to the mimetic faculty' (p. 254):

> History would seem to now allow for an appreciation of mimesis as an end in itself that takes one into the magical power of the signifier to act as if it were indeed the real, to live in a different way with the understanding that artifice is natural, no less than that nature is historicized. (p. 255)

In setting out the problematics of his study, Taussig early on makes visible the strangeness of the magical objects of non-western peoples, a strangeness that attests not to their 'otherness' and 'savagery', but to the strangeness of mimetic practices as such, practices in which, of course, 'we' are imbricated or of which 'we' are a part. At the centre of the relation between mimesis and magic, then – what makes mimesis magical – is the signifier acting *as if it were* the real. Mimetic self-awareness resides in the impossible place where the signifier is real and not real at the same time, where the mystifying practices of capital and the colonial enterprise are not merely demystified, but remade within a magical practice which explodes their claims to objective rationality – 'out-fetishizing the fetish', as Taussig describes Walter Benjamin's critical practice (p. 1).

Mimesis, then, is not the straightforward copy that Sword reads into modernism's relation with occult practices. For her, modernist form copies language's lack (the signifier is just inert tool) while thematising the occult's drive to transform. However, it is precisely modernism's mimetic practices – and not centrally its choice of theme – which make it a – however problematic – useful critical category. Modernism did not need spiritualism, theosophy or the occult generally to recognise the significatory and semantic crises of modernity, but it needed the magical practices at the heart of contemporary occult discourses in order to be experimental – precisely to treat the signifier as if it were real – to bring into existence a space that could transform the world, that could go beyond the crises and reassert the possibilities of meaning.

Taussig argues that mimesis per se is magical, but at numerous points in his book he hints at the possibility that modernist aesthetics have a particular relation to mimesis, or at least that modernist aesthetics throw up troubling questions about the relation between mimesis and magic. In asking in what precisely the power of figurines used by the Cuna people of the San Blas Islands off Panama is located, Taussig includes a set of photographs of carved wooden turtles used in magical practices to bring success in hunting the creatures. To these he compares a drawing of 'decoys' used by the Cuna in the hunt itself to attract the turtles into their nets. The magical objects Taussig sees as more realistically turtle-like, while the decoy strikes him as

> a 'modernist' and unreal turtle with neither head nor neck nor flippers yet, to my way of seeing, which should never been confused with the turtle's, this is nevertheless quintessentially turtlish and irresistible ... Is the decoy closer to the real turtle than the magically effective imitation? Or is the decoy closer to what the Indians think a real turtle thinks a real

turtle looks like? – in which case why make the magical turtle-figures look so 'real'? (pp. 11–12)

Taussig does not explicitly answer these questions, and of course the focus of his book is the ways in which so called non-modern representation makes magic, not because it is 'primitive', but because it uses and remakes the often commodified imagery of the west. So although Taussig does not elaborate on this connection as such, what is clear is that throughout the book, Taussig's argument implies that modernist mimesis is in some ways the antithesis of non-modern mimesis – the figurines look real and the decoys 'unreal' in comparison. This hesitation is found also in the writing of the Soviet film director Sergei Eisenstein as he attempts to articulate his particular practice of experiment in representation. While Eisenstein invokes the 'prelogical' thinking of pre-modern cultures, he is ambiguous about magic for precisely these reasons. He very often used the lexicon of magic to describe his theory and practice, but in notes to a lecture given in 1929 he also distances his practice from 'the magic ideologies of the most ancient peoples' because their magic is based on the principle of realism:

> This basic idea of imitation as a means to mastery crops up in the oldest ideologies . . . But this master, the magic one, is a mere fiction. Because magic imitation copies form.
> And the event as such remains as intangible to it as the pale reflection in the empty mirror. (Eisenstein 1993: 66–7)

However, as he acknowledges, it is not that imitation is discarded – 'Nonetheless imitation is the way to mastery' (p. 67) of the object being represented – but it is principle not form that is imitated. Yet Eisenstein then goes on to implicitly acknowledge that such distinctions are not the end of the matter.

> In instinctive primitive form there is however no distinction between external attribute, internal content and principle ...
> The age of form is drawing to a close.
> We are penetrating matter. We are penetrating behind appearance into the principle of appearance. (p. 68)

Behind appearance is not the essence but the principle of appearance, but what the imitation of this produces is neither the inert representations of the bourgeois world, nor the literal ones of the ancient, but a magic for a revolutionary modernity, one that allows not the repetition of the world as it is, but the creation of a new world from the hidden truths of the existing one:

> We have to create new forms because we *need* them. That is the difference between our avant-garde [i.e. the Soviet] and the other ...
> The film of fact.

'Factual' play (illusion).
Play with facts (montage of visible events). The creation of a new world.
(p. 70)

What modernist mimesis makes visible in a way that more realistic forms do not is the necessary mechanics of magical production in order to make a new world. If the copy is *more* than the original, as Taussig's theory of magical mimesis asserts, that *more* is precisely and only the formal work which has produced it as a copy. What the form of the decoy turtles makes clear is their artificiality, that their 'turtlishness' is *made*. A self-conscious drawing of attention to their own artificiality, their status as made, is of course the defining characteristic of modernism. Contrary to Sword's argument about fragments and lack, it is the gaps in the reproduction of the original that constitute the copy's magical power of recreation. The difference between the two sets of carved turtles produces only questions for Taussig; however, later, he makes this function of the elliptical clear in magical uses of language. Taussig discusses Cuna chants, which some anthropologists have seen as exhaustive in their descriptive detail. While Taussig accounts for this descriptiveness as drawing attention precisely to its 'copiedness' (1993: 108), rather than an attempt to control the spirit world, he also draws attention to the selectivity of the chants, the extent to which much is left out. That this again is significant as a making visible of the chant's status as copy is clear when Taussig describes the selectivity of the chant as making it 'a montaged unit in action' (p. 100). Later on, Taussig looks at the role of film in both the west's fascination with non-modern magic and in the creation of new forms of magic. Again, what is crucial is ellipsis, a gap which produces a magical effect. Taussig describes the contemporary viewing of an ethnographic film on the Hauka movement in Ghana before independence. Hauka was a movement in West Africa in the first half of the twentieth century in which, through dance, indigenous people would become possessed by the spirits of colonial administrators. In the film *Les Maîtres fous* (1955), a man possessed by a Hauka spirit breaks an egg over a statue of the governor. The film then cuts suddenly to a military parade in a distant city and 'the film hurls us at the cascading yellow and white plumes of the white governor's gorgeous hat as he reviews the black troops passing' (p. 242). Taussig recounts that, when he watched the film in New York City, the audience gasped at this point. This 'sudden juxtaposition' created 'a suffusion of mimetic magic' (p. 242). The power of this juxtaposition resides in what is left out in order to bring similarity to the surface. The shock of this juxtaposition resides in space, time and cultural difference disappearing into the gap of the cut. All this disappears and what remains is the dense similarity of the effect of the broken egg and the governor's hat. The sequence of images is intensely mimetic, and therefore has magical effects, because of, not despite, its use of ellipsis. Indeed, as in André Bazin's classic essay 'The Evolution of the Language of Cinema', where montage is defined as the 'creation of a sense or meaning not objectively contained in the images themselves but derived exclusively from their juxtaposition', the force of montage depends on obvious differences being left out and an impossible similarity being demonstrated (Bazin 1967: 24–5). If magic is the production of effects more astonishing than their causes, as argued by Simon During (During 2002: 5), then the selectivity and ellipsis of form which yet produce *more* are inherently magical.

In his *Reading 1922: A Return to the Scene of the Modern* (1999), Michael North sets out what he sees as the fundamental question for critics of modernism, that is, the question of mediation:

> Is modern literature to be seen as attempting to restore some of the immediacy that mechanical reproduction had stolen from experience and some of the organic unity that industrialism had qualified, or is it to be seen along with dada as a play on the artificial mediation so prominent in life? (North 1999: 139)

The question of mediation is a fundamental one, but North sets up a false opposition in response to it. Modernists themselves felt this question acutely and magic was a way of managing it that neither relied on a return to a prelapsarian past of plenitude nor necessitated a critique of mediation which at the same time denied any possibility of immediacy. The use of magic in modernist experimental work is to this extent distinguishable from Romantic aesthetics, where form transfigured matter in order to bring about immediacy. For magic and for the experimental artists I consider, form *is* matter, not in order to debase form but to show that matter does not need transfiguring but rather needs to be set free from the instrumental vision of it. As I will argue in more detail in Chapter 1, one of the ways that the magic of occult discourses of the late nineteenth and early twentieth centuries manages this is that, like the magical practices of supposedly 'primitive' cultures with which the discourses are in relation, magic is conceived over and over again as error. The use of magic and scepticism towards it, an awareness that it is error, are therefore necessary at the same time for it to be that which enabled modernist formal experiments.

The artists discussed in this book are, then, not those experimenters who showed any particular or straightforward belief in contemporary occult discourses, and indeed, some of them showed only humorous incredulity or outright distaste. However, as I argue in particular in Chapters 2 and 3, credulity is not the point; or rather, the imbrication with magic in the work of these artists depends upon their incredulity. In Chapter 2, then, I argue that the parodic nature of James Joyce's evocation of the séance in *Ulysses*, in the 'Cyclops' episode in particular, is not about the debunking of such practices so much as it claims for Joyce's experiment with writing the same structural relation to the world as that of the séance. They both claim that words magically create the things they name. Again, in Chapter 3, where I consider the use of occult notions of sound in experimental writing, magic is invoked to the extent that it makes possible the transformation denied by more limited definitions of mimesis.

It is for this reason that Ezra Pound is such an insistent presence in the book. Surette argues that Pound uses an intellectual occult tradition rather than the magical phenomenon of the contemporary occult, and in one way this is right. Pound was sceptical about Yeats's ghosts, and what he notes with appreciation in 'the old lady' – Madame Blavatsky – and her one-time secretary, G. R. S. Mead, is their sense of humour rather than their magical powers (Pound 1970: 225–6). However, Pound was the most vocal and self-conscious experimenter in English poetry, and perhaps one of the most vocal champions for aesthetic experiment in general, and because of this it is my argument that his work necessarily engages with the magic of the contemporary occult. More than this, an investigation of Pound in relation to the magic in occult discourse reshapes the consideration of the relation between fascism and the occult. Pound's politics have been subjected to much critical scrutiny over the last few decades (rather than as before left in an embarrassed silence), and links between them and his aesthetics have been extensively mined. Within this critical work, the assumption of an inherent relation between the occult and fascism has become an orthodoxy. However, as I argue in Chapter 5, a consideration of *The Cantos* with regard to magical mimesis suggests that Pound, rather than being led politically astray through an interest in the intellectual tradition of the occult, or being led to both the occult and fascism as effects of the same mistaken cause, went where he did politically because he was not magical enough. My challenge to this reading of the relation between politics and magic is pursued further in Chapters 4 and 5 through a reading of the two pre-eminent Soviet filmmakers of the period, Dziga Vertov and Sergei Eisenstein. For both, their practice as filmmakers (and their disagreements with one another) moved around the problem of the relation between the facts of the world and their status in representation. The problem for Marxism is to distinguish between that in the world as it is which holds the potential for revolution and the creation of a world other than the world that exists now, and that in the world as it is now which is the product of capitalism and must be rejected. Of course, most often, these two possibilities inhere in the same aspect of the world. The question is, then, how does the Marxist filmmaker represent the world without merely repeating the lies and obfuscations of capitalism? As I will show, although for both the magical represents in part precisely a vehicle for these obfuscations, for both too magical mimesis via contemporary occult discourses provides an answer to such questions and as such is synonymous with their idea of experiment.

In Chapters 2 to 5, then, I focus in each chapter on one aspect of occult practice, and show how its assumptions and meanings made possible a magical mimesis which would transform the relation between experimentally produced art and the world. Chapters 2 and 3 broadly consider the crisis in language apparent in early twentieth-century culture, and argue that experimental artists used magical notions of language and sound to assert their work, not as mimetic of doubt and fragmentation in response to the crisis, but as a way to claim for writing the power to create the world anew. In particular, these chapters argue that Joyce's relations to spiritualism and theosophy need to be rethought, and that in both *Ulysses* and *Finnegans Wake* Joyce does not so much debunk the contemporary occult as use its ideas to excess, taking them beyond the limits of occult conservatism. Chapter 4 argues that the idea of telepathy can be seen as fundamental to a reconsideration of mimesis as it challenges the idea of distance – between original and copy, between perceiver and perception. The chapter argues that in the work of Dziga Vertov can be seen the centrality of telepathy to the creation of representation that does more than merely reproduce the world as it is. Chapter 5 considers ectoplasm in relation, in particular, to the materiality of film, and what the visibility of the materiality of both does to questions of mimesis. It looks at Pound's conflicted attitude to film – as demonstrated in both his critical writing and in *The Cantos* – and compares it to the aesthetics and politics of Sergei Eisenstein. For both, the filmic and the ectoplasmic incarnate central questions of the relation between representation and the world, but to very different effect. The chapter argues that in the end the politics of each depends upon the extent to which they allow representation to be ectoplasmic.

The chapters that follow, then, reconsider some of the central works of both literary and filmic modernism through their relations to the magical phenomena of the various discourses of the contemporary occult. In so doing I aim to rethink and reanimate a sense of the extraordinary claims at the heart of modernist mimesis, that is, that the copying of the world inherent in aesthetic representation constitutes an act of transformation that changes not just the art but the world itself.

I

'BUT THE FACTS OF LIFE PERSIST': MAGIC, EXPERIMENT AND THE PROBLEM OF REPRESENTING THE WORLD OTHERWISE

> 'The very reason why magic is almost all bad is because when any of it becomes good it ceases to be magic.'
> E. B. Tylor, 'Magic', *Encyclopaedia Britannica*, 1883

> 'The rights of experiment include the right to be unsatisfactory.'
> Ezra Pound, *Guide to Kulchur*, 1938

The engagement of experimental artistic practices with the contemporary occult in the first half of the twentieth century was not so much the result of personal credulity, or of a search for new forms per se, or a straightforward mimesis of the failure of language, but was instead an attempt to represent the world other than the way it was through a magical mimesis. As I have suggested in the Introduction, this is already to move away from some current accounts of what modernism does with the world. In other accounts, the varieties of modernist experiment are often formed into some kind of coherent category through the suggestion that what they all do is to re-present the world; the truth of the world is re-presented to the reader or viewer in such a way that the familiar world is made unfamiliar, and that that unfamiliarity breaks apart our tired, clichéd perceptions and refreshes our sense of the world. So, for example, in *Ulysses*, Declan Kiberd argues, Joyce releases 'those elements of the marvellous latent in ordinary living, so that the familiar might astonish' (Kiberd 2009: 11). Modernism, according to this account, gives us new eyes. What I have already begun to suggest is that, rather than accounting for modernism in this way, it should be seen not just as a new set of eyes but as a reanimation of the perceived matter through the very crucial 'errors' of magic.

In establishing modernism in this way, I will in this chapter first reconsider the question of experiment itself, not primarily in terms of a moving away from previous artistic conventions, but rather in the light of scientific and philosophical assumptions and debates about the meaning of experiment in the early twentieth century. While the idea of experiment has been used widely by modernist critics to justify their always vulnerable disciplinary category, the question of what is actually meant by experiment in cultural representation has perhaps been taken for granted, especially, as we have seen, by an historicising modernism as discussed by Stephen Ross (2009). The rejection of formalist, New Critical modes of reading, and the concentration in the 'new modernist' studies on reading modernist works as 'cultural documents' which tell us primarily about the paradigms of various forms of identity during the period have perhaps had the effect of blinding us to the strangeness and power of artistic experiment.

Having established an idea of experiment and its connection to magic during the period, the chapter will then go on to think about the political implications of this. I will consider the disagreement between Theodor Adorno and Walter Benjamin and its implications for mimetic practices. I will then go on to look more particularly at how these issues play out in representation through considering the way magic marks the place of impasse for a writer, Arnold Bennett, resisting the full implications of the challenges to conventional ideas of mimesis. The chapter will end with a look at the magazine *transition*, so crucial in the construction and dissemination of the idea of an experimental avant-garde between the wars. Magic is rarely seen as central in accounts of *transition* (for an exception to this see Laura Salisbury 2011), but in the editorials and essays of *transition*'s editor, Eugene Jolas, it is possible to see how crucial the link between experiment and magic is, how indeed experiment and magic have become synonymous for Jolas.

THE PROBLEM OF EXPERIMENT

For the British anthropologists whose work contributed so much to revivals of interest in magical practices in the late nineteenth and early twentieth centuries, what distinguished their treatment of these practices from earlier attitudes to them was their elucidation of system. While anthropologists often disagreed on the relation of later religious beliefs to magic, what they did agree on was that magical beliefs and practices constituted a system. As E. B. Tylor argues in his *Primitive Culture*, first published in 1871 and running to six editions by 1920: 'Had occult science been simply framed for purposes of deception, mere nonsense would have answered the purpose, whereas, what we find is an elaborate and systematic pseudo-science' (Tylor 1920: 134). James Frazer too, in *The Golden Bough*, sees magic as a structure of thinking, as science is a structure of thinking; not only that, but magic and science, unlike religion, are concerned with a systematic investigation of the matter of the world:

> Wherever sympathetic magic occurs in its pure unadulterated form, it assumes that in nature one event follows another necessarily and invariably without the intervention of any spiritual or personal agency. Thus, its fundamental conception is identical with that of modern science; underlying the whole system is a faith, implicit but real and firm, in the order and uniformity of nature. (Frazer 1996: 58)

However, while Tylor and Frazer dignify magic as systematic, a characteristic which it shared with science, so that for them both magic differed from science neither in structure nor in its object of scrutiny, yet magic is not science because it is wrong. As Frazer explains it: 'The fatal flaw of magic lies not in its general assumption of a sequence of events determined by law, but in its total misconception of the nature of the particular laws which govern the sequence' (p. 59). For Tylor, it is this that most clearly characterises the magical thinking and practices of the societies he studies. The assertion that magic constitutes an utterly erroneous view of the world is everywhere in his work. Magic, he claims, is 'one of the most pernicious delusions that ever vexed mankind' (1920: 112). While magic is like science in that it is a systematic form of thinking, where it differs is in its incapacity in testing its assumptions. For Tylor, crucially, it is experiment that gradually erodes and combats the error of magic: 'during the ages in which progressive races have been learning to submit their opinions to closer and closer experimental tests, occult science has been breaking down into the condition of a survival' (pp. 112–13). Magic misreads the matter of the world, whereas contemporary experimental methods tell its truth.

British anthropology conceived its vision of temporal and spatial cultural change firmly within an evolutionary framework. This enabled anthropologists to allow 'primitive' culture – both contemporary and in the past – the error of magic. Anthropology, as I have suggested above, rescued primitive magic from meaninglessness, and saw in it structure and meaning which served later human culture well. Indeed, according to Frazer, the ability of contemporary anthropology to see such structures is testament to magic as the origin of systematic thought about the world, but also to the difference in modern, scientific thinking. Modern anthropology can see the system in magic precisely because it is not magic; it has evolved beyond it. The magician, argues Frazer, never sees the system, only the art. Seeing the system is part of what it means to be modern:

> It is for the philosophic student to trace the train of thought which underlies the magician's practice; to draw out the few simple threads of

which the tangled skein is composed; to disengage the abstract principles from their concrete applications; in short, to discern the spurious science behind the bastard art. (Frazer 1996: 14)

If British anthropology and its heirs could afford some generosity towards the mistakes of 'primitives', it reserved its most scathing attacks for precisely those things which challenged a straightforwardly evolutionary view; nothing attracts anthropological ire like 'survivals', that is, the continuation of magical practices and thinking into modernity. In particular, while continued 'peasant' beliefs in the form of folklore could be seen as an unbroken line leading from the primitive, what was truly distasteful was the resurgence of magical beliefs at the heart of European modernity. When it comes to contemporary occult practices and beliefs, anthropology cannot contain its anxiety and distaste. In *Primitive Culture*, Tylor explicitly asserts the links between spiritualism and primitive magic. Spiritualism is not just a response to contemporary questions of the relation between mind and matter, he says, it is a revival of 'savage beliefs' (Tylor 1920: 142, 155).

Bronislaw Malinowski's work contains an important critique of the earlier generation of anthropologists, yet it shares their animosity towards 'survivals', and expresses it with less reserve. Contemporary magical beliefs are nothing but 'stale revivals of half-understood ancient creeds and cults, dished up under the names of "theosophy," "spiritism" or "spiritualism," and various pseudo-"sciences," –ologies and –isms' (Malinowski 1978b: 69). The offence of contemporary occult beliefs and practices was that, in a society where the experimental method reigned, where it was pre-eminent because it was the only practice which could speak the truth about nature, or rather, which could claim to provide a place, the experiment, where mute nature spoke about itself, they chose instead the error of magic (see Latour 1993: 29).

Of course, as I have suggested in the Introduction, theosophists, spiritualists and in particular psychical researchers saw their beliefs and conclusions as relying precisely on an experimental method which tested facts in such a way as to determine what it was they said. Steven Connor has argued that:

> Spiritualism was not so much endangered as driven by the demand for empirical evidence, since the entire purpose and function of the séance was to provide, time and again, manifest and unignorable proofs of the reality of human survival and the capacity for communication between this world and the next ... Spiritualism shared with its opponents the language of investigation, evidence, exhibition and exposure, and the séance was seen by spiritualists themselves as a kind of laboratory for the investigation of the spirit world, a stage on which to unveil or bring to light hitherto concealed mysteries. (Connor 1999: 203)

Certainly, the aim was that experiment would eventually reveal occult phenomena as part of the laws of nature as they were being revealed by science. While anthropology distinguished magic as precisely those beliefs which do not submit themselves to experimental method, spiritualists, theosophists and psychical researchers submitted magical phenomena to experiment in order to believe them. However, the disjuncture between the idea of experiment and the phenomena themselves was often clear even to those who took the latter seriously. The psychical researcher Albert von Schrenck-Notzing, for example, argued that for experiment to work, the 'spiritist' hypothesis needed to be substituted with one that hypothesised only around the possibilities of matter (Schrenck-Notzing 1920: 28–36). The topography of this problem of experiment was set out very clearly by Henri Bergson in his Presidential Address to the Society for Psychical Research in London in 1913. Bergson begins by asking why it is that scientists, 'men ready to welcome any laboratory work, however restricted and minute it might be ... dismiss with a foregone conclusion' the Society's work (Bergson 2007: 60). He goes on: 'One is at times astonished that modern science should be disdainful of the facts which interest you, when it ought, being experimental, to welcome whatever is matter [sic] of observation and experiment' (p. 68). In trying to account for scientific scepticism towards the SPR, he goes on to delimit two ways of viewing the world that precisely differ around the idea of experiment. While the objects and phenomena on which the SPR and the scientist work are 'facts of the same kind' (p. 62), their methods of investigating them are different. The SPR, he says, 'are obliged to begin with an entirely different method, one which stands midway between that of the historian and that of the magistrate' (p. 63). This is because, Bergson argues, modern science did not discover the experimental method as the single way to establish the truth of the world, rather it created it. Western science is founded on mathematics, and from there on mechanics, and its experimental assumptions converge on one point only, measurement (p. 68). If, Bergson speculates, science had begun by investigating mental phenomena, such as those investigated by the SPR, rather than material, scientific experimental method would now be very different. Crucially, it would not just be an experiment of observation, for Bergson argues that such a method in contemporary science has already seriously misunderstood the relation between the cerebral and the mental (pp. 70ff.). It would be, he argues, 'a psychology of which today we can form no idea ... a psychology which probably would have been to our present psychology what our physics is to that of Aristotle' (p. 78). This speculative method he calls 'the science of mind-energy' and in it, matter and not mind 'would have been the realm of mystery' (p. 79).

Bergson does not say much more in his address to the SPR about what such an alternative kind of experiment might be like, but such suggestions can be found elsewhere. As F. C. T. Moore has argued, in Bergson's phenomenological approach can be seen a proposition that the very actions and experience on which all experiment depends 'prefigure or require the magical' (Moore 1999: 137). Moore argues that for Bergson, actions in the world in which objects other than the self are implicated inevitably necessitate magical thinking. In order to perform certain tasks, the individual experiences them as if the action they are producing is in fact the agent, the producer of the action. So, in his final major work, *The Two Sources of Morality and Religion* (1932/5), Bergson argues that:

> There is no proof that the child who knocks his head against the table and hits back, looks on the table as a person . . . The truth is that between the identification of the table with a person and the perception of the table as an inanimate object, there lies an intermediate representation which is neither that of a thing nor of a person; it is the image of the act accomplished by the table in striking, or, better still, the image of the act of striking, bringing with it – like luggage borne on its back – the table which stands behind . . . The fencer who sees the button of his adversary's foil coming at him knows that it is the movement of the point which has drawn the foil forward, that it is the foil that has drawn the arm forward, that it is the arm that stretched out the body by stretching out itself: he can lunge properly, and give a direct thrust instantaneously, only from the time he feels things in this order. (Bergson 1977: 125–6)

As Bergson argues, as well as the purposeful action, as in fencing, and the inefficacious one, as in hitting a table, the ascription of intention to natural phenomena is also magical. Bergson cites William James's account of his own experience of an earthquake, where, for him, 'the earthquake' was experienced not as the result of material phenomena, despite his empirical knowledge, but instead was experienced as 'the *cause* of the disturbance' (p. 155; emphasis in original). What is crucial in each of these instances is that magical thinking makes possible our interaction with the world beyond the self in a way for which science cannot account. Hence these instances of magic, which were dismissed by anthropologists as distasteful 'survivals' of a 'primitive' past, for Bergson speak an essential truth of the human mind: *'they are defensive reactions against the representation, by the intelligence, of a depressing margin of the unexpected between the initiative taken and the effect desired'* (p. 140; emphasis in original).

Magic mediates between the world as it is and the world as we would like it to be as a result of our own actions. It makes it possible to act in the world in such a way that, if successful, the action would change the world, even though we know we may fail because of the world as it exists before and beyond our action. The positing of a world other than the one that exists before our intervention therefore, for Bergson, depends upon magic. A definition of magic here would be an action that behaves as if the world were otherwise, and in as much as it is a successful action, it makes the actual world become, in some small part, that otherwise world. Magic is error, then, but it is productive error. More than this, for Bergson, the experimental method based on observation of the material world which he outlined in his address to the SPR in 1913 differs from the magical not just to the extent that it is 'right' about the world and magic is 'wrong', but to the extent that it does not attempt to intervene in that world; or at least to the extent that it does not *acknowledge* its role as anything but distanced observer.

Between British anthropology and Bergson, magic and positivist experiment dip in and out of relation with each other. The anthropologists are strenuous in their attempts to fix these terms as opposites. Positivism recognises the truth about magic (its error) to exactly the extent that it is not itself magical. For Bergson, on the other hand, engagement with the world as it is, which for science is the preserve of its own method, is possible exactly to the extent that it is magical. In the following section I will bring in to this picture another critique of magic in order to begin to see what a politics of this relation might be. For Theodor Adorno, magic and positivism are not opposites, but what they share is not productive in Bergson's sense, but is precisely their problem. However, I will argue that the debates of cultural Marxism during this period, considered alongside the anthropological and philosophical debates already covered, in their problems, assumptions and silences, can reveal why experimental representation is only possible as a magical practice.

Magic, Modernity and Marxism

For the central thinker of cultural Marxism in the twentieth century, Theodor Adorno, the failings of capitalist modernity are not revealed by magic. While magical beliefs in response to capitalism might identify the latter's lies and failings, ultimately for Adorno magic merely reinscribes it as the only possible world. Indeed, in his 'Theses against occultism' (1946–7), Adorno reserves the most extreme emanations of his not inconsiderable spleen for those with occult beliefs. For Adorno, at the mistaken heart of magical beliefs is a misconceived relation precisely between the world as it is and the world as it could be:

> The tendency to occultism is a symptom of regression in consciousness. This has lost the power to think the unconditional and to endure the conditional. Instead of defining both, in their unity and difference, by conceptual labour, it mixes them indiscriminately. The unconditional becomes fact, the conditional an immediate essence. (Adorno 1978: 238)

For Adorno, then, the occult, far from making possible a thinking of the world otherwise, merely repeats what is. Because it misunderstands what it perceives in the phenomenal world, it is finally complicit in the work of capitalism in making the present world the only possible world. Occultism is 'the complement of reification' (p. 240). The creation of a spirit world divorced from any critical relation with this world means that occultists, '[i]n pursuing yonder what they have lost ... encounter only the nothing they have' (p. 242). The insistence on the existence of this realm, then, obviates the necessity of thinking the material world. It can be merely sensed in order to be comprehended: 'Their sublime realm, conceived as analogous to space, no more needs to be thought than chairs and flower-vases. It thus reinforces conformism. Nothing better pleases what is there than that being there should, as such, be meaning' (p. 242). For Adorno, as for Tylor, magic's central characteristic is error. While magic may point to crises in capitalism, it misreads them. If it no longer misread them, it would not be magic.

The twin danger of magic and positivism is, of course, precisely that which Adorno warns Walter Benjamin against in their important exchange of letters in the second half of the 1930s. These letters contain issues central to debates about the relation between capitalism, aesthetic form and Marxist critique. The general consensus since has been that Adorno won that particular argument (see Adorno et al. 1980: 100–9), but I want to argue that magic as error was precisely the point.

Adorno's letter to Benjamin of 10 November 1938 is a response to his reading of Benjamin's study of Baudelaire, written in 1938, a later version of which was published as 'On Some Motifs in Baudelaire'. At the centre of Adorno's critique is his assertion that Benjamin's 'dialectic lacks one thing: mediation' (Adorno et al. 1980: 128). In his study, Benjamin has attempted to suggest a relation between the poetry of Baudelaire and the material culture of nineteenth-century Paris; but for Adorno that is precisely the problem. Benjamin's essay suggests relation rather than theorising it. Benjamin has omitted 'everywhere the conclusive theoretical answers to questions, and even [made] the questions themselves apparent only to initiates' (p. 127). This seeming obfuscation is the result of Benjamin's method of piling up the facts and objects of nineteenth-century culture. The obsessive collection of the objects of modernity strongly marks Benjamin's work; he is driven, as Adorno suggests elsewhere, 'to awaken congealed life in petrified objects' (Adorno 1981: 233) and the amassing of facts/objects produces such an awakening. This presentation of the objects of the world stripped bare of a theory that would reveal the processes of their production in capitalism, and from there their true relation to 'cultural traits', for Adorno means that Benjamin's work here occupies a precarious position:

> [T]he theological motif of calling things by their names tends to turn into a wide-eyed presentation of mere facts. If one wished to put it very drastically, one could say that your study is located at the crossroads of magic

and positivism. That spot is bewitched. Only theory could break the spell ... (Adorno et al. 1980: 129)

As we have seen, for anthropology, whether the British school or its detractors, magic and positivism are in opposition because of their different relations to objects in the world. At the centre of what is at stake in that difference is the question of animation. For Tylor in *Primitive Culture*, animism is at the heart of what magic is. For subsequent writers, whatever their disputes with Tylor's position, that magic constitutes a material world in some way empowered and alive is not in question. Anthropology, on the other hand, deals with inert facts and objects. Positivism asserts the inert nature of objects in the world; as it observes the operations of nature from a distance, positivism sees nothing but the mechanical operation of forces on objects. While mechanical forces can be productive they are in no way intentional, they do not have agency (see, for example, Tylor 1920: 78 on games of chance). However, Adorno's charge against Benjamin's 'bewitched' method reveals one possible reason for a positivist anthropology's obsession with magic. Adorno *accuses* Benjamin of being anthropological in that he is in thrall to facts/objects in themselves and this makes him easy prey to magic (Adorno et al. 1980: 129). Indeed, Adorno reveals that the strangeness of anthropology's obsession with facts is disavowed and projected onto 'primitive' practices and beliefs. With this in mind, it is possible to see why even the most positivist of anthropologists struggle to keep 'magical' facts on the side of the primitive. In his preface to the second edition of *Primitive Culture*, Tylor counters the charge from critics of the first edition that his work is based on a mere accumulation of facts. The effects of his work prove that such ethnological facts are:

> real, and vital, and have to be accounted for. It is not too much to say that a perceptible movement of public opinion has here justified the belief that the English mind, not readily swayed by rhetoric, moves freely under the pressure of facts. (Tylor 1920: viii)

Here, facts have their own vitality; what they produce precisely are the very effects at a distance that are attributed to magical thinking. At the same time, as we have seen, what distinguishes the scientific method, within which Tylor wishes to situate anthropology, from magic is the nature of experiment, in which objects/facts are subject to the penetrating gaze of the detached observer, but not to an internal animating force. However, the magical nature of such positivism is not lost on later anthropologists, and can be seen in Malinowski's charge that the 'often fragmentary, incoherent, non-organic nature of much of the present ethnological material is due to the cult of "pure fact"' (Malinowski 1978a: 238).

If Adorno's critique holds the assumptions of anthropology up to the light, so too anthropology makes clear submerged aspects of Adorno's argument. What is at stake for Adorno is the question of truth – 'God knows, there is only one truth' he appeals to Benjamin (Adorno et al. 1980: 131). As we have seen, anthropology constructs itself around the assertion that what distinguishes magic from science is the question of error. If magic were not in error, if it were truth, as Tylor states in the epigraph to this chapter, it would no longer be magic. Magic and error are synonymous. Magic is a description of error. For both Adorno and anthropology magic is necessary in order to clearly distinguish between truth and error. For anthropology, the matter of the world is made safe, is made useable for its categorising drive by seeing as erroneous any suggestion that such matter be itself an agent. For Adorno, the matter of the world is totally in the grip of capitalism, but the possibility for liberating it, for making a world other than the one that is, is dependent on agency residing not in that matter (how can such power reside in matter which is so totally subject to capitalism, which is in error?) but in dialectical materialist analysis. For Marxist cultural criticism in general, magic is used to describe the insidious power of capital, not the work of resistance. Despite their differences, both anthropology and Marxism are the work of modernity, and modernity, as Bruno Latour has argued, appeared to bring about 'a luminous dawn that cleanly separated material causality from human fantasy' (Latour 1993: 35).

For Adorno, then, the trouble with magic is that it is utterly complicit with the forces of reification. The root of the word 'reification' is the Latin *res*, thing. Words for reification in other languages are more explicit about the concept's enmeshment with the thing – the literal translation of German's *Verdinglichung* is 'thingification'. What the English word does make clear, though, is the link between the concept and the structures of thinking which reproduce the world as it is. *Res* is the root too for the English word 'real' and its derivatives – 'reality', realism', 'realist'. Reification is about fixing a 'real' so that it becomes *the* real. Adorno's attacks on magic throughout *Minima Moralia* and in his letters to Benjamin are concerned precisely with this – that magic fixes the world as it is by mistaking the work of culture and the work of nature. Benjamin's historical method in the Baudelaire essay is problematic for Adorno because he believes it lacks the mediation which would open out the things of the world and demonstrate that they come into being through material processes which are controlled by some human beings and imposed upon others. If such processes are made through human agency, they can be unmade, or remade. The world can be other than the way it is. Adorno's charge that Benjamin's method falls 'at the crossroads of magic and positivism' asserts that in both magic and positivism, in Timothy Bewes's words, 'the "given world" . . . is taken to be the truth of the world' (Bewes 2002: 4).

The trouble, of course, is the extent of the possibility for change present in the tradition of Marxist analysis beginning with Adorno. Bewes suggests that the concept of reification may have fallen out of use in recent theoretical analysis because we have reached a point of what Adorno called 'absolute reification'. The proletariat, who for Georg Lukács were outside reification because of their oppression, have become assimilated into consumer society (pp. 8–9). Adorno's science is melancholy for Bewes because the possibility for recreating the world has disappeared. Reification has itself been reified, 'a purely "objective" phenomenon impermeable to political intervention' (p. 9). Bewes challenges the eschewing of reification as a critical tool in response to this. For Bewes, the concept of reification is absolutely necessary in order to keep alive the possibility that the world could be other than it is. If the concept goes, so too does an awareness that the work of reification is just that, work and not nature. Without reification, capitalism itself is reified.

Adorno's charges that Benjamin's work is anthropological are right, then, but Benjamin does what no anthropology of the period could do – that is, he treats the objects of modernity as an anthropologist would the objects of primitive culture. The significance in terms of understanding the status of magic for thinkers and artists during period is that Benjamin does not take the objects of modernity to primitivism (which would indeed be reactionary, conservative and utopian, as Adorno suggests), but rather he brings magic to the objects of modernity. While he takes issue with anthropological positivism, Adorno's critique takes contemporary anthropology at its word – magic is error; Benjamin attempts an alternative anthropology which cannot help but reimport the magical. Here, magic is productive error. In particular, this productivity is clear to the extent that magic transforms mimesis.

Benjamin's fragment 'On Astrology' (1932) is concerned exactly with working towards a possible method which could envision a new kind of mimesis. Benjamin's aim is stated in the first sentence of the fragment: 'An attempt to procure a view of astrology from which the doctrine of magical "influences," or "radiant energies," and so on has been excluded' (Benjamin 2005a: 684). This de-occulted astrology is approached, or rather is created, through an idea of similarity that reveals 'an active, mimetic force working expressly inside things' (p. 684). While this mimetic force remains through time, its location changes, as does the ability to see it. Our ability to see 'mimetic resemblances' differs from that of people in antiquity, but the presence of a mimetic force which is still active in us (which Benjamin locates pre-eminently in the ability of the infant to learn language) makes it possible to deduce a use for astrology, rather than merely dismissing it as nonsense. Benjamin takes up and extends the ideas in 'On Astrology' in the slightly later 'Doctrine of the Similar' (1933), also unpublished in his lifetime. In this essay, Benjamin is not so much keen to exclude 'magical influences' as he is to see the magical as one necessary aspect of the moment of resemblance. Crucially, here it is made clearer that the perception of mimetic resemblances is dependent itself on a particular constellation in time. Again using the example of astrology, Benjamin suggests that object and method together constitute the moment of recognition:

> The perception of similarities thus seems to be bound to a moment in time. It is like the addition of a third element – the astrologer – to the conjunction of two stars; it must be grasped in an instant. Otherwise the astrologer is cheated of his reward, despite the sharpness of his observational tools. (Benjamin 2005b: 696)

For Benjamin, the similarity that is created/revealed in these moments is not one that is perceived, that is empirically established, but is rather a 'nonsensuous similarity' (p. 696), a similarity, in other words, that is magical in as much as it suggests relations between things that are beyond the empirical. He goes on to scrutinise language in these terms, as that aspect of modernity which retains, indeed acts as an archive for, nonsensuous similarities (and here rehearses many of his ideas about the relation between language and magic from his earlier essay, 'On Language as Such and on the Language of Man'; Benjamin 1979). As Benjamin notes at the close of his essay, it is crucial that this magical aspect of language be seen in tandem with its commonplace aspect, what he calls the semiotic. One cannot be present without the other:

> Thus, even profane reading, if it is not to forsake understanding altogether, shares this with magical reading: that it is subject to a necessary tempo, or rather a critical moment, which the reader must not forget at any cost lest he go away empty-handed. (Benjamin 2005b: 698)

As much as he begins in the effort to exclude magic, a consideration of mimetic objects and forces brings Benjamin back to the necessary presence of magic.

Mimesis, Magic and Experiment

The relation between mimesis and magic can be seen in the work of a non- or perhaps almost modernist, that of Arnold Bennett, famously one of Virginia Woolf's Edwardians. The debate between Bennett and Woolf, conducted from the publication of Bennett's essay 'Is the Novel Decaying?' in March 1923 (Bennett 1923) until his death in 1931 in lectures and in the pages of the periodical press, has long been seen as salient in Anglo-American modernism's argument with the conventions of realism. In 'Mr Bennett and Mrs Brown' (1924), responding to Bennett's charge that the younger novelists do not create convincing characters, Woolf accuses the Edwardians of confusing the real and the lifelike (Woolf 1966: 325). While the construction of character in Wells, Galsworthy and Bennett, Woolf argues, focuses on the surface of life, on houses, clothes and incomes, and so reproduces the lifelike, it does not animate those characters, it does not produce life. In the novel which was contemporary with his opening salvo, *Riceyman Steps* (1923), Bennett can be seen as struggling precisely at the limits of the realist ability to animate. The problem of form in Bennett's work is attested by even the most sympathetic of critics, both his contemporaries and more recent ones. Bennett notes in his journals a meeting with George Moore, who praised the objectivity and originality of *Riceyman Steps*. Moore tells Bennett that it engages through its accurate depiction of a certain sort of life rather than its artistry: 'It has no form whatever, *no* form. It is not very carefully written ... The book is the FACT ... and that's all.' Moore's delight in the novel is double-edged for Bennett, and draws his weary comment that 'in my opinion it is very well constructed' (Bennett 1971: 478). It is clear from many of Bennett's comments that he valued the challenges to mimetic conventions that he saw going on around him. He acknowledged in 1929 that he never now wrote fiction 'without thinking of Joyce's discoveries' (quoted in Mendelson 1991: xxii), yet he wrote novels which masked their representational work, even from other novelists. The extent to which Bennett acknowledged that this question is necessarily enmeshed with magic is clear from *Riceyman Steps*, the novel he wrote soon after reading *Ulysses* for the first time, where the ability of magic to bring life drenches the novel thematically. Bennett's comments on Joyce's 'Penelope' show that he could acknowledge that a certain kind of mimesis and magic were synonymous – the episode, he wrote, 'might in its utterly convincing realism be an actual document, the magical record of inmost thought by a woman that existed' (quoted in Gilbert 1952: 385) – and *Riceyman Steps* too invokes magic as that which is needed to make things live. The novel finally, though, is unable to break through a conventional realism that relies on a mediated relation to the fictional world.

The novel concerns itself with a couple, Henry and Violet Earlforward, whose early passion for each other withers due to Henry's deathly concern with money and Violet's inability to counter it and her consequent bitterness. Their early married life, their sense of the transforming possibilities of passion and their later bemused collapse are framed, and indeed in part caused, by the life-giving intervention of Elsie, their young maid. Bennett implies that Elsie's generosity of spirit, her unarticulated belief that life is more than the sum of its utilitarian parts, has the potential to transform, if only Henry, in particular, could open himself to it. On their wedding night, in a chapter entitled 'The Priestess', as Violet moves into her new bedroom, she notices that someone, presumably Elsie, has tied an old satin slipper to the marriage bed with pink ribbon:

> And the old satin shoe influenced her. There was something absurd, charming, romantic and inspiring about that shoe. It reminded Violet that security and sagacity and affectionate constancy could not be the sole constituents of a satisfactory existence. Grace, fancifulness, impulsiveness, some foolishness, were needed too. (Bennett 2003: 83)

Violet's marriage present to her husband has been to arrange for his bookshop and living quarters to be cleaned while they are out of the house getting married and enjoying their day-long honeymoon. Later in this chapter we learn that Henry's gift to Violet is a safe in which to keep her valuables. Contrasted with these prosaic gifts are the extravagantly useless gifts from Elsie to the couple. She showers them with rice, accomplishing 'this gesture with the air of a benevolent priestess performing a necessary and gravely important rite' (p. 87), a gesture which transforms the mood of the startled couple: 'It was as if a sinister spell had been miraculously lifted' (p. 87). As a climax to her generosity, Elsie presents them with a small wedding cake, and finally 'the magic of her belief' in the marriage made manifest in the cake 'compelled the partners also to see themselves as bride and bridegroom' (p. 88). Throughout the novel, the figure of Elsie is linked again and again with magic. It is Elsie alone who knows 'the mysterious spell of the enigma of life' (p. 183), it is Elsie who each morning 'breathed the breath of life into the dead nocturnal house, and revived it', and Elsie who believes in the power of magical thinking (pp. 180, 183). Indeed, while Elsie is the central magical figure in the novel, in fact all actions or desires which exceed the limits of the empirical or the assumption that matter is inert, or has only material effects, are described in the lexicon of magic. Violet's attempts to bring order to the house are described as 'magical creative power' (p. 92). When Henry agrees to act against his miserly, utilitarian instincts he was 'afraid and enchanted' (p. 175).

This use of magic to indicate something that cannot be quite accounted for is fairly conventional, but one scene in the novel makes it clear that Bennett intuits the link between all this and questions of mimesis, that is, questions of the way that representation can be seen as a process that does not make inert copies but that animates the material of which it makes use precisely through the act of copying. Crucially in this scene it is possible to read Bennett's inability to master these intuitions, and the extent to which they are linked to the very experimental practices that he acknowledges but cannot himself employ. During their day-long honeymoon, Henry and Violet visit Madame Tussaud's where, along with many in the crowds around them, Violet mistakes a wax figure for a human being and then experiences 'quite a turn' when she makes the opposite mistake, and what she had thought was a wax figure suddenly moves: 'I wouldn't like to come here alone. No! That I wouldn't' (p. 74). They go into the Hall of Tableaux, where historical scenes have been reconstructed using wax figures. In the narrative that describes this, a number of contrasting reactions to the scenes are discussed. A lengthy quote is needed here, for what is puzzling about the narrative is quite whose opinions are being articulated:

> A restful and yet impressive affair, these reconstitutions of dramatic episodes in English history. And there was no disturbing preciosity in the

attitude of the sightseers, who did not care a fig what 'art' was, to whom, indeed, it would never have occurred to employ such a queer word as 'art' even in their thoughts. Nor did they worry themselves about composition, lighting, or the theory of the right relation of subject to treatment. Nor did they criticize at all. They accepted, and if they could not accept they spared their brains the unhealthy excitement of trying to discover why they could not accept. They just left the matter and passed on. A poor-spirited lot, with not the slightest taste for hitting back against the challenge of the artist. But anyhow they had the wit to put art in its place and keep it there. What interested them was the stories told by the tableaux, and what interested them in the stories told was the 'human' side, not the historic importance. King John signing Magna Charta under the menace of his bold barons, and so laying the foundation stone of British liberty? No! The picture could not move them. But the death of Nelson, Gordon's last stand, the slip of a girl Victoria getting the news of her accession, the execution of Mary Queen of Scots? Yes! Hundred per cent, successes every one. Violet shed a diamond tear at sight of the last. Violet said:

'They do say, seeing's believing.' (pp. 74–5)

The end of this passage clearly places Violet among the uncritical crowd interested only in the human stories the tableaux tell, but whose voice do we hear before this, interrogating the pleasures of the crowd and their lack of interest in the tableaux as aesthetic constructions? Most of the chapter until this point has been focalised through Henry, and these too could be Henry's thoughts, ventriloquised by the novel's omniscient third person narrator, but if so not only is the consideration of these questions of aesthetics rather out of character, but we as reader should then treat them with scepticism. Already by this point in the novel we know that Henry is a deeply unsympathetic character, whose views and assumptions are given little or no validity by the novel itself. That these might be Henry's views, though, is supported by Henry's attitude to Violet's 'diamond tear'. The passage quoted above continues:

She was fully persuaded at last that English history really had happened. Henry's demeanour was more reserved, and a little condescending. He said kindly that the tableaux were very clever, as they were. And he smiled to himself at Violet's womanish simplicity – and liked her the better for it, because it increased her charm and gave to himself a secret superiority. (p. 75)

If this analysis of the behaviour of the crowd is Henry's, then the reader should reject it, even though it describes exactly the assumptions necessary to the reader of a realist novel. If the opinions expressed are straightforwardly those of the narrator, then they challenge precisely the contract between representation and reader upon which the success of such a novel depends. The strangeness of this passage is set in motion by questions around the nature of mimesis provoked by the wax figures of Madame Tussaud's. The success of the figures depends upon their precise repetition of the surface reality of life (Violet mistakes a wax figure for a human being), but their failure is precisely their inability to reproduce that life itself (what Violet finds more disturbing, more powerful, is mistaking a human being for a wax figure). The wax figures are only properly uncanny when Violet mistakenly thinks one of them has moved – 'It gave me quite a turn' (p. 74). While Bennett wishes to assert the ability of realist conventions to produce life itself, both the scene he chooses to demonstrate this – the visit to Madame Tussaud's – and his repeated invocation of magic when he is unable to account for an effect by using the descriptive capabilities of those realist conventions undermine his position. The strangeness of the passage is evidence that while ostensibly Bennett has faith in one version of mimesis, his aims as a novelist push him towards another. In this novel, where the repetition of the surface of life in order to speak the truth of that life fails, the transforming, animating powers of magic are invoked.

What Bennett lacks is an experimental method that would animate his novels, a method that would concern itself with a new relation, that of magic, between the world and the artist's treatment of it. The question of technique in experimental work has been seen by some critics, however, as precisely that which empties experiment of magic. Adorno cites Stéphane Mallarmé and his statement that works of literature are 'not inspired but made out of words' in his critique of Benjamin's overvaluation, as he sees it, of mechanically reproduced representation in the challenge to the cultic value of art:

> precisely the uttermost consistency in the pursuit of the technical laws of autonomous art changes this art and instead of rendering it into a taboo or fetish, brings it close to the state of freedom, of something that can be consciously produced and made. (Adorno et al. 1980: 122)

Technique, the visible process of production, therefore transforms the error of magic into something else. Indeed, Mallarmé's insistence on made words has been crucial for a number of recent critics who wish to assert, for reasons other than Adorno's, that experimental writing turns words into isolated and inert matter. In his *Gramophone, Film, Typewriter*, Friedrich Kittler argues that with the advent of reproductive technologies at the end of the nineteenth century, the ability of writing to produce 'hallucinated worlds' in the imagination of the reader was over. The phonograph and the film could reproduce the real of the world, not just its hallucinated image. The idea of a hallucinated world beyond the letter on the page was no longer possible, and experimental writing, for Kittler, is inaugurated around precisely this realisation:

> Around 1880 poetry turned into literature. Standardized letters were no longer to transmit Keller's red blood or Hoffmann's inner forms, but rather a new and elegant tautology of technicians. According to Mallarmé's instant insight, literature is made up of no more and no less than twenty-six letters. (Kittler 1999: 14)

In Simon During's study of what he calls 'secular magic' – that is, magic for the purposes of entertainment without making any claims regarding the existence of occult forces – he sees experimental writers of the late nineteenth and early twentieth centuries, influenced in particular by Edgar Allan Poe, as drawing on the techniques of secular magic precisely because they were about technique and not about occult forces. Mallarmé, along with Raymond Roussel and André Breton, 'embraced tricks and special effects because they implied a practical, demystified recognition that magic exists primarily as the effect of techniques', not as the effect of occult forces (During 2002: 196). For During, magic happens when effects are 'more astonishing than their causes' (p. 5), but the significance of secular magic is in its demonstration, rather than occulting, of its techniques of production. While During does not claim that such demonstrations are evidence of disenchantment – for him the importance of secular magic in modernity is precisely that it makes impossible a straightforward chronological move from enchantment to disenchantment – he does claim that in bringing technique to the surface, experimental writers are emptying their work of any occult force (pp. 64–5).

However, as we have seen, the use of magic always invokes error, and because of this the very nature of 'experiment' in experimental writing changes. For During, magic is just technique, but I want to argue that technique in art is necessarily magical. If we concentrate on experiment rather than technique, the possibilities of a focus on the technical expand beyond During's emptying out. Because of the ambiguous truth status of art, the appropriation of the idea of experiment from science – in parallel with the effects of psychical research's appropriation of experiment in Bergson's argument – rather than securing the status of art, had the effect of exposing the very process of experiment as magical. In Bergson's example, the fencer, in order to intervene in the world in the most efficacious way, must believe in a reversed cause and effect – the tip of the foil is the actor, pulling the hand and arm after it. What Bergson's example suggests is that *any* intervention in the world requires such magical thinking – it is necessary in order to jump the lacunae between the world as it is and the world as it may be after the intervention. Such a structure of thinking can be found too in Bewes's argument – the moment of revolutionary transformation is possible only through an erroneous, magical belief in precisely its possibility. As Joshua Landy has recently argued about Mallarmé, the purpose of his experiments was not to cut poetry off from the world, but rather to remake the possibility of engagement:

> A redemptive poetry would have not to *say* something but to *do* something, to do by saying. Or rather, it would have to permit *us* to do something by its means, just as books of spells permit their users to transform friends into gods, and foes into frogs . . . Redemptive poetry would, then, be an effective spell, *complete with instructions for its use*. (Landy 2009: 111; emphasis in original)

The experimental work of art does use magic as a technique, and this draws attention to its status as *made*, but at the same time its attempts to remake the world other than it is make necessary a magic that is not *merely* technique but technique as transformation. The place where both of these effects of magic overlap and have their being is in magic's status as error. The invocation of magic as error reveals art's status as error – a status that more conventional art attempts to cover up because it makes clear its status as made; but the invocation of error, too, makes possible the representation of a world that is not this one. In the rest of the chapter, I will look at the invocation of magic in the writing of Eugene Jolas in *transition* to explore in a little more detail the way that magic works in the creation of aesthetic experiment.

Eugene Jolas and the Experiment of *transition*

The magazine *transition* is of course well established as a key conduit of modernist and avant-garde work between the wars. The frustration of its founder and editor, Eugene Jolas, with the linguistic conventions of American journalism and his early encounter with Surrealism (in Strasbourg in 1923) gave him a strong sense of language as being at the centre of contemporary cultural malaise, and of a new language as being the only cure. With the founding of *transition*, while language remained central to his vision, this need for fundamental change was extended to the 'language' of representation generally, in film, in the visual arts and in music. Between 1927 and 1938, *transition* published an extraordinary range of work from what are now seen as the central avant-garde artists of the interwar period. Beginning with the first issue, the whole of James Joyce's 'Work in Progress', published as *Finnegans Wake* in 1939, was published in instalments, and from the earliest issues, articles and editorials appeared defending and explaining Joyce's work. Earlier avant-garde work, such as Hugo Ball's sound poetry and the writing of German expressionism, was published, sometimes for the first time in English translation, and indeed the first English translations of Franz Kafka's work appeared in *transition* during the 1930s. The magazine carried work by a huge number of visual artists, some already well established and many still unfamiliar, including Pablo Picasso, Kurt Schwitters, Wassily Kandinsky, Man Ray,

László Moholy-Nagy and Joan Miró. Critical articles on film and photography by Sergei Eisenstein and Moholy-Nagy appeared, and articles on the origins of Dada and Surrealism by Richard Huelsenbeck and André Breton. American writers published in the magazine included Hart Crane, Kay Boyle, Gertrude Stein and William Carlos Williams.

Jolas's claim in his unfinished autobiography – written between the late 1930s and his death in 1952 – that '[d]aring experimentation with words, colors and sounds was the chief preoccupation of an intercontinental avant-garde that extended across continents' during the interwar period now seems nothing more than a statement of the obvious (Jolas 1998: 87). However, the regularity of *transition*'s use of the idea of experiment, and Jolas's many editorials and articles explaining his vision for experimental work across the arts, indicate not only the insistence of the idea, and possible reasons for this insistence, but also some of the problems inherent in this use of experiment, and some of the reasons why artistic experiment as it is written of and practised in *transition*, and so as it existed for a crucial chunk of the American and European avant-gardes between the wars, is utterly enmeshed with ideas of magic.

In the decade of its existence, *transition* committed itself specifically to providing a place for experiment. Jolas's introduction in the first issue declares that the magazine 'wishes to offer American writers an opportunity to express themselves freely, to experiment'. To European writers, it offered the opportunity to publish their experimental work 'in a language Americans can read and understand' (Jolas 1927a: 137). More than this, in order to help Anglo-American audiences understand such experimental work, earlier avant-garde work – expressionism, Dada, Surrealism – was published in such a way as to give it a genealogy, to place in within a particular *idea* of the avant-garde, and this idea had at its centre the concept of experiment: 'the review gradually became a laboratory into which I tried to gather the forces that sympathized with my desire for a renewed logos' (Jolas 1998: 107).

Jolas's writing asserts the centrality of experiment over and over again, but the nature of such experiment is not always clear. If experiment consists of ventriloquising the truth of mute nature, as Bruno Latour suggests it does for science, where scientists and their methods come to 'represent the mute and material multitude of objects' (Latour 1993: 29), then Jolas's reading of the crisis of contemporary culture makes any direct transfer of the concept problematic. While Jolas's famous 'The Revolution of the Word' from the June 1929 number boldly declares that 'THE REVOLUTION OF THE WORD IN THE ENGLISH LANGUAGE IS AN ACCOMPLISHED FACT' (Jolas 1929b: 13), elsewhere Jolas makes it clear that it is the *problem* of experiment, rather than its inevitable achievement, which concerns him. In his editorial writing, Jolas sets out again and again his vision, at the centre of which is the desire to remake the relation between the 'I' and the world:

> The philosophic problem of the twentieth century-spirit seems to us to lie especially in the attempt to discover a new notion of man. The relationship between the I and the dynamic totality needs to be definitely analyzed, in order to elucidate the process of evasion from the disquietude in which we live. (Jolas 1927d: 191)

In his 'Notes' of the Fall 1928 number of *transition*, defending the magazine against its already vociferous detractors, Jolas sets out again his vision, at the centre of which is the desire to remake the relation between the 'I' and the world, but here makes it clear that what is necessary is not a ventriloquising of the world as it is, but rather that such 'facts' are themselves the problem. They need to be not ventriloquised but transformed:

> But the facts of life persist. What is the poet to do with them? Is there not a space between the subjective and the objective reality which ought to be filled? This process would lead to a marriage of reason and instinct which, with the resultant breaking up of the traditional means of expression, would open up an entirely new world. Thus the new realism synthetizing two realities should make us think in terms of both the supernatural and the natural. (Jolas 1928: 181)

The aim for aesthetic experiment, then, is the revelation of 'an entirely new world', it is thinking the world other than it is. Jolas's rhetorical questions in the extract above rather suggest a straightforwardly affirmative answer, but other attempts to outline the precise strategies of such experimentation reveal a more thorny problem. In 'Reality' (1929), Jolas rejects the realism of Émile Zola because it is about copying the world: 'Artistic creation is not the mirror of reality. It is reality itself' (1929d: 20). Throughout *transition*, Jolas is highly critical of work, particularly American writing, which is 'photographic', which is what he calls 'the sycophant of reality' (Jolas 1927d: 196). The artists who produce such work give us nothing but 'a monotonous description of their mediocre universe' (Jolas 1929c: 25).

If artistic reality is 'reality itself', however, the nature of the reality which constitutes the artistic creation is more tricky. Again in 'Reality', Jolas, while acknowledging its importance and refusing to side with 'all the snobs, who ... discuss it glibly and pretentiously', locates the failure of Surrealism in its inability to 'synthesize' reality (1929d: 19). Surrealism gets it right by privileging what Jolas calls the 'pre-logical' – taken from his reading of the anthropologist Lucien Lévy-Bruhl – but gets it wrong because it does not go beyond it. What the poet or other artist is to do with the 'facts of life' is not then as obvious as Jolas's rhetorical questions suggest. If Zola and his followers fail because in their work 'the immediate senses are celebrated as the prime factors in the esthetic organisation [so that] the enigmatic or the pre-logical is ignored'

(p. 15), and the Surrealists fail because they do not go beyond the prelogical, how then does the artist experiment with what exists to produce 'an entirely new world'?

The assertion that the magical is the goal of the new writers and artists championed by Eugene Jolas appears everywhere in his writing in *transition*. An editorial in the third issue of the magazine, which Jolas later described as his 'manifesto' (Jolas 1998: 93), has the title 'Suggestions for a New Magic'. In this, while Jolas declares that '[u]nless there be a perception of eternal values, there can be no magic' (Jolas 1927b: 178), the experiment he champions is not about the search for transcendental truth per se: 'Perhaps we are seeking God. Perhaps not. It matters little one way or the other' (p. 179). Rather, it is remaking the world in representation that needs to be magical. Jolas's distancing of himself and his magazine from formal politics can be seen in this light. It is not politics which can remake the world, it is poetry, because only poetry can remake the world magically. Poetry, a term used by Jolas to mean any art which powerfully recreates the world rather than just reproducing 'the photography of events' (p. 178), is inherently magical. As he argued in a later article:

> The poet passes from the natural order of things into the supernatural. At the extreme limits of his consciousness there is a reality that presents immediately a transfiguration of the concrete. Through his lyrical confessions transmitted in prismatic movement, we get the creative action towards a beyond. He strives for the immediacy of a metaphoric mental perception. (Jolas 1929c: 27)

Jolas rejects the value of rationalism and empiricism in his writing in *transition*, but does acknowledge the 'truth' of contemporary science as far as it can be seen as itself trouncing materialism, and its own experiment can be seen as suggestive of a world otherwise: 'In physics, chemistry, mathematics, we have witnessed the prolongations of its frontiers. The atom, once the last reality, has given way to new disintegrations which open up possibilities for tremendous evolutions' (1929d: 19).

What Jolas sees as necessary is a bridge between the self and the world; indeed the bridge was one of names originally considered by Jolas for his magazine and this bridge is a transformative representation, a magical vision of the matter of representation, of words, sound, space and matter.

> The epic writer of the future will not copy reality. He will create, with the material he possesses, another world in which he will make his own laws. This other world is not above his own world, but identical with it. (Jolas 1930: 19)

Indeed, then, the facts of life persist, but the use of magic makes of this not a problem, but a solution. The experiment of self *and* world reanimates the matter of the world such that the earth is no longer the same place. In the chapters which follow I will show that the error of magic, as found in the 'modern' discourses of the occult in the early twentieth century, offered artists the means to experiment in a way that remade the world.

2

'AND WHAT HAS ALL THIS TO DO WITH EXPERIMENTAL WRITING?': WORDS AND GHOSTS

> 'The essential business of language is to assert or deny facts.'
> Bertrand Russell, 'Introduction', in Ludwig Wittgenstein, *Tractatus Logico-Philosophicus*, 1922

> 'Inorganic and fanciful associations attach themselves to words . . . There is something eerie in the look of the silent *h* in "ghost".'
> J. P. Postgate, 'Introduction', in C. K. Ogden and I. A. Richards, *The Meaning of Meaning*, 1923

If magic is error for modernity, then the most scandalous of its errors is its collapsing into identity of words and objects. As Randall Styers argues, one of the central themes running through scholarly work on magic from the second half of the nineteenth century is the claim that magic is fixated on the power of words (Styers 2004: 219ff.). Certainly magic is often defined as that which attempts to animate matter, but again and again writers on magic assert a particular attitude to language as central to this animation. For James Frazer, if magic originates in the human fear of the dead, then the power of language is absolutely central. The most common and the most powerful word taboos amassed by Frazer are those around names and, in particular, the names of the dead are tabooed again and again in 'primitive' culture, as speaking the name of a dead person threatens to make them present in body too: 'In all cases, even where it is not expressly stated, the fundamental reason for this avoidance is probably the fear of the ghost' (Frazer 1996: 304). Of course, as Styers goes on to point out in his discussion of Ernst Cassirer's *Philosophy of Symbolic Forms* (1925), this placing of both the reanimation of matter and the power of words at the centre of magic is not contradictory or paradoxical. As I have already suggested, magic uses representation to animate matter: 'Word magic, image magic, and writing magic are the basic elements of magical activity and the magical view of the world' (Cassirer 1955: 24). Any paradox is a result of modern misreading of the magical understanding of representation:

> The mythical world is concrete not because it has to do with sensuous, objective contents, not because it excludes and repels all merely abstract factors – all that is merely signification and sign; it is concrete because in it the two factors, thing and signification, are undifferentiated, because they merge, grow together, concresce in an immediate unity. (p. 24)

As Cassirer's work demonstrates, though, the other side of this understanding of magic's obsession with the power of words is the insistent denial of such a power. For Cassirer, familiarly, magic is error. The 'progress' to religion consists in a separation of the spiritual from the material through a new relation to signs, a relation that consists in religion rising above 'mere' representation (p. 25).

This anxiety about precisely what language is, its function, its relation to the material world, is of course almost a definition of modernity. As Bruno Latour argues, the very existence of 'modernity' is premised on a (for him erroneous) distinction between nature and culture; given this, language is bound to have a very anxious and conflicted place among modernity's divisions, categories and definitions (Latour 1993). All representation, as the term suggests, puts itself in the place of the world, yet it remains distinct from it. We depend on language to know and control the material world, yet its representation of the world creates a new realm that exceeds the rules and control of the material. This excessiveness in its turn compromises the ability of language to be instrumental. This anxiety about the status of language, about its function and relation to the world it purports to describe, became central in a number of areas through the nineteenth century. While linguistics on the whole remained comparative and historical, rather than asking questions of language per se, until the beginning of the twentieth century and the work of Ferdinand de Saussure (see McMahon 2003 and Emden 2005: 35ff.), in philosophy of very different kinds, language began to take on what has been called an 'unprecedented centrality' (Berry 2006: 113). In particular, many philosophies of the period, despite their differences, came to see that the problem of language was not just in its erroneous or improper use, as it had been for John Locke, for example, but was inherent in its very form. Nietzsche's work is central here. For him, rhetoric does not represent an artificial use of language; rather language is always rhetorical and as such its relation to reality is never direct

(Emden 2005: especially 45ff.). When we speak of things, 'we possess only metaphors of things which in no way correspond to reality' (Nietzsche 1999: 144). However, in *The Gay Science*, Nietzsche's work most obviously concerned with poetic language, the fact that this disjunction between things and words is not recognised becomes, not just a source of despair, but one of possibility:

> *Only as creators!* This has given me the greatest trouble and still does: to realize that what things *are called* is incomparably more important than what they are. The reputation, name, and appearance, the usual measure and weight of a thing, what it counts for – originally almost always wrong and arbitrary, thrown over things like a dress and altogether foreign to their nature and even to their skin – all this grows from generation unto generation, merely because people believe in it, until it gradually grows to be part of the thing and turns into its very body. What at first was appearance becomes in the end, almost invariably, the essence and is effective as such. How foolish it would be to suppose that one only needs to point out this origin and this misty shroud of delusion in order to destroy the world that counts for real, so-called 'reality.' We can destroy only as creators. – But let us not forget this either; it is enough to create new names and estimations and probabilities in order to create in the long run new 'things.' (Nietzsche 1974: § 58; emphasis in original)

Nietzsche's work might hold together a pessimism about language's inability to tell the truth with an assertion of its possibilities as creative, but it is exactly this ability to create new things that other philosophers wish to disavow, to make erroneous. Other philosophical positions, responding to such a sense that language has no direct connection to the world, but unwilling in consequence to see language as beyond the supposed logical order of the world of things, attempted to confront the language problem head on, and to wrest order from it. Revealing of the anxiety about the relation between words and the things denoted by them, and the attempt to dispel such anxiety, is the extent to which numerous writers devoted their attentions to investigating and explaining the status and function of words which denote things which do not exist, in particular ghosts. After setting out some of the less commented on consequences of the sense of language discussed by Nietzsche above, I will in this chapter be arguing that the return of the dead most frequently described by the word 'ghost' is a central figure for the attempts of both theorists and experimental writers to settle for neither a naïve view of language as straightforward description, nor a pessimistic view of it as sundered from the world.

Bertrand Russell's theory of descriptions was an attempt to solve the philosophical problem of how words could exist for things which do not. Russell's famous examples – 'Unicorns don't exist' and 'the present king of France' – were possible for him because they were composed of logical relations only (see Russell 1979: 67–8 and 1919: 158–60, 168–71, 176–9). While Russell does not really address this problem in relation to literary writing, the implications of his thinking were not lost on writers. In his satire of Lady Ottoline Morrell's salon at Garsington during the First World War, *Crome Yellow* (1921), Aldous Huxley's character Scrogan – loosely based on Russell – has to admit that in his Rational State writers would be good only for 'the lethal chamber' (Huxley 2004: 127). His interlocutor, the would-be writer Denis Stone, has earlier divined just such an attitude in Scrogan and offered him an alternative view of language. Asked by Scrogan to explain the choice of word in a poem by a fellow guest, Ivor – among whose many accomplishments is that of being a medium and having 'good first-hand knowledge of the next world' – Stone answers that for writers words have an existence of their own: 'The creation by word-power of something out of nothing – what is that but magic? And, I may add, what is that but literature?' (pp. 85, 116).

Russell's one-time student, Ludwig Wittgenstein, disagreed with Russell's final faith in the artificial language of logic. For him, 'natural' language, while superficially confused, had underlying this perfectly logical forms (see Hacker 1988: 64–5). The consequences of this, as set out in his *Tractatus Logico-Philosophicus* (1921; first English translation 1922), inaugurated twentieth-century philosophy's 'linguistic turn' (North 1999: 31). Wittgenstein proposed that, by investigating language as made up of propositions, all meaningful language can be shown to be a function of logic and to do no more than describe the world as it is. What such an analysis revealed is the extent to which a sentence's meaning fits with the world: 'A proposition is a picture of reality. A proposition is a model of reality as we imagine it' (Wittgenstein 1974: § 4.01). What links a proposition and the reality ('facts' in Wittgenstein's terminology) to which it corresponds is logical structure:

> A proposition communicates a situation to us, and so it must be *essentially* connected with the situation. And the connexion is precisely that it is its logical picture . . . It is only in so far as a proposition is logically articulated that it is a picture of a situation. (§§ 4.03, 4.032; emphasis in original)

Rather than worry about what words such as 'God', 'morality' or 'beauty' meant, what their 'fit' with the world was, philosophy could simply ignore these questions as meaningless (§ 6.421):

> Most of the propositions and questions to be found in philosophical works are not false but nonsensical. Consequently we cannot give any answer to questions of this kind, but can only point out that they are

nonsensical. Most of the propositions and questions of philosophers arise from our failure to understand the logic of our language. (§ 4.003)

As Wittgenstein sets out clearly at the beginning of his preface and famously sums up his argument at the end of the *Tractatus* (§ 7): 'what can be said at all can be said clearly, and what we cannot talk about we must pass over in silence' (p. 3). So the central argument of *Tractatus* is that the 'only significant propositions (and hence thoughts) are those which are pictures of reality – that is, which are pictures of how things are in the world' (Grayling 1988: 44). However, of course, this is not to say that Wittgenstein sees religion and ethics as a waste of time; on the contrary, they are 'what is higher' (§ 6.42).

Wittgenstein in the *Tractatus* wishes to solve the problem of language by having it both ways. An identity between word and thing is necessary to make language tell the truth, but the implications of this – that, as Nietzsche realised, words can create new things – is denied. Words sundered from a relation with the facts of the world could be dismissed as 'a source of widespread nonsense and fanaticism' (Berry 2006: 117). However, the difficulty of this position can be seen within the *Tractatus* itself. In its last few pages, despite what he has said before, Wittgenstein indicates in language – in what Grayling calls 'brief and unsystematic remarks' (1988: 47) – something of the content of that silence. Speaking of the will, Wittgenstein claims: 'The world of the happy man is a different one from that of the unhappy man' (§ 6.43). This is very different use of 'world' from the use at beginning of the *Tractatus* – where 'The world is all that is the case' (§ 1).

Wittgenstein's ambiguity in the *Tractatus* over language and its possibilities has of course been noted by many critics, and linked by them to the experimental writing of the period, but an attention to Wittgenstein's understanding of magic of the 1920s and early 1930s is suggestive of another way of reading this ambiguity. Richard Sheppard, in his *Dada-Modernism-Postmodernism* (2000), sees the ambiguity of the *Tractatus* as a doubleness in that it 'both sets out and simultaneously deconstructs' the assumption that language has an 'isomorphic' relation to 'atomic reality' (Sheppard 2000: 105). Sheppard argues that this doubleness, along with the theories of Henri Bergson and Ernest Fenollosa, is an admission that 'the loss of confidence in ordinary syntax, linear logic, and the power of reason to grasp reality in any final sense' (p. 116) is actually a gain, in particular for those radical experimenters with language who celebrate the 'free play of the signifier' (p. 135). For him, Dada poetry distinguishes itself from other, more conservative, kinds of experiment, such as that of Rainer Maria Rilke or F. T. Marinetti, because it joyfully acknowledges 'the arbitrary and mutable nature of the linguistic sign' (p. 139). That this is an accurate description of Dada experiment is contestable (see Wilson 2013) because Sheppard does not consider the existence of a third position; that is, neither a complacent belief in words as descriptors of reality nor an acceptance of the sundering of word and world. It is this third possibility that hovers around the edges of the *Tractatus* and emerges more explicitly in Wittgenstein in the early 1930s.

What is missing from the ostensible argument of the *Tractatus*, then, is not so much magic but a particular attitude to error that would see magical mimesis as productive; that is, the error of using words which do not fit with the world as it is. Michael North puts this, rather than Sheppard's doubleness, at the centre of his rereading of the *Tractatus* beyond its ostensible argument. He sees in the struggles around the translation of the work the central role of misunderstanding that was to become so important to Wittgenstein's thinking about language in the *Philosophical Investigations*. This move from an implicit to an explicit engagement with mistakes and misunderstandings North specifically links to the 'anthropological method' developed by Wittgenstein in the 1930s, and he suggests that his later work looks 'a great deal like armchair anthropology' (North 1999: 32). Rather than the perfect language that seems to be the aim of the *Tractatus*, North argues that Wittgenstein's later method 'suggests that understanding is brought most successfully to the level of reflection *by* misunderstanding' (p. 39; emphasis in original). In the anthropological method, Wittgenstein thinks himself into the position of an anthropologist hearing and experiencing a foreign language, but the language that he is actually considering is his own. The method attempts a place where 'the philosopher is so thoroughly estranged that he can imagine imagining his normal, everyday life as if it were the life of some remote tribe' (p. 41). Despite this acknowledgement of the centrality of an anthropological notion of error in Wittgenstein's thinking about language, North stops on the edge of acknowledging magic as that which would provide a language that is in the world but not just a descriptor of it. What neither Sheppard nor North include in their accounts of the *Tractatus* and its place in Wittgenstein's changing view of language is his engagement in the early 1930s with James Frazer's *The Golden Bough*. North cites Wittgenstein's own acknowledgement that his anthropological method came about through his conversations with the Marxist economist Piero Sraffa, but Wittgenstein's response in the 1930s to the work of James Frazer makes clear the extent to which his own intellectual struggle over language is enmeshed with the period's obsession with magic.

Wittgenstein began reading Frazer's *The Golden Bough* around 1930, and began writing his responses to the work in his manuscript books in the summer of 1931. He then dictated to a typist the greater part of the manuscript books, rearranging and editing his original notes as he went. His preliminary remarks on Frazer in the manuscript books were not, however, transferred to the typed versions; as the editor of Wittgenstein's notes on Frazer laconically notes, 'I think we can see why' (Wittgenstein 1979: v). Wittgenstein's manuscript notes on *The Golden Bough* begin:

> I think now that the right thing would be to begin my book with remarks about metaphysics as a kind of magic.
> But in doing this I must neither speak in defence of magic nor ridicule it. What it is that is deep about magic would be kept. -----
> In this context, in fact, keeping magic out has itself the character of magic.
> For when I began in my earlier book [the *Tractatus*] to talk about the '*world*' (and not about this tree or table), was I trying to do anything except conjure up something of a higher order by my words? (p. v; emphasis in original)

The very 'higher order' which in the *Tractatus* Wittgenstein had asserted was beyond language – it could only be shown, not stated – here is *created* by language. This is different from Sheppard's opposition between language as a perfect fit with the world or language as post-structuralist linguistic autonomy. Language here does not merely denote, it does not even connote, rather it produces the thing it names.

In Wittgenstein's notes on Frazer which were transferred to the typescript version, he acknowledges here too the link between language and magic – 'And magic always rests on the idea of symbolism and of language' (p. 4e). Wittgenstein's consideration of language via Frazer overturns his view of the correspondence between language and the world as set out in the *Tractatus*:

> If we hold it a truism that people take pleasure in imagination, we should remember that this imagination is not like a painted picture or a three-dimensional model, but a complicated structure of heterogeneous elements: words and pictures. We shall then not think of operating with written or oral signs as something to be contrasted with the operation with 'mental images' of the events.
> We must plough over the whole of language. (p. 7e)

In his study of Wittgenstein on Frazer, Brian Clark tries to account philosophically for Wittgenstein's ambiguity toward magic in his *Remarks*. It is certainly true that his notes criticise Frazer for his positivist designation of magic as error, but this is because Wittgenstein sees the attempt to explain magic in language as misconceived (p. 1e). It is language that is the problem, and he does see magic as error when it comes to language (Clark 1999: 125, 128):

> We should distinguish between magical operations and those operations which rest on a false, over-simplified notion of things and processes. For instance, if someone says that the illness is moving from one part of the body to another, or if he takes measures to draw off the illness as though it were a liquid or a temperature. He is then using a false picture, a picture that doesn't fit. (p. 5e)

However, as we have seen, Wittgenstein's notes which were not transferred to the typescript version reveal that it is precisely this error that is crucial, as he will go on to see of mistakes in language in his *Philosophical Investigations*. In the notes on Frazer, we see Wittgenstein struggling with how to acknowledge magic as something other than error – to allow it into the world of philosophy – but at the same time wary of it exceeding what is true in the world.

While Wittgenstein challenges Frazer's designation of error – 'Frazer's account of the magical and religious notions of men is unsatisfactory: it makes these notions appear as *mistakes*' (p. 1e) – what he describes as magic is precisely error according to the *Tractatus* and to the positivism which informs it and was influenced by it. For the *Tractatus*, magic is error in that language can only represent that which exists in the world, but its attempt to make sense of the relation between the word and the world leads it back to magic, hence Wittgenstein's allowing in his manuscript notes that he might have 'conjured' the world in the *Tractatus*, that his words, rather than describing, created or summonsed. The linguistic turn, then, while it intended to rationalise language, to bring language within the remit of scientific methodology and positivist assumptions, instead leads to a confrontation with magic in which magic cannot be dismissed or disavowed, but must be admitted. At the centre of this admission are ghosts. It is the return of the dead, for Frazer, which most clearly shows the magical sense of the relation between language and the world, and it is ghosts who haunt attempts during the period to address the crisis of this relation and to remake it.

The English translation of the *Tractatus* was published by Routledge and Kegan Paul in 1922 in a series – the International Library of Psychology, Philosophy and Scientific Method – edited by C. K. Ogden. The following year, Ogden published his own contribution to the 'linguistic turn' in collaboration with I. A. Richards, *The Meaning of Meaning: A Study of the Influence of Language Upon Thought and of the Science of Symbolism* (1923), in the same series. Ogden and Richards criticise Wittgenstein's work for its 'curtain of mysticism' and for its too easy assumption of the fit between words and things. They argue that Wittgenstein's 'fit' between simple propositions and states of affairs ignores precisely what is of interest to them, that is, the damage done by 'fictions', words – like Russell's unicorns – which stand for things whose existential status is debatable. However, while this critique seems to oppose the positions of Ogden and Richards on one side and Wittgenstein on the other, the place of the word 'ghost' in their works muddies this distinction and suggests again that all 'linguistic turns' lead to an acknowledgement, however unwanted and however resisted, of language as magic.

In the introduction to the first edition of *The Meaning of Meaning*, J. P. Postgate opens the subject of the relation between words and things: 'That a name is in some way implicated with the essence of an object or thing is an error indeed; but an error which, as the authors of this book show, is dangerously alive' (Postgate 1994: xxxi). However, Postgate's example of the complex relation between written and spoken words implicitly admits that even he was not immune to the magic of words: 'Inorganic and fanciful associations attach themselves to words ... There is something eerie in the look of the silent *h* in "ghost"' (p. xxx). The presence of ghosts in the development of the 'linguistic turn' is clear too from the book that followed Postgate's introduction. The work was very influential during the interwar period. In her memoir, Sylvia Beach, a friend of Ogden who introduced him to James Joyce, remembered that in the mid-1920s *The Meaning of Meaning* was 'much in demand at my bookshop' (Beach 1960: 176). Ogden's connections at Cambridge from before the war included Richards, Russell, Wittgenstein and T. E. Hulme, and his work is indeed at the centre of the 'linguistic turn' during the period. Ogden's concerns can be seen as provoked by a sense of the gap between the precision of thought and the vagueness of language, and resulted from the late 1920s on in his development (again in collaboration with Richards) of Basic English, a much reduced version of English which aimed at making it easier for non-native speakers to learn the language, and more grandly, at becoming a universal lingua franca and at reducing conflicts both political and martial through a reduction of intra-linguistic misunderstandings (see Thacker 2006 and Shiach 2007).

While Basic presented itself as a solution to the conflicts and chaos that imprecise language use created in the world, in *The Meaning of Meaning* and in his later essays in his journal *Psyche*, Ogden associates the problems which Basic will solve very explicitly with magic. The aim of *The Meaning of Meaning* is to establish two clear functions of language – the symbolic and the emotive. Any confusion of these two functions, the authors argue, leads to '[m]any notorious controversies in the sciences', but a rigorous demarcation of their separate functions would lead to a resolution of such controversies (Ogden and Richards 1994: xl). At the centre of the misuse of language identified by Ogden and Richards is the confusion between word and thing, a confusion that, as their use of Herbert Spencer and their inclusion of a supplementary essay by Bronislaw Malinowski, 'The Problem of Meaning in Primitive Languages', makes clear, is at the heart of magic. For them, almost all difficulties in language occur because of the assumption that words and things have a direct relation, whereas, they argue, with the exception of a small number of onomatopoeic words, the only direct relations are between words and thoughts, and between thoughts and things (pp. 15ff.). If the relations, real or imputed, between words, things and thoughts can be represented by a triangle, with the points representing each of the above, then among the problems of language the 'fundamental and most prolific fallacy is, in other words, that the base of the triangle ... is filled in' (p. 21) (see Figure 2.1). This is the basis of Ogden's and Richards's critique of

THOUGHT OR REFERENCE

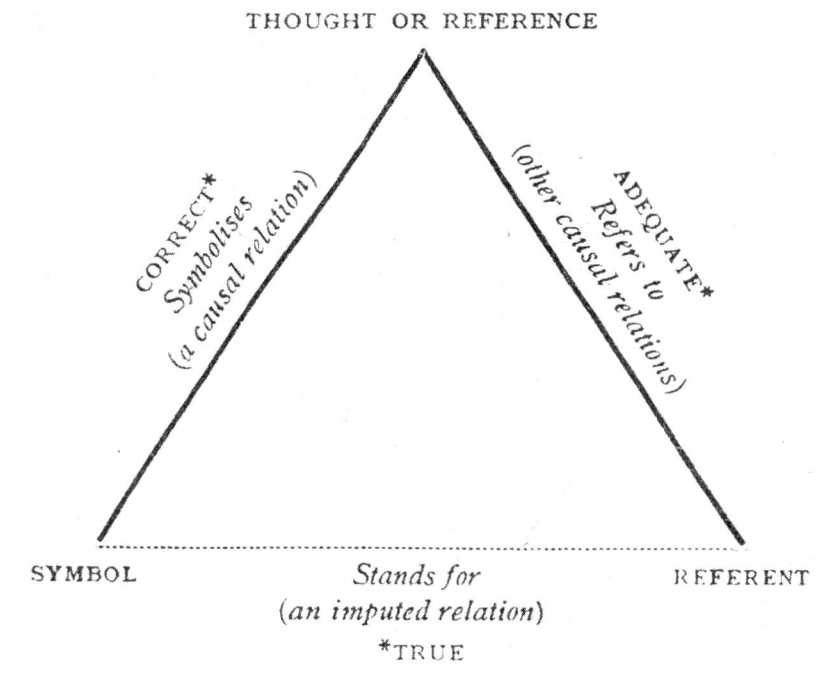

CORRECT*
Symbolises
(a causal relation)

ADEQUATE*
Refers to
(other causal relations)

SYMBOL — *Stands for* — REFERENT
(an imputed relation)
*TRUE

Figure 2.1 The relations between words, things and thoughts
(Ogden and Richards 1994: 16)

Saussure. Whereas more recent accounts of Saussure have focused on his sundering of signs from their referents, they argue that his creation of '*la langue*' in fact depends upon exactly an implicit belief in the unity of words and things. For them, '*la langue*' is a 'fiction' in the same way that 'ghost' is (pp. 8–10).

The second chapter of the first edition of *The Meaning of Meaning*, entitled 'The Power of Words', was written by Ogden alone (on its publishing history, see W. Terrence Gordon 1994a: 33). This lengthy chapter sets out the reasons for this 'prolific fallacy'. Human beings have always, Ogden argues, attributed to words 'occult powers' (Ogden and Richards 1994: 35). In his critique of this, Ogden follows the assessment of magic of Tylor, Frazer and their followers discussed in Chapter 1; this power is dangerous because it is 'the most conservative force in our life' (p. 37). We are forced to use a language that had 'developed to meet the needs of arboreal man' (p. 37) and, as a consequence, we still think like him. Ogden cites numerous examples of such word magic in contemporary, 'civilised' life, from Hegel to the work of Cambridge logicians, from theosophy to the therapies of suggestion, from government propaganda to Jung.

It is in the second chapter of *The Meaning of Meaning* that Ogden first uses the term 'fictions' to describe words which, because they exist, are assumed to denote an object in the world, but in fact denote nothing. This term originates in the work of Jeremy Bentham and, while Ogden had not made a systematic study of Bentham at the time of his work on *The Meaning of Meaning*, he went on to do so in the second half of the 1920s (Terrence Gordon 1994b: vii), and Bentham's ideas about language can be seen as determining in the development of Basic English.

In an article from 1929, 'Ghosts, Fictions, and Incomplete Symbols', Ogden argues for the centrality of the 'Theory of Fictions' in Bentham's thinking, and not just in his work on language. Fictitious entities are, to quote Ogden quoting Bentham in another article in *Psyche* from 1932, 'those necessary *products of the imagination*, without which, unreal as they are, *discourse* could not, scarcely even could *thought*, be carried on, and which, by being *embodied, as it were, in names*, and thus put upon a footing with real ones, have been so apt to be mistaken for real ones' (Ogden 1994: 72; emphasis in original). Bentham has italicised the fictitious entities in his own sentence, making it clear both that they are vital to language but that they need to be recognised for what they are. Indeed both Ogden and Bentham admit that such fictions are vital in producing a language that produces the possibility of human culture, but the problem arises when the fictitious status of these entities is forgotten, when they are mistaken for real entities. In 'Ghosts, Fictions, and Incomplete Symbols', Ogden recounts a number of early experiences given by Bentham to account for his sense of the danger of such fictions. As a child, Bentham endured terrors on account of the usual childish confusion between real and fictitious entities, and again this confusion centres on the (non)existence of ghosts. His grandmother had seen a ghost, and told her young grandson about it, producing a paralysing terror in him. The servants in his grandmother's house got to know of his terror of ghosts and, for them:

> It was a permanent source of amusement to ply me with horrible phantoms in all imaginable shapes ... At Barking [his grandmother's house], in the almost solitude of which so large a portion of my life was passed, every spot that could be made by any means to answer the purpose was the abode of some spectre or group of spectres. (p. 20)

Even as an old man, Bentham still felt the effects of this:

> [T]his subject of ghosts has been among the torments of my life. Even now, when sixty or seventy years have passed over my head since my boyhood received the impressions which my grandmother gave it, though my judgment is wholly free, my imagination is not wholly so. (p. 19)

These early experiences create in Bentham, then, a heightened sense of the ability of language to create that which does not otherwise exist. It is this crucially which Ogden takes from Bentham, which develops his thinking beyond that in *The Meaning of Meaning*, and dominates it for the rest of the interwar period. In an article from *Psyche* in 1928, 'Bentham's Philosophy of As-If', Ogden concludes with the approving use of Bentham's conclusions: 'To language, then – to language alone – it is that fictitious entities owe their existence, – their impossible yet indispensable existence' (Ogden 1994: 16).

While in the *Tractatus*, Wittgenstein suggests that all things beyond this world are beyond articulation, in his *Remarks on Frazer's Golden Bough* he sees as especially significant the fact that Frazer uses the word 'ghosts' (as he does again and again in *The Golden Bough*) to describe primitive fears around the return of the dead. That Frazer uses this word, Wittgenstein believes, should have suggested to the positivist anthropologist that, while we moderns might not believe in ghosts, the fact that we have such a word suggests a language-use compatible with that of the 'savages' (Wittgenstein 1979: 8e):

> I wish to say: nothing shows our kinship to those savages better than the fact that Frazer has to hand a word as familiar to us as 'ghost' or 'shade' to describe the way these people look at things.
>
> ... What is queer in this is not limited to the expressions 'ghost' and 'shade,' and too little is made of the fact that we include the words 'soul' and 'spirit' in our own civilized vocabulary. Compared with this, the fact that we do not believe our soul eats and drinks is minor detail.
>
> A whole mythology is deposited in our language. (p. 10e)

For Wittgenstein here, it is precisely language which, rather than enacting the rationality of scientific method, links modernity to magic: 'And when I read Frazer I keep wanting to say: All these processes, these changes of meaning, – we have them here still in our word-language' (p. 10e). Wittgenstein covertly acknowledges the link between language and ghosts in his *Remarks* in that both exceed modernity's sense of the world. It is this link that makes ghosts, and their return in the séance, such productive subject matter for experimental writers intent on transforming language in order to transform the world.

Ghosts and Experimental Writing

One much debated effect of the *Tractatus*, along with the general anxiety around language in the period of which it is a symptom, was to steer philosophy towards the sciences, via logical positivism, and away from culture (Berry 2006: 117). In the *Tractatus*, however, what lies on the other side of what can be said is not just, famously, silence, but nonsense and the mystical. While the Wittgenstein of the *Tractatus* insists that what cannot be said can only be shown, this grouping of silence, nonsense and the mystical nevertheless indicates clearly what indeed all this has to do with experimental writing. Literary modernism has been defined as a writing that is profoundly troubled by language. Indeed, as we have seen in my discussion of various readings of

Mallarmé, it is argued that it is in writing specifically, in its materiality, that the non-transcendence of language becomes apparent. However, as I have argued, modernist artistic practices do not deny referentiality, but use magic to make such practices possible. At the centre of magic is the collapse of identity between representation and the thing in the world being represented in order to transform the original, not a sundering of representation from the world. While contemporary critics may read such attempts as really an admission of a loss of faith in referentiality, for experimental writers in the first half of the twentieth century magic was important precisely because it offered to ground representation in the world and so to give it power within that world. In his autobiography, Eugene Jolas quotes James Laughlin's admission that experimental writing, while painfully aware of the linguistic crisis which challenged language's ability to describe the world and so threatened to sunder language from the world, needed a different response:

> And what has all this to do with experimental writing? Just this: that the writer, the serious writer, is rendered by his occupation most sensitive to language deficiency. It is not by accident that Stein and Joyce, that Cummings and Jolas, that basic English and surrealism are coeval to a major crisis of civilization. Working intimately with words, the writer becomes aware of their bad habits as well as their persuasive power. (Quoted in Jolas 1998: 115–16)

Post-structuralism is concerned with the bad habits of language, and indeed with its 'persuasive power' as one of its bad habits, but for experimental writers it was precisely the persuasive power of language that needed to be remade, and as we have seen, for Jolas it was magic that would remake it.

Such misreadings of modernist practice as post-structuralist *avant la lettre* abound in modernist criticism since the 1980s, even when, as with Sword, the critics themselves are not paid-up post-structuralists. As Berry argues in his survey of modernist engagements with language, it is eminently possible to see numerous 'Saussurean affinities' in modernist writing, many of them predating Saussure's structuralist work. Prufrock's 'It is impossible to say just what I mean!' is hard to read now without thinking about a Saussurean analysis of the arbitrary relation between signifier and signified. However, it is possible to see in Berry's examples of this a misreading which points us elsewhere. William Carlos Williams's remark that the 'word must be put down for itself, not as a symbol of nature but a part', from *Spring and All* (1923), is quoted as evidence of a modernist tendency to claim linguistic autonomy. This Berry describes as 'treating words themselves as material realities', and again we see a confusion between language as materiality and language as split off from the world (Berry 2006: 117). Williams's words can more convincingly be read as an assertion that language takes its place as part of the world, as having its own agency which can intervene in the world of which it is a part, and change it. The section of the work from which the quotation comes argues against symbolism. It is empty language because it keeps apart the thing itself from the words or images used to represent it. The alternative is a striving to fit word to thing, to make them one:

> Composition is in no essential an escape from life. In fact if it is so it is negligible to the point of insignificance. Whatever 'life' the artist may be forced to lead has no relation to the vitality of his compositions. Such names as Homer, the blind; Scheherazade, who lived under threat – Their compositions have as their excellence an identity with life since they are as actual, as sappy as the leaf of the tree which never moves from one spot. (Williams 1970: 101)

Berry does go on to acknowledge, however, that while these Saussurean readings seem to have purchase, 'the concern with language among English and American modernists probably owed more to Wittgenstein's early philosophy than to linguistics' (Berry 2006: 116–17). Berry sees evidence of this in a suspicion of articulation among numerous modernist characters (p. 117). However, I would argue that while Prufrock and the rest articulate this tendency to the inarticulate, their creators shared with early Wittgenstein a sense of the identity of word and thing which is necessary to creation and which, as we have seen, led both writers and philosopher to magic and to ghosts.

In a lecture from 1953, T. S. Eliot described imagism as the 'starting-point of modern poetry' (Eliot 1978: 58). More recently, imagism has been seen as interesting by numerous critics primarily as a salient example of the materiality of language in modernist thought and practice (Thacker 1990 and 2006). Such materiality, as I have suggested above, is often seen as splitting writing off from the world, as part of modernist aesthetic autonomy. However, if imagism is foundational in terms of modernist poetics, and hence modernist writing as a whole, then one of the things this reveals is the extent to which modernist practice is rooted, not just in the collapse of the word with the thing, but in magical mimesis; that is, that imagism points toward not just perfect description but magical creation. In her defence of imagism in *The Egoist* in 1915, the novelist May Sinclair uses the example of the Eucharist to distinguish the imagists' attitude to language from that of their predecessors:

> The Victorian poets are Protestant. For them the bread and wind are symbols of reality, the body and the blood . . . The Imagists are Catholic; they believe in Transubstantiation. For them the bread and wine are the body and the blood. (Sinclair 1915: 89)

Transubstantiation has historically been the main element of Catholic dogma which has drawn the charge of magic from Protestants. Indeed, one suggested, although probably erroneous, etymology for the term 'hocus-pocus' is in the words of the Latin mass, '*hoc est enim corpus meum*' (this is my body). However, while Timothy Materer has suggested that some of the many sources for the term 'vortex' were esoteric and theosophical (Materer 1979: 15, 20), its predecessor imagism (and Pound's work more generally) has been most often seen as a rejection of the 'slushy' late romanticism evident in the symbolist fascination with the occult. While Materer argues for the centrality of the occult in Pound's work generally, for him imagism presents a problem for this argument (Materer 1995: 46). Modernism has often been defined through reference to its 'hard' and 'soft' varieties, terms which act in part as shorthand for modernism's off/on relation to romanticism. One of the origins of 'hard' modernism generally, and imagism more specifically, is often located in T. E. Hulme's essay 'Romanticism and Classicism'. Here, Hulme contrasts the classicist acknowledgement of boundaries and limits with the romanticist yearning for the infinite and the beyond. These contrasting attitudes produce two different varieties of language. Classicist language is 'hard and dry' (Hulme 1924: 126), its aim is, famously, 'accurate, precise and definite description' (p. 132); romanticist language is damp, and yearns towards a beyond (p. 127). However, the position of imagism here is less certain than its conventional place in literary history allows. In her article on imagism, May Sinclair reverses the terms of Hulme's essay. While he associates his hard, dry, precise language with fancy, and against imagination, Sinclair, in defending the imagists against charges of imitation, contests that, because the creation of images in imagist poems are a unique welding together of word, thing and thought, they must be the products of imagination, and therefore creative rather than merely descriptive:

> the Imagist who *is* an Imagist cannot imitate. It is fancy, not imagination that is concerned with symbols and with imagery. You can analyse its processes. You can also imitate them. But Imagination which alone creates Images is an indivisible act. For each imagination its image is ultimate and unique. (Sinclair 1915: 89)

Hulme's championing of fancy has been seen as leading, in his poetics and his influence on imagism, to an aesthetic of description, whereas Sinclair's contention is that imagism is an aesthetic of creation. In 'Notes on Language and Style', Hulme says 'Nothing new under the sun', his quotation of the much-quoted phrase speaking of and enacting the impossibility of creating beyond what already is (Hulme 1994: 31). However, it is also the case that in these notes this impossibility is not total but an effect of language that can be resisted. While language moves inexorably toward platitude – words become mere 'counters' which are artificially placed over the things they purport to describe – nevertheless, for Hulme, the possibilities for newness and truth are located clearly in poetic language:

> The art of literature consists exactly in this *passage from the Eye to the Voice*. From the wealth of nature to that *thin* shadow of words, that gramophone. The Readers are the people who *see* things and want them expressed. The author is the Voice, or the conjuror who does tricks with that curious rope of letters, which is quite different from real passion and sight.
> The Prose writer drags meaning along with the rope.
> The Poet makes it stand on end and hit you. (p. 31; emphasis in original)

Hulme's use of the magical lexicon here may seem to provide evidence for Simon During's assessment of the relation between experimental writing and magic discussed in Chapter 1. The conjuror only *seems* to produce magical effects. However, the poet produces effects which do not just seem, they have a real existence in the corporeal world, they 'hit you'. Description, then, rather than being the mere imitation suggested by 'fancy', demands a belief that language *can* express 'the wealth of nature' precisely because accurate description *is* creation.

In imagist poetry we can see a movement from a fairly conventional use of metaphorical tropes to exactly an enactment of description as creation, as indeed metaphor as magic. Hulme's own pre-imagist poems often have at their centre a 'like' which carries the burden of poetic meaning. In 'Autumn', the possibility that the speaker's night-time stroll will produce a conventional vision of nature is undermined by the last lines, where the stars are described as having 'white faces like town children' (Hulme 1972: 48). Such a central use of simile continues in many of the poems from the imagist anthologies, but in those poems considered most imagist the explicit 'like' has disappeared, and the poems depend on a closer and closer relation between the two elements that make up a metaphor. We only assume that the first line of Pound's 'In a Station of the Metro' is what is actually seen, and the second line tells us what this is like, because the title of the poem suggests the literal location. But, of course, the 'literal' description of the poem's first line is itself a metaphor. The description of what is actually seen figures the faces as that most fictional of beings, the ghost (Pound 1972: 95).

Hulme's second brief stay at Cambridge coincided with Wittgenstein's arrival there, and both had close ties with C. K. Ogden, the former through the Heretics Club and the *Cambridge Magazine*, the latter, as already discussed, through Russell and the publication of the *Tractatus* (see Thacker 2006: 39–55). Despite their differences, each of the three shares a distrust of generalised words which make great claims for themselves, words such as 'God', 'beauty' and 'truth' (see Hulme 1994: 8), and yet for each, their sense of language as an object of study, their sense of it as a problem, as a thing in itself with 'persuasive force', leads them all to the very thing they have been trying to avoid, language as magic.

In Hulme and Wittgenstein, their attempts to struggle with the nature and status of language lead both to insisting on its visual nature. Andrew Thacker links Wittgenstein's 'picture theory of language', which is at the heart of the argument of the *Tractatus*, to imagism (Thacker 2006: 43). Indeed, he goes further, to suggest that it 'is perhaps not too fanciful to view the *Tractatus* as a form of imagist prose' (p. 46). While in one way this is self-evident, in another it is paradoxical, and this suggests how the focus on the visual, while it is supposed to free both Hulme and Wittgenstein from a language of imprecision and transcendence, takes them to magic. In the *Tractatus* and in Russell's theories, propositional language is as far from poetic language as can be imagined. Such a language denotes the world through its utter identity with the object, whereas poetic language is traditionally seen as connotative, the relation is one of suggestion or association rather than identity. More particularly, poetic language, as conventionally understood, is able to airily speak of that which does not exist – it is language divorced from the world as we know it. However, this transcendental language is more religious than magical according to the distinctions made between them in the early twentieth century. Romanticism is famously 'spilt religion' for Hulme, but that does not mean that the language of classicism is limited to the inert matter of positivism and scientific materialism: 'It would be a mistake to identify the classical view with that of materialism' (Hulme 1924: 117). The animation of nature is precisely what distinguishes magic from religion for Tylor and others. In Hulme and in imagism, the object, the thing, is crucial because it is matter *alive*. In 'Notes on Language and Style', Hulme's aphoristic juxtapositions, like the images of imagist poetry, suggest this truth that cannot be said explicitly, but it is rather demonstrated in concrete things:

> *Visual Poetry*
> Each *word* must be an image *seen*, not a counter.
> That dreadful feeling of cheapness when we contemplate the profusion of words of modern prose.
> The true ideal – that little statue in Paris. (Hulme 1994: 25)

This unity of word and thing which animates the world is central to the sources for Pound's later poetic practice too. While propositional language is conceived by Wittgenstein as pictorial, its visuality has to be literal rather than figurative: 'In order to understand the essential nature of a proposition, we should consider hieroglyphic script, which depicts the facts that it describes' (Wittgenstein 1974: § 4.016). However, in the work of Ernest Fenollosa, the American sinologist whose literary executor Pound became, the identity of word and thing is precisely the point of metaphor. In his essay 'The Chinese Written Character as a Medium for Poetry', edited by Pound and published in 1919, the identity of language with the world, seen most perfectly (according to Fenollosa) in Chinese characters, is what produces the metaphorical. Fenollosa does not struggle with the relations between words, things and thoughts as Hulme, Ogden and Wittgenstein do, because for him thought is not abstract but concerns concrete things; language, thought and the world are indivisible. The abstractions of thought are not separate entities, but are 'folded in concrete things' (Fenollosa and Pound 2008: 47). Crucially for him, the truth of language resides in the sentence, not in the word or the name:

> A true noun, an isolated thing, does not exist in nature. Things are only the terminal points, or rather the meeting points of actions, cross-sections cut through actions, snap-shots. Neither can a pure verb, an abstract motion, be possible in nature. The eye sees noun and verb as one: things in motion, motion in things, and so the Chinese conception tends to represent them. (p. 46)

It is this focus on relation that means that Fenollosa's concrete language is not literal but inherently metaphorical. The relations at the heart of metaphor are inherent in the world, which is constructed through 'homologies, sympathies, and identities' (p. 54). Fenollosa's thinking here is magical, as is acknowledged later on in the essay. Poetry tells the truest truth about the world because its rhetorical structure is identical with that of the world: 'Metaphor, [poetry's] chief device, is at once the substance of nature and of language ... Poetry only does consciously what the primitive races did unconsciously' (p. 54). This focus on relation rather than on the discrete object gives a vitalist slant to Fenollosa's analysis. Verbs, not nouns, become primary, and matter comes alive: 'Like nature, the Chinese words are alive and plastic, because *thing* and *action* are not formally separated' (p. 50).

In the best imagist poetry, and in the work of Pound most obviously influenced by Fenollosa, *Cathay* (1915), there is a very strong sense of what the poem does not say, of what is left out. In 'The Jewel Stairs' Grievance', one of Pound's translations of a poem by the eighth-century Chinese poet Li Po, the speaker is a woman whose lover has failed to appear. In his note to the poem, Pound remarks that the 'poem is especially prized because she utters no direct reproach' (Pound 2001: 136). The silence which surrounds the poem is not, however, the result, as in Wittgenstein, of a delimiting of that which is beyond language. In Fenollosa's terms, if objects in the world are defined by their relation, then any object is in connection with all others. The limited objects of this poetry act as mediums to those which are not in the poetry. The object animated by a language which collapses word and thing is itself in metaphorical relation with the rest of what is.

In Paul Ricoeur's *The Rule of Metaphor*, his analysis of Aristotle ends with the claim that, because of its relation to metaphor, mimesis is not just referentiality. Rather, it serves 'as an *index* for that dimension of reality that does not receive due account in the simple description of that-thing-over-there' (Ricoeur 2003: 48). As I have suggested above, Pound effects the powerful collapse of the elements of metaphor in 'In a Station of the Metro' in part through his description of the faces in the first line as 'apparitions'. Certainly, as Derrida has so famously punned, ghosts are the acme of ontological instability. Their presence in the world perhaps more than any other explodes the limits of a 'simple description of that-thing-over-there'.

While Pound's brief interest in spiritualism during the Stone Cottage years (see Longenbach 1991; Liebregts 2004) gave way to his dismissal of 'Yeats' ghosts', the link between ghosts and the remaking of metaphor in the precise, accurate description inaugurated by Hulme and practised by the imagists is not, as I have already argued, a matter of belief. As Hulme's notes make clear, it is a matter of technique. The difference between the Romantic and the modern does not here consist in a denial of magical belief, but in the latter making it more real:

> The contrast between (i) a firm simple prose, creating in a definite way a fairy story, a story of simple life in the country (in the old country). Here we have the microcosm of poetry. The pieces picked out from which it comes. Sun and sweat and all of them. Physical life and death fairies. And (ii) on the other hand, genteel poetry like Shelley's, which refers in elaborate analogies to the things mentioned in (i).
> Gibbering ghosts and Morris's tales seem *real*, as (i). Transmigration of souls seems a drawing-room thrill, compounded of good-will and long words. (Hulme 1994: 25)

Ghosts, then, haunt thinking during the first half of the twentieth century about what words can do, about how exactly they are connected with the world of people and things. While Hulme claims in 'Notes on Language and Style', 'Dead things not men as the material for art' (p. 27), it is in the particular *mise en scène* of the spiritualist séance that the distinction between them breaks down.

Literary Experiment and the Séance

As I have argued in the Introduction, the séance is a place of magic. What anthropologists of the period keen on establishing distinctions between magic, science and religion were clear about, in a way that undermines the disavowals of practitioners, is the extent to which spiritualism was a magical practice. As James Frazer argued, calling the dead back to the world of the living is the thing most feared and most avoided by 'primitives' because of the magical belief in the identity of word and thing. Spiritualist practice then, at every séance, asserts this identity against the central orthodoxies of modernity. It is the figure of the ghost recalled by the words of the séance that acts out, that incarnates, the agency and power of language. The séance, then, became *the place* for the demonstration of the power of language to create that which is other than the world as it was.

Pericles Lewis has argued that the modernists preferred classical models of interaction with the dead over those of either Christianity or spiritualism, but the distinctions are not so clear, and early twentieth-century spiritualism and psychical research made much of the link between classical *apophrades* and their own practice (Lewis 2010: 172; see Myers 1883: especially 76ff.). It was difficult to consider one without the other, however distressing that may have been for many classicists. All of those modernists that Lewis cites, while certainly engaging with classical models, also engage with the séance, and often depict them in their novels. While these depictions are usually in part parodic, and certainly almost always show an ambiguous attitude toward the séance, they are there because experimental writing and the séance both depend on magical language. The séance stands thematically for what is happening formally in modernist literary experiment. The return of the dead – ghosts – are the most powerful enactment of the ability of language to create.

Lewis reads *À la recherche du temps perdu* (1913–27) as a, for him, familiar modernist remaking of religious experience. He acknowledges the importance of magic for Proust – his 'totemic distribution of narrative force' and his animation of objects (Lewis 2010: 83, 104ff.) – but sees magic as a pre-Christian religion, rather than part of a contemporary debate about what distinguishes magic from religion: 'Whereas Durkheim excludes magic from religious life, Proust finds in magic and in animistic theories of the soul more authentic forms of religious experience than in the empty structures offered by religious organizations and social sects' (p. 86). However, Lewis later acknowledges that the centrality of magic for Proust does involve a distinction between magic and religion – 'for Proust, art is closer to magic than to religion' (p. 104) – but the possible consequences of this are not followed through. What Lewis also does not notice in Proust is the link between magic, the return of the loved one after death and *writing*. Lewis is of course correct that contact with the dead is at the heart of Proust's novel, but he reads Proust's treatment of actually existing spiritualism as dismissive. However, formally Proust's novel insists again and again on language as creating the world. As Lewis notes, on the death of the writer Bergotte, the narrator is certain that 'experiments in spiritualism offer us no more proof than the dogmas of religion that the soul survives death', but while Lewis notes a number of the other things that the narrator suggests as substitute evidences for survival, he does not mention the centrality of artistic creation to this. The narrator argues that, among other things, it is artistic scrupulousness that provides evidence for immortality and connection to the world of the dead. Nothing in this world provides a reason for 'an atheist artist to consider himself obliged to begin over again a score of times a piece of work the admiration aroused by which will matter little to his worm-eaten body' (Proust 1989, vol. 3: 186). For Proust, practising a certain sort of writing, a technical scrupulousness, is a magic that both returns the dead and connects us to their world. While Proust's narrator suggests that the belief that 'one gives a thing real existence by giving it a name' (vol. 1, p. 98) is confined to childhood, later the relation between the existence of things and objects is made clearer to him. While walking the Guermantes Way with his grandfather, the narrator, despairing of ever achieving a vocation as a writer, is pleased to be distracted from his hopeless thoughts:

> Then, quite independently of all these literary preoccupations and in no way connected with them, suddenly a roof, a gleam of sunlight on a stone, the smell of a path would make me stop still, to enjoy the special pleasure that each of them gave me, and also because they appeared to be concealing, beyond what my eyes could see, something which they invited me to come and take but which despite all my efforts I never managed to discover. (vol. 1, pp. 194–5)

While the narrator assures the reader that these experiences could in no way 'restore the hope I had lost of succeeding one day in becoming an author and poet, for each of them was associated with some material object devoid of intellectual value and suggesting no abstract truth' (p. 195), a few pages later both the narrator and the reader learn that this is far from the case. Being given a lift home from a walk in a neighbour's carriage, the narrator sees again the objects that had produced such effects in him, and attempts to capture that effect in words, though still resisting the truth about the power of these impressions:

> Without admitting to myself that what lay hidden behind the steeples of Martinville must be something analogous to a pretty phrase, since it was in the form of words which gave me pleasure that it had appeared to me, I borrowed a pencil and some paper from the doctor . . . (p. 197)

Later, the links between the power of words, artistic experiment and the séance are suggested in part of Swann's story. Swann is enraptured by a phrase in a sonata by the composer Vinteuil, and sees in it an expression of his love for Odette. The narrator describes Vinteuil's phrase as 'supernatural' (vol. 1, p. 381), and Swann sees Vinteuil's experiment as 'discovering the secret laws that govern an unknown force, driving, across a region unexplored, towards the one possible goal, the invisible team in which he has placed his trust and which he may never discern' (p. 382). The body of the violinist is possessed by the phrase 'like a medium's' (p. 383) and during the performance a dazzled *comtesse* confides to Swann that 'I've never seen anything to beat it . . . since the table-turning!' (p. 384). While Swann is amused by this, he 'perhaps also found an underlying sense' (p. 384). Later, when he learns at last from Odette that she had had erotic experiences with women 'two or three times', he marvels that these words – 'nothing more than words, words uttered in the air, at a distance' (p. 395) – could so lacerate his heart, and remembers 'instinctively' the remarks that linked Vinteuil's musical phrase to table-turning. This link is not explained by Proust's narrator; neither the narrator nor Swann want to fully articulate the relation between the power of words, artistic experiment and the séance, but this is the link which *produces* Proust's novel. It is unspoken because the novel itself is the testament to it.

A similar relation between narrative silence, thematic rejection and formal enactment can be read in Thomas Mann's *The Magic Mountain* (1924). The *mise en scène* of the novel – the sanatorium on the mountain – is established as a topsy-turvy underworld, drawing on classical allusions. When he arrives at the sanatorium to visit his cousin, Hans Castorp is compared by Settembrini to Odysseus descending to Hades: 'You are bold indeed, thus to descend into these depths peopled by the vacant and idle dead—' (Mann 1983: 57). Later, of course, Hans takes part in two séances, related in the section entitled 'Highly Questionable'. During the first séance, the narrator tells us, those involved are aware that any phenomena would be the result of 'an unclean traffic with their own natures, a fearsome prying into unfamiliar regions of themselves', and that using the séance to contact the dead was little more than 'for form's sake' (p. 661). Very soon, the phenomena of the séance outstrip their expectation, and they seem to contact the medium's spirit guide, who tells them that in life he was a poet. The narrator maintains that still the 'manifestations' came from 'the uncharted regions of their own inner, their subjective selves' (p. 662). The narrator, who links the world of the magic mountain to the world of the reader, the word to the world, repeats the 'truth' that the manifestations are performances. When, during the second séance attended by Hans, the sitters are asked which 'departed' person they would like to contact, they are all uneasy, reluctant to speak the name, even though, as the narrator tells us, 'it was here simply a question not of an actual return, but merely a theatrical staging of one' (p. 675). It is Hans who eventually speaks a name, 'in a husky voice', the name of his cousin, Joachim Ziemssen. However, the outcome of this second séance is a vision of Hans's cousin whose status, without comment from the narrator, is highly ambiguous. Hans does see Joachim, and whispers 'Forgive me' in response, but it is impossible to know whether this response is directed to the ghostly presence of Joachim, or to the still absent Joachim, whose memory has been sullied by Hans's participation in base and fraudulent goings-on (on the links between this experience and the materialities of film, see Chapter 5). On this the narrator is mute, but elsewhere the ability of storytelling to produce such magical effects is admitted. In a discussion of time and its relation to narrative, the narrator eventually concludes that, while narrative is inseparable from the flow of time, like music, unlike music 'the contentual time of a story can shrink its actual time out of all measure' (p. 542). In these cases, where the time of the narrative is radically different from the time of its content, 'the story practises a hermetical magic', which the narrator likens to the experience of opium dreams (p. 542). This image returns at the very end of the novel as the narrator says goodbye to Hans on the battlefield of the First World War: 'Your tale is told. We have told it to the end, and it was neither short nor long, but hermetic' (p. 715). The séance then acts out what cannot be fully said in the narrative, but which the narrative fully contains, that is, that fictionality operates via a narrator who conventionally unifies word and world, and who in experimental writing does this not through imitation but magic.

James Joyce has always been seen as a sceptic, as more interested in the magic of everyday than with a Yeatsian traffic with the other side. As Pericles Lewis has claimed, Joyce 'offers perhaps the best candidate for interpreting the modernist novel as essentially secular' (Lewis 2010: 177) and cultural and literary historians interested in spiritualism and modernism have on the whole steered clear of reading his work in relation to it. Some critics have read Joyce in relation to theosophy, but with sometimes strange results because of their desire to protect Joyce from the embarrassment of contagion. Len Platt has argued that Joyce's engagement with theosophy in *Finnegans Wake* is deeply critical, because theosophy 'demonstrated the irrationality of the modern, and the turn that contemporaneity had taken away from the originary egalitarian instincts of a progressive order' (Platt 2007: 97). Platt rejects the idea that theosophy is representative of modernity (p. 100), and argues that *Finnegans Wake* critiques it for its betrayal of the Enlightenment project, for its status as 'rationalism gone wrong' (p. 103). However, Platt also acknowledges that Joyce's work shares much with theosophy – 'theosophy is embedded in the detail of the *Wake*' (p. 106) – but sees this primarily in terms of content, of '[r]eferences and allusions' (p. 108), rather than form. Platt does not really consider the relation between theosophy and the form of *Finnegans Wake*, surely its most crucial aspect. Later he does acknowledge that theosophy and Madame Blavatsky's *Isis Unveiled* have a '"structural" significance on [*sic*] the wake' (p. 112), but insists this is purely ironic. Platt sees that correspondence, the underlying formal principle of *Finnegans Wake*, could well come from Blavatsky's work and theosophy more generally, but continues to insist nevertheless that Joyce's engagement with theosophy is purely dismissive, that it is part of the *Wake*'s 'rationalist assault on modern irrationality' (p. 116). This desire to protect Joyce from the silliness of theosophy results in *Finnegans Wake* being held up as 'rationalist', a very odd place to end.

Joyce's formal experiment must be at the centre of our critical reading of him. I am not claiming that Joyce entertained any occult beliefs per se; I am claiming that his commitment to remaking (the English) language made inevitable a practice of language as magic, for all the reasons discussed above. As for Wittgenstein, Ogden and Hulme, this is nowhere better demonstrated than in writing of the return of the dead in the séance. While Joyce is a sceptic, what his writing demonstrates is the magical word at the heart of literary experiment and that language is so powerful that it can make ghosts. In particular, the function of the séance in Joyce can be seen, not solely as a parody of irrational beliefs, but as evidence that Joyce too, in his exploration of language and linguistic experiment, arrived at a magical mimesis.

In *Dialectic of Enlightenment* (1944), Adorno and Horkheimer read the *Odyssey* as demonstrating the dialectical dynamic between myth and enlightenment, and as evidence that such a dynamic was present at the inauguration of European culture. Odysseus is a hero because of his cunning, and cunning is that which both uses and denies the imbrication of that which is ostensibly in opposition. One of the central enactments of this for Adorno and Horkheimer is Odysseus's encounter with Polyphemus the Cyclops in Book 9. For the older mythic world, and the representatives of it who impede Odysseus on his journey home, word and object are one. Odysseus, as rational man, knows that this is not the case. He defeats the Cyclops with the duplicity of cunning – he knows that this is not the case but acts as if it is. Odysseus tells the Cyclops that his name is 'Nobody', '*Udeis*', which in Greek sounds very like Odysseus. Puns reveal that phonemes have no automatic relation to their referents – the same sounds have different referents – but Cyclops, with his assumption of the identity between word and object, is excluded from the joke. When he tells his fellow Cyclops who rush to his aid that 'Nobody' has blinded him, they return to their caves, assuming that he is merely suffering from a sickness sent by Zeus. Through Odysseus's trick:

> a change is effected in the historical situation of language, which begins its transition to description . . . The sphere of ideas to which the decrees of fate irrevocably executed by the figures of myth belong, is still innocent of the distinction between word and object. The word must have direct power over fact; expression and intention penetrate one another. Cunning consists in exploiting the distinction. The word is emphasized, in order to change the actuality. In this way, consciousness of intention arises: in his distress, Odysseus becomes aware of the dualism, for he learns that the same word can mean different things. (Adorno and Horkheimer 1997: 60)

Odysseus acts as if the identity of words and things were true while knowing that it is not the case. Joyce's scepticism is no bar to him writing as if words were magical in order to carry out the revolution of the word. In writerly practice, Joyce is not a sceptic, and indeed, in *Ulysses* the centrality of the magical word in experimental writing is enacted precisely through the séance.

A theosophically inflected spiritualism, we should now not be surprised to learn, makes its strange appearance in the 'Cyclops' episode, the episode that has been seen 'as marking a turning point in Joyce's literary practice' (Tadié 2003: 47). The technic of 'Cyclops', as given by Joyce to Stuart Gilbert for the latter's 1930 reference work on *Ulysses*, is gigantism. The episode's narrator, who is never named, is an ordinary Dublin man, rather gruff, 'simple and bibulous', as Gilbert has it (Gilbert 1952: 259), whose concerns are, in the main, casting a suspicious eye over his fellow drinkers, reporting their conversation, and displaying as many synonymous terms for the acceptance of a drink as possible. This aspect of the book is ordinary, quotidian, if not downright vulgar and acerbicly factual. The 'gigantism' of Gilbert's schema comes in interpolated episodes which re-narrate the action or the subject of the drinkers' conversation in hyberbolic language and style. So, in the first instance of this, the narrator, having met a friend, Joe Hynes, on the street, has just related to him his latest job as a collector of bad debts in an earthy vernacular, chasing one 'old plumber named Geraghty ... that's the most notorious bloody robber you'd meet in a day's walk and the face on him all pockmarks would hold a shower of rain' (Joyce 2000a: 377). This narration is then repeated in legalese, contrasting greatly with the first narrator's pithy precision. The narrator and Joe then decide to go to Barney Kiernan's pub for a drink, and the control of the narrative switches to the second narrator, the narrator of gigantism, which begins as follows: 'In Inisfail the fair there lies a land, the land of holy Michan. There rises a watchtower behed of men afar. There sleep the mighty dead as in life they slept, warriors and princes of high renown. A pleasant land it is in sooth of murmuring waters, fishful streams where sport the gunnard, the plaice, the roach, the halibut, the gibbed haddock ...' (pp. 378–9), and so it goes on listing, in the language of the Irish revivalists, the abundance and plenitude of a past time, brought freely to 'a shining palace' to the chieftain, O'Connell Fitzsimon. The purpose of this passage seems to be to effect a contrast with the present, as represented by the preceding anecdote of the first narrator. While the 'extremely large wains' (p. 379) of time past bring 'strawberries fit for princes' (p. 380), among many other things, graciously to their chieftan, the plumber Geraghty is a mean and small-minded thief. Of course, the 'past' of the passage is ridiculously idealised, and it is this vision of the past that is really being undercut here, not the quotidian events of Dublin in 1904.

All the subsequent interpolations bar one follow this pattern – that is, a re-narrating of events in the world of the first narrator and Barney Kiernon's, or of events of which the drinkers are speaking, idealised, hyperbolised in the dreamy language of the Irish revival, in legalese, or later in the more cynical hyperbole of the provincial newspaper (pp. 396, 410, 412), or the even more cynical puffed rhetoric of the House of Commons (p. 409). What seems to be happening in each is a construction of the mock-heroic, particularly, in this episode so concerned with Irish politics, a parody of claims to greatness and heroism at this late point in Ireland's history. The material of the episode is re-inscripted, re-covered with conventionalised language. Joyce mocks the ability of these kinds of language to connect with and describe the world. However, this is not Joyce as a Saussurean, as insisting that language per se does not connect with the world. Thomas Docherty has argued that the 'wrong turn' in Joyce criticism has been to read him in relation to Saussure rather than in relation to Fenollosa's linguistic theories. While Docherty suggests that in Joyce words are still sundered from reference – what we get is 'the word in itself, without reference but with volume' (Docherty 2003: 123) – as my reading of Fenollosa above suggests, his theories centre on reconnecting language and world. This question of the structuralist or post-structuralist reading of modernist experiment is at the heart of any reading of the latter's relation to the occult. For Helen Sword, as we have seen, modernism's central concern is the inability of language to communicate effectively, its sense of the troubling gap between words and the world, and this accounts for its relation to the occult. She sees in early twentieth-century spiritualist practice a shift around the expectations of communication. Rather than a reaching for the transcendent, 'modernist-era spiritualists seem almost to revel in the fact that the dead, like us, are mired in the materiality of the written word' and Sword sees the early twentieth-century mediumistic practices she discusses as enacting this materiality (Sword 2002: 20). It is this shift in spiritualism which accounts, for Sword, for the modernist attraction to it, however embarrassed and disavowed that attraction may have been. While, as we have seen, Sword criticises the appropriation for purely metaphorical use of the tropes of spiritualism by her more theoretically inclined peers, this account of the attractions of spiritualism seems to suggest a strong continuity between the modernist work she looks at and the post-structuralist borrowings she critiques.

Indeed, Sword's fundamental conception of language derives from post-structuralism. She suggests that accounts of literary activities in the afterlife communicated via mediums such as Hester Dowden 'call into question the timeless literary values they seem to celebrate, foregrounding the contingent nature of signification and the stubborn materiality of language' (p. 12). A little later she claims that the mediumistic practices she is considering enact 'the disintegration of the speaking self in a complex, heteroglossal, stubbornly materialistic modern world' (p. 31). While Sword does not say what exactly she means by materiality, its most usual recent use in criticism is to suggest that, rather having a direct relation with the objects to which they ostensibly refer, words in fact have relations, continually unstable and always in question, only with other words. Post-structuralist language is one sealed off from the world, able finally to speak only about itself. Sword's tacit accommodation with post-structuralism can be seen later on, when she argues that the spiritualist medium:

> anticipates the central innovations not only of modernist literary aesthetics – its fragmentations of identity, subversions of literary tradition, and celebrations of intersubjectivity – but of postmodern textual criticism as well, which teaches that literary masterpieces once considered eternal and immutable are in fact indeterminate, endlessly malleable, and circumscribed by contingencies of production, editing, reception, and interpretation. (pp. 23–4)

While Sword's reading suggests that modernism and post-structuralism see similar attractions in spiritualism and the séance and make similar uses of its tropes, one with justification and the other without, my reading of the use of the séance by modernists suggests otherwise. Here is a materiality of representation not in the post-structuralist sense used by Sword – where materiality denotes an autonomy from the idea of reference – but in a sense that dispenses with the need for such a distinction.

While most of the interpolated sections in 'Cyclops', then, demonstrate the failure of various kinds of language to represent the world, in one section, the relation between the events of the episode as narrated by the first narrator and their hyperbolic retelling is not so straightforward, and it is in this episode that we can see Joyce using the séance to insist that language connects with the world in order to create and transform. Towards the beginning of the 'Cyclops' episode, Alf Bergan enters Barney Kiernon's and claims to have just seen Paddy Dignam on the street. The others round the bar tell him that Dignam is dead and has been buried that morning, as the reader well knows, his funeral having been narrated in 'Hades', episode 6 of *Ulysses*.

> – Dead! says Alf. He is no more dead than you are.
> – Maybe so, says Joe. They took the liberty of burying him this morning anyhow.
> (Joyce 2000a: 388)

Alf is, as the narrator tells us, 'what you might call flabbergasted' (p. 388). Immediately following this another interpolation begins, a parodic narration of a theosophically inclined séance, with its toolkit of coloured auras, pseudo-eastern philosophy, neologisms and nonsense. Paddy Dignam returns to the bar to speak with his friends and pass on messages from beyond. The parody exists in the attention drawn to the banal and tedious nature of the séance, with its message of lost boots and request for a drink of buttermilk:

> Interrogated as to whether life there resembled our experience in the flesh he stated that he had heard from more favoured beings now in the spirit

that their abodes were equipped with every modern home comfort such as tālāfānā, ālāvātār, hātākāldā, wātāklāsāt and that the highest adepts were steeped in waves of volupcy of the very purest nature. (p. 389)

The beyond here is a thinly veiled version of the here and now, its concentration on domestic amenities making it little more than an upmarket hotel, and testament to the restricted desire and imagination of the sitters. Joyce's attitude to spiritualism here matches that of nearly all of the central Anglo-American modernists: the quotidian corporeality of Madame Sosostris with her bad cold in *The Waste Land*; the *Four Quartets*' comparison between communication with spirits and the vocation of the saint 'to apprehend / The point of intersection of the timeless / With time', in which the saint clearly comes off better (Eliot 1985: 212); Pound's dismissal of Yeats's ghosts; Woolf's linking of communication with the dead via spiritualism with the lower classes and artistic failure (see Woolf 1988: 237 on the return of Katherine Mansfield's ghost). So, spiritualism is linked with venality, credulity, stupidity, vulgarity. Indeed, for Eliot in *Four Quartets*, magical thinking seems to be a kind of shorthand for all of the degradations of mass culture: 'all these are / usual / Pastimes and drugs, and features of the press' (Eliot 1985: 212). In this context, Joyce's parody here may seem straightforward enough. In a novel obsessed with the dead, he is here obviously distancing himself from spiritualist practices and beliefs. However, this reading does not notice clearly enough the very technic of the episode, that is the way it makes its experiment. The series of 'gigantic' interpolations throughout 'Cyclops' all foreground the relation between precisely the world and the word. They re-narrate in hyperbolic language the actions or topics of conversation of the Dubliners in Barney Kiernan's bar and show the failure of these languages to connect with the world. This interpolation does not work in the same way. While the drinkers talk about Paddy and his death because of Alf Bergan's mistaken belief that he had just seen Paddy on the street, the substance of their conversation is that Paddy has *not* returned and could not have been on the street. While Joe Hynes sardonically answers Alf's insistence that he has just seen Paddy by saying 'You saw his ghost then' (p. 388), there is no real suggestion that Dignam has returned; his tone is sarcastic. What is asserted in the conversation is his *absence*, not his presence. This interpolation has a different relation to the world of the bar then from each of the other interpolations in the 'Cyclops' episode. So formally, quite apart from its subject matter, the interpolation speaks of absence not of presence, that is, what is not happening in the bar, rather than what is. Of course, the calling up of what is absent is exactly the purpose of a séance. The interpolation's relation to the main narration acts out spiritualism's purpose. Joyce here uses spiritualism formally in a way that is not parodic. While his representation of the contents of the séance *is* parodic, his repetition of the séance's function is not. What the interpolated séance suggests is that there is a relation between spiritualism and its return of the dead and Joyce's sense of the relation between writing and the world. The hyperbole of the other interpolations mocks any language which constructs the quotidian present as conventionally heroic, not from an Eliotic deprecation of the present, but to assert the idea that the present is enough, that it has its own, other heroism. What Paddy's séance suggests, though, is not the extent to which all language falsifies the event or even the extent to which a remade language can recreate the real as extraordinary, but that the present moment lacks something, and that lack is compensated for in writing; language has the ability to create above and beyond the material world precisely because of its particular relation to it. The 'tālāfānā, ālāvātār, hātākāldā, wātāklāsāt' are, of course, parodic. The inherent joke in the change in the orthography of these words is the paucity of this particular example of spiritualist practice in using language to express that which is beyond what is – the beyond is nothing but a badly disguised version of the banality of the here and now. But *structurally* what this episode speaks is exactly the possibilities of language to create beyond the world as it is.

Eugene Jolas saw Joyce's 'Work in Progress' as the greatest example of his own belief that magic was both the modus operandi and final aim of experimental writing. As is clear in Jolas' editorials on Joyce, the focus on language and the desire to remake language to meet the contemporary situation did not have magic as an optional extra, but was for him the very definition of experimental writing:

> By publishing and defending Work in Progress, the new creation of James Joyce, *transition* established a basis for a literary insurrection that included a radically new conception of the processes of consciousness and of the development of language. Like the second Faust, Work in Progress will, I am very sure, continue to baffle the non-visionary minds, although the immensity of its plan and execution as well as the magnificence of its humor and cosmic imagination cannot fail to interest those who do not see in creative expression merely a means for communication ... (Jolas 1930: 14)

In *Ulysses*, as I have argued via the reading of the Paddy Dignam séance, this is particularly clear in those episodes where the language, instead of being hyper-real, as in the use of stream of consciousness in the earlier episodes, starts to split apart from the 'real' of the scene, and in these moments very often the *mise en scène* of the séance returns. 'Circe', whose 'art' is given by Stuart Gilbert as 'magic', is an exploration of the link between what exists and what does not. The hallucinations experienced by Bloom and Stephen are hyperbolic representations of their usually hidden fears and desires. The form of the episode – the play – links it to the séance in its focus on dialogue and performance, as does the hallucinated return of various dead. However, while a focus on the séance as performance was a regular feature of the debunkers of spiritualism, Joyce's pastiche of the conventions of the symbolist play undermine such easy demarcations between the real and the not-real. The hallucinated events of 'Circe' are rooted in the real, but transform the latter into the terrifying, the pleasurable and the consolatory. The relation between words and the world is iterated formally in the magical hyperbole and in the words of the players: 'In the beginning was the word, in the end the world without end' (p. 626). It is difficult not to read Stephen's drunken 'Kings and Unicorns!' (p. 689) as a disparaging reference to Bertrand Russell's anxious attempts to stave off the logical impossibilities of mythical creatures and 'the present king of France'. As magic insists and the séance enacts, language creates because it part of the world, because it is one with the things it describes. As William Carlos Williams argued, words are not 'a symbol of nature but a part' (Williams 1970: 102).

The 'gigantism' of 'Cyclops' marks the split between event and representation, and is itself expanded further, of course, in *Finnegans Wake*, both in its subject of the slumbering giant and its linguistic excess. Joyce credited Harriet Weaver with the giant theme of his new work, but it is clearly a subject that had interested him in the writing of *Ulysses* too. A postcard from Joyce to Sylvia Beach in 1924, from a trip to see the menhirs at Carnac, spoke of 'Cyclops' (Beach 1960: 189).

Book III.iii of *Finnegans Wake* is now usually seen as containing a séance, as the interrogators' questions are answered by a range of figures speaking through the mediumistic body of Yawn. Jean-Michel Rabaté has linked this section of the *Wake* to 'Circe'; both recapitulate the themes of the sections which have preceded them through 'the densest climax of the dream', and of course the ghost, and the séance in its attempts to call ghosts forth, have been seen by many as powerful tropes of history as recurrence and repetition (Rabaté 2007: 385). Indeed, it has been suggested by Jane Lewty that the *Wake* in its entirety can be read as a séance; as the dreamer sleeps, the disembodied voices of EVP are produced by the radio in his room:

> I contest that *Finnegans Wake* is a continual séance, conducted through a stationary figure whose 'Hearsomness [. . .] facilitates the whole of the polis' (FW 23, 14–15). A *necropolis*, where all the speakers are dead but amplified, accessed and energised through a wireless set. (Lewty 2002: 112)

Lewty convincingly amasses spiritualist themes from III.iii, along with instances of Joyce's contact with spiritualist thinking and practice, but Joyce's language in the *Wake* is not a screen that separates the reader from the truth taking place beyond it. As the reader of the *Wake* has been told almost from the beginning, Joyce's writing in his 'Work in Progress' 'is not *about* something; *it is that something itself* (Beckett 1983: 27; emphasis in original). Lewty suggests that *Finnegans Wake* turns readers into 'psychical researchers', but our task as its readers is not to investigate strange phenomena with the aim of providing a rational, scientifically valid account of them (Lewty 2002: 156). The magic of Joyce's language consists in it *being* the world, not separating us from it. If one of the many phrases for which HCE stands is indeed *hoc corpus est* (see Lewis 2010: 179), Joyce retains enough of his Catholic heritage to insist on the truth of transubstantiation. Thing and representation are one in Joyce – this is what, for Jolas, makes 'Work in Progress' the acme of experiment – and the unity of the two is the basis of the ability of magical mimesis to create and transform the original. In the next chapter I will consider how the insistence on language as sound in *Finnegans Wake* suggests further links between Joyce and the magic inherent in theosophical belief and practice.

3

A 'SUBTLE METAMORPHOSIS': SOUND, MIMESIS AND TRANSFORMATION

'Lokk for himself and see the old butte new. Dbln. W.K.O.O. Hear?'
James Joyce, *Finnegans Wake* (13.13–14)

'[V]ibration in the air is sure to awaken corresponding powers, union with which produces good or bad results, as the case may be.'
Madame Blavatsky, *The Secret Doctrine*, 1888

If the experiment of *Finnegans Wake* is the harnessing of a magical understanding of transformation through a renewed relation between word and world, one of the central mechanisms for this transformation is sound. The importance of sound in *Finnegans Wake* is well known, and has been insisted on from Beckett's famous assertion in 'Dante . . . Bruno. Vico . . . Joyce' (1929) that Joyce's novel is not to be read, or rather is not only to be read; it 'is to be looked at and listened to' (Beckett 1983: 27). Another early admirer, Sergei Eisenstein, went further, suggesting that sound is at the heart of the transformatory power of the novel: 'The effect at times is astounding, but the price paid is the entire dissolution of the very foundation of literary diction, the entire decomposition of literary method itself; for the lay reader the text has been turned into abracadabra' (Eisenstein 1977f: 185). The word 'abracadabra' is not a description of a particular referent, but a release of the power of sound in order to bring something about, to effect change. It must be spoken to have its effects, and it is its sound and not its referential meaning which produces them. The implications of Eisenstein's reading of *Finnegans Wake* is suggestive of the extent to which sound is involved in the limits and possibilities of experiment during the period more widely, and the extent to which that involvement is founded on sound as magic. In this chapter I want to extend my reading of Joyce via the contemporary occult to suggest that in *Finnegans Wake* Joyce's experiment is made possible by using a theosophical understanding of sound which, unlike theosophy itself, believes in the transforming effects of sound without reservation. In other words, Joyce's experiment works, not in its disavowal of theosophical beliefs around sound or its attempt to put in their place a 'rationalist assault on modern irrationality' (Platt 2007: 116), but to the extent that in its form it believes in the magic of sound even more than the theosophists and spiritualists. I will first look at the status of sound in experimental writing during the period to show both its centrality and its difficulty, and then go on to look in detail at its place in theosophical beliefs. My assertion that in *Finnegans Wake* we see the transformatory powers of sound so strongly claimed by the contemporary occult taken seriously, but then taken beyond the conservative limits of the occult, will be framed by a reading of another novel which deals in the relation between sound, experiment and transformation, Thomas Mann's *Dr Faustus* (1947). Mann's novel admits the need for magical transformation in order to make artistic experiment possible, and sees this most powerfully in music's use of sound, but is paralysed by the possibilities that such transformations may bring what is unwelcome into the world. Mann sees the need for experiment and all it implies, but also links the transformations of aesthetic experiment to the horrors of the political experiment of National Socialism. Joyce, on the other hand, uses as a model for transformation an idea of unceasing change that does not rest after the first 'abracadabra'. Transformation for Joyce does not end in fixity, but is continuous.

Experimental Writing and the Problem of Sound

As we have seen in Chapter 2, for Hulme and the poetry shaped and influenced by him, while poetry asserted its power to create and transform by returning the dead, what it seemed to move away from was that other element of the spiritualist séance, sound. Steven Connor has argued that the nineteenth-century séance came to privilege the phenomena of voice over all other (Connor 2000), and while this rather ignores the power of the other magical phenomena associated with the séance, it is certainly the case that it was more often the voice that called the dead back, not writing. However, in 'Notes on Language and Style', Hulme's images for what language, and especially poetry, should be again and again privilege sight and touch over hearing: 'With perfect style, the solid leather for reading, each sentence should be a lump, a piece of clay, a vision seen; rather, a wall touched with soft fingers' (Hulme 1994: 25). Where the sound of language is acknowledged, again as we have seen in Chapter 2, it is as a falling away '[f]rom the wealth of nature to that *thin* shadow of words, that gramophone' (Hulme 1994: 31; emphasis in the original). Visuality, plasticity, and sculptural forms were used in the resuscitation of poetry, so transforming it from a 'thin shadow' to a thing of flesh and substance (on the link between this and other aspects of occult magic, see Chapter 5). While Pound begins his 'Vorticism' (1914) by saying that he supposes that the claims that all art works as music does are 'self-evident', his apologia for the poetry associated with vorticism marks its distance from French experiment of the late nineteenth century in that to which it aspires. The poetry he defends in 'Imagisme' and 'Vorticism' has an 'inner relation' not with music but with 'modern paintings and sculpture' (Pound 1916: 94, 95). For Pound and Hulme, the visual and plastic arts are used to give poetry a substance, a body that can be seen and touched. The unity of word and thing is asserted, not by linking poetry with the conventional representational possibilities of the visual arts, but by associating it with the avant-garde's insistence on the primacy of the material of art, Pound's 'primary pigment' (p. 101). Pound links experiment in poetry to experiment in the plastic arts which foregrounds material existence, which sees the work as not just using colour and form, but as about them. Once colour is admitted as the point of a painting, 'you let in nature and truth and abundance and cubism and Kandinsky, and the lot of us' (p. 98).

However, it is of course the case that Pound was deeply engaged in sound as music, attempting in 'I Gather the Limbs of Osiris' (1911–12) to settle the relation between music and poetry once and for all, a project that is evident too in his *Antheil and the Treatise on Harmony* (1924) and in his collaboration with George Antheil on the opera *Le Testament de François Villon* (1923). Brad Bucknell sees in Pound's engagement with music an acting out of the tension in Pound more generally between a commitment to the primacy of technique, which champions the visual and the materiality of form, and an inability to give up the centrality of the subjectivity of the poet, most clearly demonstrated in the expressiveness of music: 'Behind his desire to establish a poetics of concreteness, be it imagist, vorticist, ideogrammatic, the importance of music in poetry stands always as an expressivist shadow' (Bucknell 2001: 53). Bucknell acknowledges that Pound's particular approach to music and its relation to poetry 'forms part of the substructure of his attempt to make poetic language both concrete and spatial' (p. 54), but nevertheless his engagement with music remains for Bucknell a marker of conflict between what we might call Hulme's visually inflected classicism and an older romanticism that sees music as the highest art precisely because it is the least engaged with the material things of the world but expresses a pure subjectivity. However, if the place of sound is considered in Pound's work rather than music per se a different picture emerges, of Pound's relation to mimesis, of his relation to the magic of the contemporary occult, and of the relation between these things and experiment in the arts more generally. Bucknell suggests that music functions for Pound as part of the solution to the problem of mimesis, by which, Pound says, 'every art' is 'damned and clogged' (Pound 1973a: 42). However, it is sound rather than music per se which seems useful to Pound in freeing art from a particular version of the mimetic, and freeing it in order, not to transcend, but to be more real, to have substance. Poetry, says Pound:

> is an art of pure sound bound in and through an art of arbitrary and conventional symbols. In so far as it is an art of pure sound, it is allied with music, painting, sculpture; in so far as it is an art of arbitrary symbols, it is allied to prose. (p. 33)

Sound links poetry with music *and* the visual arts precisely because it is neither mimesis as straightforward copy nor is it part of a sundering of the symbolic and the thing itself. Here music and the visual are on the same side to the extent that each is able to be the thing itself. Music is not expressivist but is rather a kind of magical mimesis, a copy of the world in its materiality, but a copy that transforms rather than repeats that world. This suggests that music (via the emphasis on sound) can have significance for Pound and for artistic experiment generally beyond the expressiveness focused on by Bucknell. While music remained for the nineteenth-century the art of transcendence, sound, on the other hand, became increasingly a thing of substance. While the transcendent possibilities of 'absolute music', music which is entirely non-referential, 'without programs or words or other extra-musical devices and reference points' (Bucknell 2001: 23), link it to religion according to Styers' definition (Styers 2004), sound, according to nineteenth-century science, is linked to the material. Rather than the transcendence of music, sound becomes enmeshed with technological appropriations of the mechanism of the ear. As Jonathan Sterne has argued, through the nineteenth century sound lost its connection with inwardness as it shifted from being an effect of the voice and the mouth to being an object of investigation in itself (Sterne 2003: 33). This changing conception of sound moved it from a relation with the transcendent and the religious to a relation to the material world. Sound became substance, and so became an object of scientific investigation – measurable and quantifiable (pp. 44–5). In Edison's phonautograph from 1874, for example, vibrations passed through an excised human ear and produced tracings on a sheet of smoked glass via a stylus. The substantial existence of sound was both a cause and effect of its technological enactment (pp. 31, 44–5).

However, sound as substance also links it not just to science and technology but to magic in Styers' definition, and this reading of sound indicates the complexity of its relation to mimesis. 'Absolute music' eschews the conventional mimesis of programme music for non-referentiality, but so does avant-garde experiment which brings non-musical sound into music. At the same time, musical experiment, such as Schoenberg's, which took music back to its mathematical bedrock eschewed both the conventional mimesis of programme music and the transcendent aims of 'absolute music'. As such, the transforming powers of sound, their effect on the workings of mimesis, are complex and contradictory. As Douglas Kahn has noted, the place of sound in relation to music makes it clear how the former disturbs mimetic relations, how it swings back and forth between its function as insubstantial disturber of relation and its tendency to destroy representation per se, to return representation to the all too substantial matter of the world:

> The main avant-garde strategy in music from Russolo through Cage quite evidently relied upon notions of noise and worldly sounds as 'extra-musical'; what was outside musical materiality was then progressively brought back into the fold in order to rejuvenate musical practice. This strategy was, of course, exhausted at the point when no audible sound existed outside music. But for a sound to be 'musicalized' in this strategy, it had to conform materially to ideas of sonicity, that is, ideas of a sound stripped of its associative attributes, a minimally coded sound existing in close proximity to 'pure' perception and distant from the contaminating effects of the world. (Kahn 1992: 3–4)

The embrace of sound as sound here disturbs stability, and sets in motion a back and forth between the world and a closed off aesthetic autonomy. Although Kahn suggests that this led to a 'discursive block' in music (p. 3), at the same time this sense that sound sets things in motion pervades discussions of its possibilities among other experimental artists during the period. Sound plays a crucial part in the conceptions of mimesis that experimental artists engaged with during the first half of the twentieth century. Indeed, it could be argued that sound occupied the crux of the complex and sometimes contradictory thinking about the relation between the work of art and the world. Works of art were experimental to the extent that they attempted to undo and remake this relation, and their difficulty – in terms of their production, their legibility, their political position – was located in the problematics of such a transformation. At the heart of this difficulty is the fundamental question of how one thing turns into or produces another. Experimental critics and artists recognised that notions of the behaviour of matter, of the substantial, were both of the essence but precisely their problem. To challenge representational conventions required a remaking of the form of works of art, a remaking of the points at which the work of art claimed to touch the real, the world of matter and substance, to overlap with it and to share its truths. Nineteenth-century representational conventions valued the extent to which works of art repeated the substance of the world – how flesh-like were the tones of painted skin, how much did writing reproduce a world of familiar names, physiognomies, and spatial and temporal relations? While such representational laws were for a few evidence of the cultic, magical origins of artistic forms – they spoke of the animistic intentions of art forms, their attempt not just to copy but to bring to life – the complaint of experimental artists of the early twentieth century was that such practices had lost all traces of this originary power; that animation needed to be reimported into artistic practice because such animation was the precursor for the transformatory powers of art. Paradoxically, the repetition of substance no longer demanded to be read as transformation, and instead was dead, lifeless, incapable of producing the transforming effects that were art's function. Paradoxically again, to remake art as transformatory involved making visible those aspects of art that were previously least visible, that is, the properties and capabilities of form. Form, however, was envisaged as an insubstantial thing. This paradox is attested to in numerous early defences of Joyce's 'Work in Progress', which make clear the centrality of this question for all experiment and for Joyce in particular. Writing in *transition* in 1927, William Carlos Williams admits this paradox, but insists nevertheless on the possibility of remaking the substance of art through the insubstantial operations of form:

> I see no other approach, at least, to the difficulties of modern literary styles than to endeavor to find what truth lies in them. Not in the matter of writing but in the style. For style is the substance of writing which gives it its worth as literature.
>
> But how is truth concerned in a thing seemingly so ghostlike over words as style? . . . . (Williams 1927: 149)

Two years after Williams's intervention, Eugene Jolas locates the possibilities for such transformations in sound:

> The sound of the word which we elicit following an instinctive law becomes new to us, even with old words. If we repeat, for instance, a familiar word long enough we gradually discover that the rhythmic quality dominates us. If we keep on repeating it we find that it will lose its primal etymological meaning. There occurs a subtle metamorphosis. The transmuted meaning approaches an almost abstract concept. (Jolas 1929c: 29)

Here, sound detaches form from conventional meaning, and allows a remaking precisely of the transformatory possibilities of words. The 'subtle metamorphosis' in the meaning can only produce a metamorphosis too in the effect of such words. The transformatory possibilities of sound are multiple. Such multiple possibilities are the effect of its mobile flexibility, its liminal position between substance and non-substance, between representation and object, between culture and nature. Where this is precisely its importance for experiment in Jolas, this was its problem too. Such transformations could produce 'good or bad results', as Madame Blavatsky airily puts it in the quote used as an epigraph to this chapter. However, much theosophical work, including Blavatsky's own, is less airy in its acknowledgement of this. While theosophy is central in its articulation of the magic of sound, providing a model for a magical understanding of it and its transformatory powers, its own anxiety around this is revealing of the problem of sound in wider artistic experiment.

Theosophy and the Troubling Transformations of Sound

In a letter while in St Elizabeth's, Pound, going beyond his earlier dismissive humour in response to Madame Blavatsky, surprisingly defends her: 'queery as to whether the Blavat/ wasn't a super Gertie [Stein] dealing in *Upanishads* rather than Picassos' (Pound 1984: 40). While Picasso may have been Stein's touchstone for experiment once in Paris, her earlier research into automatic writing at Harvard must certainly have alerted her to the links between occult beliefs and practices and the transformatory possibilities of a remade mimesis (see Armstrong 1998, Chapter 7). A central strategy of Stein's experiments in language is to draw attention to the materiality of the word through repetition which forces the reader to hear the word rather than just read it for meaning. As is suggested by Eugene Jolas, the 'subtle metamorphosis' of sound transforms both the reader/hearer's sense of the meaning of a single word and their sense of the functioning of language per se. This notion of sound, as bursting the semantic constraints of language in order to spread its transformatory power, is indeed central in theosophical conceptions of language from Madame Blavatsky on, but theosophical thinking is also acutely aware of the danger of sound magic.

In his chapter 'The Power of Words' in *The Meaning of Meaning* (1923), C. K. Ogden cites the work of Madame Blavatsky to show that the misuse of words he calls 'word magic' – the belief, as we have seen in Chapter 2, that words have anything but an arbitrary link to the things they describe – is still alive in the modern world (Ogden and Richards 1994: 70). Ogden fixes on Blavatsky's claims, in various of her writings, that underlying all varieties of occult belief and practice is the idea that a spoken word, a sound, which though unspeakable does sound, is responsible for all magical transformation:

> Magicians, Kabalists, Mystics, Neo-platonists and Theurgists of Alexandria, who so surpassed the Christians in their achievements in the secret science; Brahmans or Samaneans (Shamans) of old; and modern Brahmans, Buddhists, and Lamaists, have all claimed that a certain power attaches to these various names, pertaining to one ineffable Word ... the Word works 'miracles' and is at the bottom of every magical feat. (Blavatsky 1877: 370)

Blavatsky gives evidence of the power of such secret words in *Isis Unveiled*, recounting the story of a Russian peasant who passed on magic words to a sceptical young doctor before dying. The doctor, on hearing the words, rushed out and committed suicide (p. 370). Indeed, Blavatsky argues in *The Secret Doctrine* that the truths of past religions are embedded in written symbols, not in spoken words, precisely because of the pre-eminent power of the spoken word. Inscription is a preferred method of the communication of such truths:

> Because *the spoken word has a potency unknown to, unsuspected and disbelieved in,* by the modern 'sages.' Because sound and rhythm are closely related to the four Elements of the Ancients; and because such or another vibration in the air is sure to awaken corresponding powers, union with which produces good or bad results, as the case may be. (Blavatsky 1888: 307; emphasis in original)

Blavatsky acknowledges that the transformatory effects of sound can produce the bad as well as the good, and it is inscription which can contain sound's unruly power. Inscription, as Douglas Kahn has argued, contains the otherwise infinite relational effects of vibration. Kahn categorises the history of sound in avant-garde work using three figures: vibration, inscription and transmission. These three, he argues, 'begin to account for how sounds are located or dislocated, contained or released, recorded or generated' (Kahn 1992: 14). Kahn sees vibration as central to experimental work with sound in the late nineteenth and early twentieth centuries that focused on the productive possibilities of synaesthesia, and hence borrowed obviously from mystical and occult sources (see Dann 1998). Within the figure of vibration, what mattered was the relation between objects in space, rather than the autonomous, material existence of the objects:

> Vibrations through their veritable movement generated a structured space and situated bodies and objects in that space. This process of situating did not outwardly transform the bodies of objects themselves, however, it just placed them in an ever-dependent relation within a larger system. (Kahn 1992: 15)

Inscription, on the other hand, turned attention to the object itself. As Kahn distinguishes them, while 'figures of vibrations head for the heavens, figures of inscription pull sounds down to earth ... Inscripted sounds were ... apperceptual, empirical, scriptural, and technological, capable of being seen, read, written, and drawn directly' (p. 17).

In Blavatsky's formulation, writing plays the part that reproductive technology does for Kahn. In the relation between writing and sound, rather than, as for Kittler, writing being displaced by sound technologies, for Blavatsky writing functions as a container for the fundamental, though potentially dangerous, vibratory truths of sound. Her primary evidence for this are systems of inscription which involve non-phonetic symbols; that is, where sound is utterly contained and silenced. According to her, the 'hieratic symbols' of 'old Egypt' and Chinese characters, both so divorced from sound that they can be 'read in any language' (as Pound claimed too), were the result of a prohibition on narration, 'lest the powers connected with the event should be once more attracted' (1888: 307). Blavatsky's reasoning around sound here is, of course, a straightforward use of contemporary conceptions of magic, as Ogden's despair makes clear:

> All this was written not in the Dark Ages, but in AD 1877, by one whose followers to-day number hundreds of thousands, the founder of a great organization, with Headquarters in London and active branches in every city in India as well as throughout Europe and America. It is difficult to treat a belief of this kind as a mere 'survival', though even in England there are many such. (Ogden and Richards 1994: 72–3)

Blavatsky links sound to transformation in a way that horrifies Ogden; however, both the implications of such theosophical ideas for artistic experiment, and the tension made obvious in Ogden's ideas by this, are revealed in Ogden's rather unexpected association with Joyce in the late 1920s, and in particular in his 'Preface' to three fragments of the 'Work in Progress' published in 1929. Ogden's championing of Joyce's 'Work in Progress' begins with his argument that experiment is needed to break the power of those who have kept language static and inflexible, particularly through the straightjacket of inscription:

> The perseveration of Print, the authority of the Authorised Version, the convenience of Dr. Johnson's Dictionary, the standardization of the English Public Schools, and the exigencies of Fleet Street. If we are looking for the chief historical influences which have somewhat over-conventionalized the English language, we shall find it hard to add a sixth of equal significance. The power of print over simple minds, the clichés engendered by doctrines of verbal inspiration, the lexicographical rally against the cursory and the colloquial, the tyranny of grammatical good form, and the scurry of late extras; all are still with us. It is not surprising that after five centuries the resentment of those who decline to play the game according to the rules of the schoolmaster is overt and vocal; or that Mr. Joyce appears as a promised liquidator where the machinery of literature has been clogged by the ministrations and minutiae of an ossified propaedeutic. (Ogden 1929: i–ii)

His reading of Joyce makes it clear that it is sound that will do the unclogging. While most writers, he says, have not yet started to chafe under these linguistic constraints, in the other arts the rebellion has already begun, and in particular, '[i]n music alone are stirrings heard which may affect fundamental notation in the near future' (p. ii). However, music as inherent form is also part of his apologia for Joyce. Ogden suggests that Joyce will have to bear the experience of other artistic experiments because '[w]hoever flouts, parodies, or evades linguistic conventions, will seem to the magistrature to have something in common with those whose inhibitions or social ties have broken down'. He recoups the experiments, however, by noting that 'even the musical innovations achieved by a reversed gramophone, in spite of analogies with the mirror-speech of certain asylum cases, have a structural and melodic significance for persons of understanding' (p. xi). For Ogden then, sound in music is both the place for innovation and so transformation, but it is also a place of form within which the dangers of experiment can be contained and remade into the legible, at least for 'persons of understanding'.

While Ogden is horrified at Blavatsky's magical beliefs about sound, then, he acknowledges too its transformatory possibilities, if only to the extent that he acknowledges its need to be contained, to remain in the end within conventional modes of legibility. Paradoxically, and in not the only imbrication, as I have argued in Chapter 2, of those who dismiss magic with the magical itself, for theosophists too, while sound is the most magical thing, and is connected with transformation per se, it is a dangerous power that needs to be controlled. Theosophical works, from Madame Blavatsky on, show a similar ambiguity around these transformatory powers. While sound may be the foundation of every 'magical feat', these very powers threaten to go beyond the control of the initiate. The power of occultism without the constraining function of theosophical disinterest and morality is for Madame Blavatsky a 'dangerous enemy to the world' (Blavatsky 1893: 18), and the extent to which sound must be controlled is clear in much theosophy and its offshoots, particularly in numerous references to a much-repeated experiment, that of the famous Chladni's plates. Ernst Chladni, a German physicist and musician, first demonstrated his experiments in 1787 in his book, *Entdeckungen über die Theorie des Klanges* ('Discoveries in the Theory of Sound'). His experiment consisted of drawing a bow over a piece of metal whose surface was lightly covered with sand in order to show the nodal patterns produced by sound vibrations. Chladni's work is, as Sterne argues, 'considered to be the founding moment of modern acoustics' (Sterne 2003: 43), in particular because he 'correctly constructed an analogy between sound and magnetism as waves as a prior condition to undertaking his experiments' (p. 44). While this analogy may have suggested a more mobile sense of the transformations of sound, that sound transforms things – unpatterned sand into a range of complex patterns – it also gave Chladni's 'perfectly respectable scientific investigations' (Ringbom 1986: 147) significance for occult thinking, but in occult thinking, and in particular in theosophy, the transformation rested, indeed stopped, on the creation and conception of form. However, at the same time, the implications of Chladni's experiments for what sound is, how the connections between things are constituted, and how this links to an understanding of representation are also clear in theosophical uses. Chladni's plates demonstrate the unstoppable transforming power of sound and also, in their assimilation by theosophy, the need to contain and control this. In *The Hidden Side of Things* (1913), the theosophist C. W. Leadbeater cites this experiment as evidence that it:

> was long ago shown that sound gives rise to form in the physical world by singing a certain note into a tube across the end of which was stretched a membrane upon which fine sand or lycopodium powder had been cast.
>
> In this way it was proved that each sound threw the sand into a certain definite shape, and that the same note always produced the same shape. (Leadbeater 1913: 267–8)

In his chapter on sound, Leadbeater uses this as a starting point to suggest that all music creates formal structures, visible to the clairvoyant, who is able to see that organ music, for example, 'builds up gradually an enormous edifice in etheric, astral and mental matter, extending away above the organ and far though the roof of the church like a kind of castellated mountain-range, all composed of glorious flashing colours coruscating and blazing in a most marvellous manner' (p. 269). The work *Thought-Forms* (1905), written by Leadbeater and leading theosophist Annie Besant, contains colour paintings of the forms created by the music of Wagner, Gounod and Mendelssohn (Besant and Leadbeater 1905: 75ff.). Again, here sound produces visible forms in the material world, it transforms from the invisible to the visible, but its effects are predictable. In *Thought-Forms*, Leadbeater and Besant use Chladni plates too to demonstrate that vibration gives form and structure on both the higher and lower planes, one of the indications that theosophy 'gave the lead' (Ringbom 1986: 147) in the use of acoustics to remake the relation between the visible and the invisible, that which could be represented via a conventional idea of mimesis and that which could not.

For theosophy, then, sound accounts for the vital element within the forms of the material world and, because of this, effects its transformation, but it must be subjected to the containing processes of categorisation and measurement. This power of sound – magically creative and to that extent in need of constraining – can also be seen in other, theosophically inclined practices and groupings. The strain of this conception runs through Margaret Anderson's account of her experience with the Russian mystic G. I. Gurdjieff. Anderson, who had been the editor of the *Little Review*, argues that both Gurdjieff and his teachings are difficult to write about because they are so linked to speech: 'it is difficult to write about him. His science belongs to the knowledge of antiquity, and this knowledge is transmitted by word of mouth, never written about except in general terms' (Anderson 1991: 6). Gurdjieff is Kurtz-like;

the power of his voice and spoken words is the most important thing about him, and, like Marlow in his inability to communicate the power of this voice in his own narrative in *Heart of Darkness*, Anderson cannot reproduce this in writing. Even Gurdjieff's own writings, she says, are 'incomprehensible to anyone who hasn't studied with him' (p. 5). Anderson's writing, despite all she tries to do to communicate Gurdjieff, in the end performs the task of Blavatsky's hieroglyphics and contains and limits his power instead.

An ambiguous response to the fundamental, transforming power of sound can also be seen in the linguistic theories of the one-time theosophist Rudolf Steiner. From 1902, Steiner was the head of the German section of Blavatsky's Theosophical Society, but his disagreements with the society, and in particular with Annie Besant, led to him leave it and go on to form the Anthroposophical Society in 1913. Steiner's occultism was shaped by his training in German idealist philosophy and his resistance to scientific materialism (see Washington 1995: 145ff.), but led him to very material experiments in education and architecture. Underlying many of his theories and his attempts to practise them was his philological work, and what is clear in this is an anxious movement between a certain magical idea of sound and a sense of the need to contain it. While Leadbeater and Besant contain sound in the final, fixed forms of shape or colour, Steiner goes further. In his lectures given between December 1919 and January 1920, collected together as *The Genius of Language* (1995), Steiner argued that sound is the origin of language, an origin lost in contemporary language, and that sound is the active, transformatory element in language. Dialects, he argues, show this in particular as they:

> still reach back to word-forms within which there is an echo of the happenings outside us in nature. This is always the case in the inmost kernel of a language, where the conceptual or ideational element is much closer to the element of sound. (Steiner 1995: 24)

Steiner charts the development of language through time as a movement from the concrete to the abstract. At its origin, language consists of sounds which are the external world – consonants – and sounds which are the internal world – vowels:

> Consonants express for us what we have experienced inwardly of outside events. To put it more graphically: If you are setting in a fence post, you can feel this action inwardly by bearing down on your foot. This is the perception of your own act of will. We no longer feel this inner act of will in the sound ... of *aufstemmen*, but in the early age of language development, you did feel in your acts of will an imitation of what was happening outside yourself. The consonant element has thus become the imitation of events outside the human being, while the vowel element

> expresses what is truly an inner feeling. 'Ah!' is our astonishment, a standing back, in a sense. The relationship of the human being to the outer world is expressed in the vowels. (pp. 27–8)

In its second stage, language then moves inward, and is formed not according to the outer world, but to the internal demands of human beings. During the third stage, language becomes abstract, furthering distancing itself from the original relation to the outer world and from the human being's experience of it (p. 45). In his first lecture, Steiner discusses his attempt to create neologisms that would return German to its origins in the concrete, although the difficulties in doing so are evidence of finding less and less in German 'the inner, living forces able to continue forming the language' (p. 16). One of the ways, he argues, that German has become so abstract and inflexible is through the importation into it of foreign words. Foreign words form the 'outer layers' (p. 23) of a language, which stop us from reaching the 'kernel proper' of it, that is, the sound that links it to the world. It is for this reason that:

> Almost all the specifically foreign words must be lifted off, because they do not express what comes out of the German folk soul but have been poured over its real being, forming a kind of varnish on its surface ... Whatever has been accepted as a foreign element from another language cannot cause in us as sensitive a response as a word, a sound combination, that has been formed out of our own folk-cultural relationship to nature or to the world around us. (pp. 19, 47)

The word genocide that Steiner advocates here is an indication of his sense of the importance of an unconstrained sound necessary for vitality and growth. Yet there is a tension in Steiner between the need to return to the origins of language in sound, and his acknowledgement that later abstraction is a necessary, safer limit on the work of the concrete via sound; indeed that the work of what Steiner calls the 'spirit' is in part a defence against it. Steiner's anthroposophy saw human beings as made up of three elements, the body, the soul and the spirit: 'Through the body, we are capable of linking ourselves for the moment to things outside us. Through the soul, we preserve the impression things make on us. Through the spirit, what the things themselves contain is disclosed to us' (Steiner 1994: 24). The schema here has clear links to the three stages in the development of language set out by Steiner in his lectures, from the concrete, to the inward, to the abstract. While abstraction in language is seen negatively at times in the lectures, the spirit links human beings to the 'higher order' (p. 30). In Steiner's work on language, the ambiguity of this can be seen in his treatment of the German language that is analogous to the level of the spirit:

> Hence the peculiar, often remote, abstract element in the German language today, something that presses down on the German soul and

that many other people in the rest of Europe cannot understand at all. Where the High German element has been wielded to a special degree, by Goethe and Hegel for instance, it really can't be translated into English or into the Romance languages. What comes out are merely pseudo-translations ... Works that belong permanently to this German organism are penetrated by a strong quality of spirit, not merely a quality of soul. And spirit cannot be taken over easily into other languages, for they simply have no expressions for it. (1995: 45)

Sound is crucial for Steiner because it links humans to the world of things, but in the multiplicity of that is suggested a loss of identity, in this case national, that needs to be reasserted by an abstract, non-identical language. This uncomfortable response to sound – an acknowledgement of it as the magical power of transformation and a recoil from the consequences of this – can be seen in Mann's novel *Doctor Faustus* (1947) as fundamentally implicated in artistic experiment. In *Doctor Faustus* we can see Mann taking seriously the link asserted by the contemporary occult between sound and magic, but we can also see his unwillingness to go beyond the occult's sense of the dangers inherent in this, and the extent to which he links this danger to the idea of experiment per se.

Doctor Faustus, the 'old-new' and Transformation

Both the dangers and possibilities of sound are explored encyclopedically by Thomas Mann in his late work, but what Mann's novel shows is a terrified impasse for the artist, between sound as a transforming power that brings the possibility of destruction and an old conception of the mimetic which fails to bring any kind of transformation at all. That Mann should make his Faust figure a composer is an indication of the extent to which artistic experiment across all mediums was linked to the risky, overreaching experiments of magic, and of the fundamental position of sound and its power in transformatory moments which can only be described as magical.

The novel has, of course, been predominantly read as a painful response to Germany's embrace of fascism and its subsequent disastrous defeat in 1945. The experiment of fascism – its utopian desire – is linked with the desires and fortunes of its central character, the composer Adrian Leverkühn, whose pact with the devil in order to achieve a 'breakthrough' in musical experiment appears to link both sound and experiment to magic, the occult and evil. However, it is possible to see the novel as asking a more complex question, and one that acknowledges the attractions of experiment – of the transformation that produces the new – both in politics and aesthetics: can experiment and the bringing of the new into the world be anything but dangerous? Mann has been seen as anxious regarding the experimental in his own work, and as essentially a literary traditionalist, and his status as a modernist remains problematic (see Lehnert and Pfeiffer 1991). His response to the work of James Joyce attests to his conflicted attitude to experiment. As Hans Rudolf Vaget has written, while Mann read neither *Ulysses* nor *Finnegans Wake*, after reading about Joyce in 1942 he noted in his diary that Joyce was '[u]ndoubtedly a brother' (quoted in Vaget 1991: 167). However, reading Joseph Campbell's *Skeleton Key to Finnegans Wake* (1944) tipped this regard into anxiety. Mann then feared comparison with Joyce, anxious that it would show Joyce, as he wrote in a letter, as 'in every respect much better, more daring, and greater' (quoted in Vaget 1991: 168). It was during this time that Mann was writing *Doctor Faustus*, a novel that, as I have suggested, explicitly links experiment with transformation, with bringing into the world that which has not existed before, and via its narrator appears to be a warning against the dangers of experiment. What is at stake in the novel is the question of how aesthetic experiment is related to other kinds of experiment, most pressingly political experiment, and the place of magic in each.

In *Doctor Faustus* this question of the consequences of experiment are displaced away from writing and on to sound. This may be partly to allay Mann's own anxieties about the mix of tradition and experiment in his work; but more significantly it is because, following occult thinking, sound was *the* mode of transformation for early twentieth-century experiment. *Doctor Faustus* is an acknowledgement of the problem of creation and experiment in the twentieth century; that is, that it requires the magical, but that the magical is dangerous. Crucially for Mann, the limit case of this is the transformation of sound into music.

The danger and the attraction of Leverkühn's experiments are presented to the reader through the first person narration of his childhood friend, Serenus Zeitblom, now teacher, doctor of philosophy and humanist, writing Leverkühn's story in his study in Germany through the last two years of the war. This splitting of the narrative between narrator and protagonist is significant; in it we see not the championing of Zeitblom's rationalist humanism over Leverkühn's dangerous and irrational experiment, as is sometimes suggested, but rather Mann's radical ambiguity in his own attitude to each position which indicates exactly the role of sound as magical transformation in the experiment of the period. As Zeitblom tells us very early on, the power and force of the magical – in his terms 'the daemonic' – he has 'at all times found utterly foreign to [his] nature' (Mann 1985: 2). At this very early stage, the link is made between the 'daemonic' in Leverkühn's genius, and the 'daemonic' in Germany's social and political situation. Late in the novel, Zeitblom's discussion of Leverkühn's *Apocalypse* is interspersed with the narrator's visits to the house of Herr Sextus Kridwiss, an art expert whose evenings attracted 'the initiate members of the intellectual life of Munich' (pp. 348–9).

The *Apocalypse* is a musical experiment, a 'tone-picture' (p. 345), in which magic, 'blood-boltered barbarism', is mixed with the 'bloodless intellectuality' (p. 369) of the explicit use of the mathematical basis of tonality. The piece is a 'frightful and consummate work of tonal art' (p. 345) for Zeitblom because it makes clear the transformatory forces of sound; something new is produced precisely through the mixture of the cultic and materiality that is magic. Zeitblom confesses that the characteristics of the piece 'absorbed my attention even while they disturbed my mind', and these he connects with 'the abstract speculations to which I was exposed in the house of Herr Sextus Kridwiss' (p. 348). Zeitblom dislikes the other attendees at these evenings, although he cannot quite articulate the reason for this. His attitude to the Kridwiss circle suggests a more complex view than that of Zeitblom as stalwart against Nazi intellectual degradation and violence. It is not, Zeitblom tells the reader, that he objects to the intellectual work of a number of the attendees, despite the fact that, although not acknowledged by the narrator, their 'very worthy, strong-minded, fit and proper' work is exactly of the sort used by the Nazis to justify their racial position. Professor Georg Vogler, for example, is a literary historian who has written:

> a much esteemed history of German literature from the point of view of racial origins, wherein an author is discussed and evaluated not as a writer and comprehensively trained mind, but as the genuine blood- and soil product of his real, concrete, specific corner of the Reich. (pp. 349–50)

Zeitblom struggles to articulate his criticism of the Kridwiss circle – anti-democratic, arrogant, elitist, enamoured of violence and destruction – because he does not fully connect these intellectual and aesthetic positions with the circle's dismissal of bourgeois political assumptions and its subsequent blithe attitude to the violence and destruction in contemporary life as it is actually being lived. The Kridwiss circle champions revolution, not as a bringer of freedom, but as a bringer of 'absolute power' (p. 351). Zeitblom tells us that the circle is indebted to the work of Georges Sorel and his *Réflexions sur la violence* (1908), which proposed that in the age of the mass, political decisions should be made not through a democratic parliament but through the construction of popular myths, 'devised like primitive battle-cries, to release and activate political energies' (p. 352). Zeitblom is clear in his antipathy to this, but still acknowledges his at least partial sympathy for the more intellectual and artistic work of members of the circle which themselves are complicit with such ideas. Zeitblom acknowledges, for example, the 'considerable verbal power' (p. 350) of the poetry of Daniel zur Höhe, and is less worried by its call to arms because it is 'only symbolic poesy' (p. 351). While Zeitblom abhors the championing of such atavistic energies against rationality, science and truth, he fails to acknowledge that the very function of art is implicated in them. His critique fails because it does not link the aesthetic and the political.

Susan von Rohr Scaff has claimed that Zeitblom's role as a 'sympathetic bystander' leaves him untainted by the severe scrutiny of values that the novel enacts: 'Zeitblom goes out of his way to set himself apart from his milieu as an observer and to express his sorrow for its casualties. If anyone has escaped the plight of the times it is this benign humanist' (von Rohr Scaff 2002: 172). However, Zeitblom's position as narrator does not place him as the straightforward moral guarantor of the novel; rather his untenable position is an indication of Mann's impossible position. It is not that Zeitblom's critique of the Kridwiss circle is unjustified, more that his critique stops short of its full implications. Zeitblom laments the circle's championing of irrational belief, but does not fully see that his own position fails as a riposte. If the Kridwiss circle's embrace of experiment and newness is unpalatable, Zeitblom's attachment to tradition is untenable. The 'problem' of *Doctor Faustus* is not only that Leverkühn's experiment to bring about new, like those ideas championed by the Kridwiss circle, involves destruction (of self and much else) and inhumanity, but that Zeitblom's 'old' is useless. If others in the Kridwiss circle look on at change and newness with approbation – 'an old-new revolutionary reaction', as the narrator calls it (Mann 1985: 354) – Zeitblom's disapproval is ineffectual. As Zeitblom again and again bemoans the difficulty of telling his story, we see that the method to which he is wedded – a chronological, seamless articulation of the 'truth', the mimetic practice of realism – fails. While a number of critics have argued that Zeitblom's conservatism, the conservatism of the novel's form, and Mann's own traditionalism are congruent (Vaget 1991), in fact the status of such conservatism in general is questioned by Zeitblom's position.

At the centre both of this position and of its ambiguous challenge by the novel is the juxtaposition of the narrator as intellectual, wedded to a certain tradition of textuality, with Leverkühn as musician and composer. It is possible to read the novel as an attempt, in a similar vein to Blavatsky's theory in *The Secret Doctrine* and Steiner's final recourse to spirit, to use writing to hold off the dangerous, transformatory effects of sound. However, imagining the changes that the ideas championed by the Kridwiss circle would bring about, 'how the old-new would in this and that field systematically transform life' (p. 355), elsewhere Zeitblom has to uncomfortably acknowledge that his own humanism, rooted in a reading of the classical world, is itself complicit with the very magic that makes Leverkühn's experiment in sound dangerous. Early in the novel Zeitblom recalls, as a young man travelling in Greece, looking down from the Acropolis and seeing evidence of magical rites. This experience has lodged with him a persistent question about the relation between the rational, the progressive, 'the noble pedagogic world of the mind' and 'the powers of the underworld' (p. 14):

> When from the Acropolis I looked down upon the Sacred Way on which the initiates marched, adorned with the saffron band, with the name of Iacchus on their lips; again, when I stood at the place of initiation itself, in the district of Eubulus at the edge of the Plutonian cleft overhung by rocks, I experienced by divination the rich feeling of life which expressed itself in the initiate veneration of Olympic Greece for the deities of the depths; often, later on, I explained to my pupils that culture is in very truth the pious and regulating, I might say propitiatory, entrance of the dark and uncanny into the service of the gods. (p. 15)

Here we see the problem at the heart of Zeitblom's untenable position. What he has experienced 'by divination' his subsequent belief and practice would explain through rational pedagogical methods. Further, while Zeitblom makes from his observation a lesson for his pupils on the taming effects of art – that it turns cult into culture – his experience with Leverkühn indicates that his classical model may in fact suggest a less comforting lesson. Leverkühn's final piece of work, composed and presented to his friends just before the seizure which renders him childlike and leads to his death, is a cantata, *The Lamentation of Dr Faustus*. Representing finally the artistic 'breakthrough' for which the composer has been striving, and for the achievement of which he has made his pact with the devil, the piece manages to bring together the two sides of modern music, the expressive and the foregrounding of technique. *The Lamentation* has a strict form – based on the final words of the original Faust, 'For I die as a good and as a bad Christian', the twelve syllables of which are joined to the twelve notes of the chromatic scale, which are then reordered and repatterned over the fundamental order of the syllables:

> a formal treatment strict to the last degree, which no longer knows anything unthematic, in which the order of the basic material becomes total, and within which the idea of a fugue rather declines into an absurdity, just because there is no longer any free note. But it serves now a higher purpose; for – oh, marvel, oh, deep diabolic jest! – just by virtue of the absoluteness of the form the music is, as language, freed ... that is, it can give itself over to expression, which, thus lifted beyond the structural element, or within its uttermost severity, is won back again. (p. 468)

While Zeitblom acknowledges that what the piece gives expression to is lament (p. 466), he attempts to rescue the piece from utter despair, and suggests that 'out of the sheerly irremediable hope might germinate':

> For listen to the end, listen with me: one group of instruments after another retires, and what remains, as the work fades on the air, is the high G of a cello, the last word, the last fainting sound, slowly dying in a pianissimo-fermata. Then nothing more: silence, and night. But that tone

> which vibrates in the silence, which is no longer there, to which only the spirit harkens, and which was the voice of mourning, is so no more. It changes its meaning; it abides as a light in the night. (p. 471)

If Zeitblom's position is untenable, that to which it is problematically opposed has both magic and sound at its centre from the beginning. Zeitblom describes the occult powers as 'utterly foreign to my nature' (p. 10), and admits his sympathy with Christian suspicion of scientific exploration, because it so quickly approaches dangerous areas: 'Nature itself is too full of obscure phenomena not altogether remote from magic – equivocal moods, weird, half-hidden associations pointing to the unknown – for a disciplined piety not to see therein a rash over-stepping of ordained limits' (p. 18). In narrating those aspects of Adrian Leverkühn's childhood which he shared, Zeitblom recounts Leverkühn's father's desire to 'speculate the elements' through scientific study. While Zeitblom suggests that these studies uncomfortably approached the occult (p. 21), what he shows too is the seductions of such study and the link between it, aesthetic experiment and sound. Zeitblom gives as an example of the dangerously ambiguous line between science and magic the 'experiment in visible music', a demonstration of Chladni's plates, which Leverkühn senior performed for the delight of his son and his friend. At the centre of a sense of the power of nature, experiment, magic and transformation is sound:

> To the small amount of physical apparatus which Adrian's father had at his command belonged a round glass plate, resting only on a peg in the centre and revolving freely. On this glass plate the miracle took place. It was strewn with fine sand and Jonathan, by means of an old cello bow which he drew up and down the edge from top to bottom made it vibrate, and according to its motion the excited sand grouped and arranged itself in astonishingly precise and varied figures and arabesques. This visible acoustic, wherein the simple and the mysterious, law and miracle, so charmingly mingled, pleased us lads exceedingly ... (pp. 22–3)

Of course, the experiment in 'visible music' which entertained Zeitblom and Adrian Leverkühn as children prefigures the latter's own musical experiment in later life, experiment which entwines the transforming possibilities of sound with insanity and death. Much later, Zeitblom admits that his friend 'strongly reminded me of the older Leverkühn's musing mania for "speculating the elements"' (p. 257). The memory of Jonathan Leverkühn's interests provoke in Zeitblom the admission of the inseparable relation between magic and creation, between magic and transformation. What the witches' kitchen, the alchemist's vault and the Eucharist, all of which Zeitblom links to magic (p. 21), have in common are their transformatory claims. The new comes into the world, or the new world is begun, only through transformation which, in its seeming dislocation between what was and what comes out of it, can only be seen as magic. The Faust model used by Mann places speculation against goodness and grace. In the climactic scene just before Leverkühn's collapse, he makes his confession to his friends. It is speculation that has caused his damnation:

> My sin is greater than that it can be forgiven me, and I have raised it to its height, for my head speculated that the contrite unbelief in the possibility of Grace and pardon might be the most intriguing of all for the Everlasting Goodness, where yet I see that such impudent calculation makes compassion impossible. Yet basing upon that I went further in speculation and reckoned that this last depravity must be the uttermost spur for Goodness to display its everlastingness. And so then, that I carried on an atrocious competition with the Goodness above, which were more inexhaustible, it or my speculation – so ye see that I am damned, and there is no pity for me that I destroy all and every beforehand by speculation. (p. 482)

However, this speech is set within the context of Zeitblom's suggestion that *The Lamentations of Dr Faust* is Leverkühn's triumph. The triumph may have been bought at the price of his soul, but what the music possibly achieves is a solution to the dilemma of contemporary music and aesthetics more generally – the split between expressiveness and formal construction. Susan von Rohr Scaff suggests that the *Lamentation* can be read either as a triumph or as the devil's victory – it marks the moment of his claim for the composer's soul (von Rohr Scaff 2002: 181–2) – but it is more interestingly read as both. Such a musical achievement cannot happen without an occult understanding of the power of sound, without the 'daemonic' in Zeitblom's terms. This is what reveals Zeitblom's position to be as problematic as his friend's. He clings to a position which cannot bring newness into the world; he recognises the power of such newness, as in his admiration of Leverkühn's work, but rejects the occult power which is necessary to bring it into being. Early in the novel Zeitblom describes the technical terms used in a lecture by Leverkühn's first teacher, Kretschmar, as magic – 'all that was just magic spells to us' (pp. 58–9) – but reluctantly the teacher in Zeitblom acknowledges that the impact of Kretschmar's words were greater for his listeners' lack of understanding. The power and danger of the magical are one. This worries Zeitblom, but he still acknowledges it. However, even more important and more troubling to the novel's narrator is music's role as transformative, for this inevitably involves the daemonic. In his discussion of Leverkühn's *Apocalypsis cum figuris*, Zeitblom recognises that the section of the piece which is ostensibly on the side of the angels – a children's chorus – in fact repeats the diabolism of the previous section. While the transformation of the children's chorus seems angelic, what the piece shows is that no transformation is without the daemonic:

Every word that turns into sound the idea of Beyond, of transformation in the mystical sense, and thus of change, transformation, transfiguration, is here exactly reproduced. The passages of horror just before heard are given, indeed, to the indescribable children's chorus at quite a different pitch, and in changed orchestration and rhythms; but in the searing, susurrant tones of spheres and angels there is not one note which does not occur, with rigid correspondence, in the hellish laughter. (p. 364)

Again the question arises of whether artistic transformation is more likely to threaten culture (because of its link to the cultic) or whether it is more likely to make the cultic less dangerous by appropriating it for culture. This is the central question of the novel. These aesthetic questions are not analogous to the political situation represented in the novel. The implication of the question is that the aesthetic has a causal relation to the political. Mann's novel is a tortured engagement with sound because it acknowledges its power to transform, but is terrified that such transformations will be violent and destructive. In *Finnegans Wake* (1939), the 'more daring' novel which gave Mann such anxiety, the risk taken is precisely around the transformatory possibilities of sound. While Mann, like theosophical understanding of Chladni's plates, sees transformation as one way, as producing final forms, Joyce's sense of the relation of sound and transformation, while rooted in theosophical understandings, goes beyond them.

Finnegans Wake and the 'old butte new'

As we have seen in the previous chapter, numerous critics have noted theosophy's presence in both *Ulysses* and *Finnegans Wake*, but the majority have focused on Joyce's comic undermining of theosophical beliefs, from the lampooning of George Russell and Dublin occultism in 'Scylla and Charybdis' to what Helen Sword calls the 'hilarious parody' of spiritualistic rhetoric in the Paddy Dignam séance in 'Cyclops' (Sword 2002: 68). However, both Sword and Len Platt acknowledge that spiritualism and theosophy are structurally significant for *Finnegans Wake* (Sword 2002: 68; Platt 2007: 112). As I have already suggested, Platt's attempt to acknowledge this but distance Joyce from theosophy has strange effects. Sword allows more contagion, but retains parody as a central way of understanding the relation, even if it is a parody that is 'not only a haunted literary form but also, perhaps, a form of haunting' (p. 72). I want to suggest that in *Finnegans Wake*, Joyce uses theosophical conceptions of sound, not in order to parody them as such, but in order to take them to their logical conclusion, a conclusion, which, as we have seen, theosophy itself could not bear.

In his lecture on 'The Transforming Powers of Language in Relation to Spiritual Life', Rudolf Steiner suggests a number of ways that the contemporary world can reconnect with the sound that is the kernel of all language. Two of the linguistic practices that most successfully make this reconnection, he argues, are expletives and exclamations:

> How close we come to what we want to express with such words! And what a difference you find when you're in school and take up a subject – it needn't even be logic or philosophy – but simply a modern science course. You will immediately be confronted with words that arouse soul forces quite different from those that let you sense, for instance, the feeling you get from *Moo!* that echoes in a 'word' the forming of sounds you hear from a cow. When you say the word *Moo*, the experience of the cow is still resounding in you. (Steiner 1995: 48)

The 'Moo' here recalls the opening of Joyce's *Portrait of the Artist as a Young Man* (1916), where origins, both phylogenic and ontogenic, are rooted in an onomatopoeic language. The ventriloquising, by the narrator, of Stephen's childish language in the first lines of the novel – 'Once upon a time and a very good time it was there was a moocow coming down along the road and this moocow that was coming down along the road met a nicens little boy named baby tuckoo' (Joyce 1991: 3) – suggests that Joyce's experiment here consists in a return to the immediacy of the 'primitive', and shares with Steiner the idea that sound reconnects us to the world. However, while the 'moo' reproduces the world of things in our bodies, foreign words for Steiner have the opposite effect. The importation of foreign words into a language, as I have suggested above in my discussion of Steiner, abstracts the language, taking it away from its concrete sound origins:

> When you hear a word in a foreign language, a very different kind of inner activity is demanded than when you merely hear from the sound of the word what you are supposed to hear. You have to use your power of abstraction, the pure power of conceptualizing. You have to learn to visualize an idea. Hence a people that has so strongly taken up foreign language elements, as have the Central Europeans, will have educated in itself – by accepting these foreign elements – its capacity for thinking in ideas. (Steiner 1995: 49)

At the same time, an abstracted language, for which Steiner gives the examples of Hegel and Goethe, as we have seen, because of its attainment of the level of spirit rather than either soul or body, is impossible to translate. For Steiner, in modern German, two things – the importation of foreign worlds and the movement towards abstraction – lead to 'INNER WORDLESS THINKING' (p. 49; emphasis in original). As we have seen, the tension here is a result of the acknowledgement that the power of sound is linked to the substance of the world, but a fear of this and a move to the transcendent, to that which is beyond substance, to ultimately control it.

What Joyce does in *Finnegans Wake* is to link those things Steiner argues are inimical to the power of sound in language – foreign words – precisely to sound. Sound here, rather than reconnecting to 'our' past, takes us to the unfamiliar, but only via delight in play with sounds because all sounds, like Steiner's 'moo', make the world resound within us. So Joyce uses theosophical ideas of transformation but takes them further. This answers the problem in Len Platt's argument which I discussed in Chapter 2. Platt can see the link between Joyce and theosophy but does not want to tar Joyce with theosophy's brush. But Joyce's point is precisely Steiner's but to different effect – it is not possible to have transformatory art without the transformatory power of sound magic. This is dangerous, but the antidote to danger is reversibility of change; change is continual, never ending. Joyce's experiment, rooted in the transformatory power of sound, avoids Mann's troubled response to sound, magic and artistic experiment by extending the idea of this transformation rather than contracting it. Joyce's model for this experiment is not the final pictures in the sand of Chladni's plate, or at least takes the obvious truth of Chladni's plate (that the sand can be shaken back into no form and then formed again), and sees it in a more recent example of technological experiment with sound, the physicist E. E. Fournier d'Albe's optophone. The optophone used the photosensitive properties of the metal selenium to convert light into sound. The earliest demonstration of the device, reported in both the *New York Times* and the *Scientific American* in 1912, allowed a blind operator to hear what was in front of him by slowly moving a cardboard cylinder around. This cylinder was connected to the selenium cell, housed in a small box, and that in turn fed a telephone receiver held to the operator's ear. Distinctions between light and shade were marked by changes in the sound coming from the receiver. The device could be adjusted so that either light or darkness was made audible, but in the demonstration as reported in the *New York Times*, it was shadows created by significant objects, such as a table or a person, that led to a diminution of sound or to silence, whereas areas of light, such as a window, increased the noise (*New York Times* 1912: 5). By 1920, and responding to the enormous increase in the number of blind people following the war, the optophone had been refined to convert letters into sounds, allowing a kind of reading through sound. However, the basis of the technology was the reversibility of this process. Rather than Mann's old-new, then, Joyce's 'old butte new' speaks of continual transformation.

The harnessing of the reversibility of light and sound in Fournier d'Albe's invention led to his demonstration and patenting of an early, though doomed, version of television in 1923 and 1924. Fournier d'Albe's place on the cutting edge of technological uses of recent discoveries in physics would seem to place the optophone far from occult thinking about sound. However, his other interests connect him firmly both to occult thinking and to Joyce. He lived in Dublin between 1890 and 1909, and, although not Irish, took up the cause of the Celtic Revival with gusto, wearing 'traditional' Irish dress, and founding the Pan-Celtic movement at the turn of the century. As part of his work in this, he became fluent in Irish, Welsh, High Scots, Breton, Manx and Esperanto, compiling an Anglo-Celtic dictionary in 1903. Fournier d'Albe became well known in Dublin and gave lectures at University College while Joyce was studying there. In 1908 he became the honorary secretary of the newly formed Dublin section of the Society for Psychical Research. He investigated a haunted house with W. B. Yeats in 1909 (McCorristine 2011), and investigated (and revealed as fraudulent) the famous Goligher spiritualist circle in Belfast in the early 1920s (Fournier d'Albe 1922). He wrote a biography of William Crookes, the physicist and spiritualist, and translated into English the investigation by the German Baron von Schrenck-Notzing of ectoplasmic phenomena (Fournier d'Albe 1923 and 1920). While Fournier d'Albe, like Schrenck-Notzing, was sceptical about the spiritualist explanation for extraordinary phenomena, his understanding of contemporary physics and his experiences as a psychical researcher combined to lead him to the magical, that is, to the belief, not that the material world was a bridge to the immaterial, but that the material world itself was the location for the supernatural. Writing of the discovery of fire as an example of scientific progress, Fournier d'Albe suggested that the use of fire by human beings 'represents the transcendence of man from the ordinary scheme of Nature and his ascent into a sort of supernatural, or at least super-organic realm' (Fournier d'Albe 1925: 24–5). For Fournier d'Albe, the changing conception of matter in the early twentieth century made possible the transporting of the supernatural world into the world of material reality. The optophone, within this schema, takes part in a magical physical world.

As Kaori Nagai has argued, Joyce may have been horrified at any linking of him with Fournier d'Albe, who in so many ways resembles the Dublin occultists made fun of in *Ulysses* (Nagai 2011: 58). However, as she also argues, for both Joyce and Fournier d'Albe, the sound of language was a place of transformation, and Joyce's use of the optophone in *Finnegans Wake* I.i 'is often identified as expressing a key motif of the novel: the marriage between vision and music' (p. 59). This 'marriage' is not the end of the story, though; rather here light and sound shiver between each other in never-ending transformations via the optophone.

> Behove this sound of Irish sense. Really? Here English might be seen. Royally? One sovereign punned to petery pence. Regally? The silence speaks the scene. Fake!
> So This Is Dyoublong?
> Hush! Caution! Echoland!
> How charmingly exquisite! It reminds you of the outwashed engravure

> that we used to be blurring on the blotchwall of his innkempt house. Used they? (I am sure that tiring chabelshoveller with the mujikal chocolat box, Miry Mitchel, is listening) I say, the remains of the outworn gravemure where used to be blurried the Ptollmens of the Incabus. Used we? (He is only pretendant to be stugging at the jubalee harp from a second existed lishener, Fiery Farrelly.) It is well known. Lokk for himself and see the old butte new. Dbln. W.K.O.O. Hear? By the mausolime wall. Fimfim fimfim. With a grand funferall. Fumfum fumfum. 'Tis optophone which ontophanes. List! Wheatstone's magic lyer. They will be tuggling foriver. They will be lichening for allof. They will be pretumbling forover. The harpdischord shall be theirs for ollaves. (Joyce 2000b, 12.36–13.1–19)

In this passage the optophone takes its place among a flood of associations and images that suggest relations between sound and constant change, and a playful demonstration of the relation between visual mimesis as description and aural as transformation. The optophone is crucial here because, as I have suggested, its technology is based on the possibility of continual transformation. In his work on Alexander Scriabin for the lay person, published just after the First World War, Eaglefield Hull begins his defence of the avant-garde composer with the description of a familiar experiment:

> Have you ever considered what a truly wonderful and deeply mystical thing a musical sound is? If you sprinkle some light sand on a pianoforte lid or, better still, on a specially arranged vibration plate, and strike a complete chord, the sand will begin to dance about and finally settle down into a beautiful geometrical pattern; strike another chord and the gyrating sound will finally dispose itself into a set of four roses or something equally interesting. Now thump the piano lid with your fist and the sand will heap itself up anyhow. That represents the difference between musical sound and noise. (Eaglefield Hull 1920: 1)

While Eaglefield Hull repeats the conservatism of theosophist uses of the experiment in suggesting that the right kind of sound produces fixed, legible forms, that it is contained by inscription, he is cool regarding Scriabin's theosophy, suggesting that only in *Prometheus* do his theosophical insights seem to have been productive (p. 257). But it is here, interestingly, that he sees Scriabin's work as showing his experimental pre-eminence, precisely because it is here that the implications of these theosophical insights become apparent. Hull links these experiments of Scriabin not to Chladni's plates, but to the scientific experiments which more obviously demonstrated the reversibility of sound transformations, from Alexander Graham Bell's telephone to Fournier d'Albe's optophone which, as we have seen, transforms form, '*alias* light and shade' (p. 218), into sound and vice versa:

> Here, then, at last would be physical outline-form recording its own correlative music ... the science-germ at least is there present, whereby, if a powerful searchlight were thrown on a rose tree, a Venus statue, or a mountain crag, each would emit and make audible its own music. (p. 219)

The optophone reproduces at either end of its process mimesis as pure copy – the material which exists at beginning is reproduced exactly at other end – and so would seem to reproduce Hull's conservative version of musical form as the reproduction of perfect copies of things in world. However, its mode of operation trounces this idea of mimesis. The optophone reveals that such mimesis never rests but is always on the verge of a new transformation, from light to sound, from sound to light.

Aids for the blind must have had a particular resonance for Joyce as his eyesight worsened in the late 1920s and 1930s, but for him the optophone was not about turning sound into writing or about turning writing into sound. The experiment of *Finnegans Wake* is not so much about what the transformatory possibilities of sound can bring about; it *is* those transformatory possibilities, from its beginning/ending to its ending/beginning, in a continuous loop. In *Finnegans Wake*, both the history which the novel is to tell and indeed human history itself begin with a sound. The fall – into sin, into language, into history, in consciousness – is represented in a way that draws attention to the tension between sound and writing: 'The fall (bababadalgharaghtakamminarronnkonnbronntonnerronntuonnthunntrovarrhounawnskawntoohoohoordenenthurnuk!)' (Joyce 2000b: 3.15–17). The fall cannot be read without being sounded. This preposterous word forces itself, and words per se, into sound. Word becomes sound; but following this sound is also the word. It is sound that brings the novel into being, that brings the new into the world. What is enacted on the first page of *Finnegans Wake* is the reversibility of word and sound, of that connected with meaning and that which shatters meaning, of semantics and onomatopoeia. In Madame Blavatsky, sound is constrained by writing, but in Joyce writing pours forth sound which then returns to writing which returns to sound and so on.

While Mann's fear of the 'old-new', which he links with both the Kridwiss circle and with Leverkühn's experiment, comes from a sense of transformation as in the end reaching a stasis, here, the visual and the acoustic, the legible and the audible, are mixed together so that what is seen is heard and what is heard seen. The description of the 'two mounds' (p. 12.20) made in the Irish landscape by the body of the sleeping Finnegan/HCE, lying 'dormont from the macroborg of Holdhard to the microbirg of Pied de Poudre' (p. 12.35–6), following, as it does, the tour round the 'museyroom' (p. 8.9) in the park, and its testament to war, strife and colonial force, leads into a passage which links

Ireland and sound and England and sight. A differential in the value of the two senses which follows colonial privilege is of course conventional, but Joyce does not leave it there. In the 'sound of Irish sense' (p. 13.1) we already have an intimation that the relation between sight and sound (and of course Ireland and England) is not going to be as straightforward as conventional aesthetics (or the ideology of the colonisers and the mirroring resistance of the colonised) would have us believe. The 'sense' of language is not utterly separate from its sound; rather sense is sounded. It is an ambiguous sense, of course, the adjective 'Irish' associated with the topsy-turvy for English and consequently Irish ears, is seen in the source for these lines, Swift's satiric poem on Wharton's Folly, the redundant Magazine in Phoenix Park. But that is the point; Ireland, and Dublin in particular, undoes the conventional, mixes and messes up. The visual – the 'outwashed engravure' (p. 13.6–7) – reminds the speaker of that which sounds.

Synaesthesia has a long history in both occult thinking and aesthetic experiment in the nineteenth and twentieth centuries. In both, however, it is most commonly associated with the Romantic (see Dann 1998). Synaesthetic abilities mark the individual as in contact with a beyond which can in its turn produce artistic genius. However, in Joyce, synaesthesia is not Romantic. In this passage and in the *Wake* more generally, the loss of distinction between senses, hearing and sight in particular, is the mark not of subjective experience or individual genius but of the dynamics of a sound which moves between substance and non-substance, the material and the immaterial, between itself and another, that is, light. In the long passage from *Finnegans Wake* quoted earlier, sound-producing machines cluster together, dominating those sound-producing tools which need a person to play them, that is, musical instruments. The magic lyre, invented and demonstrated by Sir Charles Wheatstone in the early 1820s, marked a crucial moment in the technologisation of sound making, a crucial stage in the transition from instrument to machine. Wheatstone's father had a musical instrument making business, and he was later influenced by Ernst Chladni, whose figures has so fascinated Jonathan Leverkühn, refining Chladni's experiment to demonstrate the existence of minute vibrations not observable in Chladni's figures. Wheatstone too was convinced that sound behaves like light, and can be refracted and polarised, and his experiments to demonstrate this added to the case of those who supported the wave theory of light in opposition to Newton's corpuscular theory (Bowers 2001: 18–19), a belief demonstrated finally and conclusively in the optophone. The lyre was suspended by a brass wire from the sound boards of a piano, harp or dulcimer in the room above. When the instrument in the room above was played, the lyre would produce sound, as if by magic. Wheatstone called his invention the 'acoucryptophone', meaning 'hearing a hidden sound' (p. 8). Of course, it is not the sound that is hidden, but the producer. The demonstration is indeed a 'lyer', as Joyce has it; the human operator is present if not visible. However, in the optophone, the human operator is finally disposed of. The technology of the optophone demonstrates that it is in the machine that the reversibility of sound and sight, and its consequent possibilities, reside. Sound does not just behave like light, but becomes it, or vice versa and therefore transforms the visible into the invisible, the symbolic into the thing itself, escaping the theosophical attempts to contain sound by inscription.

In this passage from *Finnegans Wake* full of sound and music, it is the 'optophone which ontophanes'; that is, it makes visible that which is, it brings things to light (see Mahon 2007: 153). This is a strange claim. As I have suggested, the optophone was usually understood at the time as a machine which converted text to sound for the blind. Here, though, the optophone as making what is invisible visible is stressed. Of course that is precisely what it does do for the blind – what does not exist for them visually is made to exist aurally – and Joyce had good reason to speak of the optophone from the perspective of its blind user rather than his seeing reader. But what this revisioning of the optophone also does is stress the circularity of the optophone's transformations. Sound can be transformed into text in the same way that text can be transformed into sound, and the process is never-ending. The 'old butte new' can be *seen* only when magically transformed by sound, but that visibility immediately begins the process of the return to sound.

4

'HERE IS WHERE THE MAGIC IS': TELEPATHY AND EXPERIMENT IN FILM

'We rise against the collusion between the "director-enchanter" and the public which is submitted to the enchantment.

The conscious alone can fight against magical suggestions of every kind . . .

Down with the scented veil of kisses, murders, doves and conjuring tricks!'

Dziga Vertov, 'Kino-Eye', 1926

'The reaction to a film play by Vertoff may be as strong, but as removed from the conscious intelligence, as that to any nightmare.'

C. J. Pennethorne Hughes, 'Dreams and Films', 1930

The cultural history of film has often been rooted in the shifting conceptions of and metaphorical uses of light. Film produces life, movement and action from light, making it seem organic (as light produces life and growth in the natural world), but also uncanny (the creation of life and movement from nothing). That the world is reproduced through the effects of light in photography and film has led numerous critics recently to reassert the uncanny and occult status of the media (Gunning 1995). Indeed light has many occult resonances, from Emanuel Swedenborg, through theories of vitalism, to the metaphorical uses of light and electricity in occult and spiritualist discourse. However, in this chapter I want to argue that spatiality, specifically the question of distance, engaged experimental filmmakers and theorists in the first half of the twentieth century as much as did light, and that this question of distance again and again entangled them with a central magical practice of the period.

I have argued in the preceding chapters that modernist experiment with language yearned to reconnect words to the world in new and more vital ways, and that in order to do this it drew from contemporary discourses of the occult a fundamentally magical practice, one which remade ideas of mimesis. As I have argued in the Introduction, in magical mimesis, the reproduction of the world does not merely confirm the world as it is, but in the very act of copying it creates the possibilities for the world to exist otherwise. The problem with such experiment (and indeed for readings of such experiments, as I have argued in Chapter 2) is that language, however pushed toward picturing or sounding the real of the world, retains a semiotic element that appears to reinscribe its separation from the world, its status as representation rather than the real. Anxiety about this residue can be seen in modernist thinking and practice, from Hulme's desire in 'Cinders' that words be rescued from becoming mere counters – 'Language becomes a disease in the hands of the counter-word mongers' (Hulme 1994: 8) – through Ogden's troubled struggle with the power of language to Eugene Jolas's insistence that language needs 'new words, new abstractions, new hieroglyphics, new symbols, new myths' that should be 'organically evolved and hostile to a mere metaphorical conception' (Jolas 1927b: 178). As many have noted, and as is made clear in Jolas's use of the hieroglyph, this anxiety is often expressed in a turn to the visual. For those intent on reproducing the world via a medium less fraught with dangers from the symbolic, from a language which threatened always to misrepresent, as again has been noted by many critics, words as pictures offered less a solution than pictures themselves, and specifically the pictures produced by the new technologies of film. As Laura Marcus has argued, the 'dream of recapturing a prelapsarian, universal, pictographic language fed directly into early film aesthetics' (Marcus 1998: 103). Like photography, film's power was seen by many critics and practitioners between the wars as residing in its avoidance of the symbolic, in its mechanical eye, in its operation as not a representational but a recording medium (Moore 2000; Trotter 2007: 3; see also Kittler 1999). As Annette Michelson has argued, despite the many differences between experimental filmmakers and between theorists in the interwar period, what links them all is: 'the recognition of a new instrument facilitating critical inquiry with unprecedented immediacy and power, articulated in both theory and practice by René Clair, Jean Epstein, Elie Fauré, Walter Benjamin, Béla Bálasz, Fernand Léger, Laszló Moholy-Nagy, and Vertov' (Michelson 1984: xli). Immediacy, then, is at the centre of experimental filmmaking and theoretical conceptualisations of the significance of film in the period and immediacy lies at the heart of conceptions of magic as they were developed through the nineteenth century. In *Savage Theory: Cinema as Modern Magic* (2000), Rachel Moore suggests that:

> [t]he most striking and most consistent concern of early film theory was the way modern language was seen as an impoverished expressive form whose arbitrariness and imprecision could be overcome by the moving picture. The space between the word and the thing is not arbitrary but magical. From Benjamin to Brakhage, this is the magical realm that cinema inhabits. (Moore 2000: 7)

While not considering film in terms of magic, Michael North has argued that film's claims to an immediacy that is beyond representation between the wars was problematic, embroiling the progressive agendas of *transition* and *Close Up* in less than progressive positions around race and class, and obscuring the truth that in the end 'direct inscriptions of real phenomena' must 'nonetheless be read' (North 2005: 104). However, a related problem at the centre of film during the period has been less often articulated. It may be taken for granted now, following Tom Gunning's seminal work (Gunning 1990), that early and avant-garde film share a desire to show rather than tell, to privilege spectacle over diegesis, but what is less clear is what it is that these film practices show. In other words, the focus on showing obscures some problematic questions around what kind of visual image the 'film of attraction' is. Robert McAlmon's description of photography as an 'esperanto of the unconscious' (quoted in North 2005: 72) expresses a difficulty at the heart of such thinking. The power of both photography and film for many theorists and practitioners was that they hovered on the border between what could and could not be seen, that they showed what could otherwise not be seen. It has often been asserted that film, for example, captures truths of the world that the human eye misses. However, McAlmon's claim goes beyond this; for him photography shows what cannot be seen because it has no material existence. Here, in order to suggest the ability of the two media to show that which has no material existence, McAlmon likens photography, against the thrust of most interwar theorising, to language, the very form whose ability to suggest the existence of what could not be seen, and perhaps did not exist, was so problematic for Russell and Wittgenstein, Ogden and Richards. In both *transition* and *Close Up*, as North has shown, and in the experimental practices they featured and discussed, we can see a fascination with forms of representation beyond human perception as it is conventionally understood. This is certainly linked in both cases to ideas of universal language, but, in both, other discourses are also used to explain and make possible these aims, discourses whose occult origins spoke to and of the possibilities of making the invisible visible. The occult discourses used in early and experimental film help us to see that the mimetic issues thrown up by the medium are more complex than the idea of the 'recording eye' would suggest.

As we have seen in Chapter 1, magic is central to the attempts to construct the possibilities of experiment in *transition*, and in North's analysis a particular kind of magic hovers at the edges. It was not just universal language projects in the late nineteenth and early twentieth centuries that made manifest this fantasy of unmediated communication. North quotes Antonin Artaud, writing in *transition* on the visual language of film. It is, for Artaud, 'an inorganic language which works on our minds by an osmosis and demands no translation into words' (quoted in North 2005: 65). He analyses the reproduction in *Close Up*, with captions, of two stills from the film *Wing Beat* (1927), starring H. D. and Kenneth Macpherson, and reveals the paradox inherent in captions which are there to insist on the autonomy and eloquence of the visual image (pp. 96–7). However, both Artaud's description of film generally and the *Close Up* description of *Wing Beat* – 'A Film of Telepathy' – suggest the centrality of a discourse that eschews the mediated even more than a universal language and its tricky paradoxes. In the remainder of this chapter I want to show that it is in telepathy and its relation to debates about the mimetic possibilities of film between the wars that the necessary imbrication of ideas of experiment and a magical mimesis is revealed.

Dziga Vertov, Conjuring, Magic and Telepathy

The most famous film of the Soviet documentary filmmaker Dziga Vertov is *Man With a Movie Camera* (1929), his joyful celebration of both life under communism and the possibilities of film for revealing it. Vertov's film can be seen as firmly part of the interwar crisis of faith in language, and investment in film as its more truthful replacement. The first and only set of intertitles at the beginning of the film declare that: 'This experimental work aims at creating a truly international absolute language of cinema based on its total separation from the language of theater and literature' (dir. Dziga Vertov, 1929). Here film is complicit with all the varieties of language reform existing in the period. However, it is also the case that questions of truth, of the status of the mimetic, and a complex dialectic between the visible and the invisible are all central to Vertov's theory and practice too, and indeed inherent in the central paradoxes of his work. Like other European avant-garde filmmakers, Vertov rejected the validity of the conventions of mainstream film, but he also rejected the conventions, as they had been developing since the end of the First World War, of many western European avant-garde practices. His kino-eye methods, eschewing fictional scenarios, scripts and actors, were committed to revealing new truths about the world rather than obscuring them. For Vertov, the camera and the world were enough to make truth visible, and this is the reason for his rejection of the 'director-enchanter' in the quotation used as an epigraph to this chapter. In his writings on kino-eye from 1924 on, Vertov sets his practice against the film of fiction whose essential method is, he suggests, 'to intoxicate and suggest' (Vertov 1998: 237). The 'director-enchanter' lulls the viewer into a 'permanent state of over-excited unconsciousness', whereas it is the 'conscious alone' which can 'form a man of firm convictions and opinions' (Vertov 1984e: 63). It is the 'scented veil of kisses, murders, doves and conjuring tricks' which effect this unconsciousness, and produce an 'unconscious mass' rather than 'conscious people' who can see the truth.

In opposition to the scented veils and 'sleight-of-hand' (Vertov 1984e: 63) Vertov criticised in the early 1920s, the practice of kino-eye was to reveal the truth, 'kino-pravda', but here his commitment to the truth takes him towards precisely an occulted perceptual practice. Again and again in his writings, Vertov asserts that kino-eye is the means to a different kind of perception, a seeing that goes beyond the ordinary and can see the truth beyond the mendacities of the bourgeois world. Speaking in the voice of the kino-eye camera, Vertov claims: 'My path leads to the creation of a fresh perception of the world. I decipher in a new way a world unknown to you' (Vertov 1984a: 18). Kino-eye is compared to the microscope, the telescope and the X-ray, all of which made visible things previously invisible (Vertov 1984c: 41).

Vertov's commitment to the machine truth of the camera, while the reason for his rejection of the tricks of the 'director-enchanter', takes him to precisely the point of magic, however. This paradox can be seen in critical responses to his work from his contemporaries onwards. Whereas Vertov wishes to banish the director-enchanters and their lulling of the audience into unconsciousness, Pennethorne Hughes, writing in *Close Up* in 1930 and quoted at the beginning of the chapter, asserts the links between dreams and films and cites Vertov's work approvingly as working on the unconscious level, the level of the nightmare (Pennethorne Hughes 1998: 261). Sergei Eisenstein too, though with much less approval, accused *Man With a Movie Camera* of being based on just such conjuring tricks as Vertov accuses his 'director-enchanter' of using. The film, he says, uses slow motion 'simply for formalist jackstraws and unmotivated camera mischief' (Eisenstein 1977a: 43). Annette Michelson has argued that Vertov's 'concern with technique and process' led to a 'disdain of the mimetic' (Michelson 1984: xxv), despite his concern with the truth. Presumably here she means a disdain of realism in favour of recovering the real of the world, but again this takes Vertov towards the conjured rather than the real, a move which Vertov's own comments on mimesis both back up but also problematise:

> Observations made of the peasant viewers during film showings in remote villages showed that the distinction that the peasant makes between the stylized artistic drama and the newsreel is a very deep one.
>
> It can be compared to the difference in the perception of a rag doll and a real child, or the drawing of a horse and the horse itself. (Vertov 1984d: 51)

The real objects of the world are linked to newsreel footage. However, neither Vertov nor his 'peasant' viewers are naïve enough to believe that what exists on the screen is the actual object. In all Vertov's work, even if it does not contain footage of cameras and editing processes, as in *Man With a Movie Camera*, that the viewer is watching a film can never be forgotten. In *Kinoglaz* (1924), his first major film, animation, slow motion, reverse motion and superimposition are all used.

Rachel Moore has argued that film's particular connection to the real event – that it both is and is not it at the same time – accounts not for its disappointment, as it did famously for Gorky when he first saw Lumière *actualités*, but for its magic: 'The film image can be seen in the spirit double of the real thing it shows, always independent of that thing, an exact copy that is thoroughly autonomous and exists as part of the spirit world that is cinema' (Moore 2000: 87). Indeed, in her work, Moore establishes the extent to which early theorisations of film are utterly dependent on an idea of magic:

> Early theorists' dependence on primitive beliefs in animism, the sacred, ritual sacrifice, idol worship, and sympathetic and homoeopathic magic to interpret the cinema's power for a modern audience suggest that technology did not lay the irrational to rest for good. On the contrary, the 'metal brain' prompted a fascination with the very primitive against which it is customarily shown in such sharp relief. (p. 2)

However, in her brief consideration of Vertov, Moore too finds a paradoxical problem in Vertov's position between the real and the magical. She acknowledges the way that Vertov transforms coal in *Enthusiasm* (1931), his first sound film and a 'paen to the working men of the Donbass coal mines' (p. 43), rather than just presenting it as inert matter. Here, however, Moore speculates that Vertov's magic might be too much magic, or magic of the wrong sort:

> The question remains, however, whether Vertov, while making the mysterious world of technology and industry available to human perception so as to imbue the human senses with the very technology that would define human society, did not, at the same time, create another form of mystification. (p. 43)

On the other hand, Slavoj Žižek has recently argued that *Man With a Movie Camera* is an 'exemplary case of cinematic communism' in that in it, oppositions, hierarchies and conflicts are 'magically suspended' (Žižek 2010: 378). The magical practice here is precisely about opening a space for the radically new, but also about representing life as it exists for the senses:

> In this utopian space of 'communism now,' the camera is again and again directly shown, not as a traumatic inscription of the gaze into the image,

> but as an unproblematic part of the picture – there is no tension between the eye and the gaze here, no suspicion or urge to penetrate the deceptive surface in search of the secret truth or essence, just the symphonic texture of life in all its positive diversity . . . (pp. 378–9)

This reading of Vertov shows his work as existing beyond the split between film as attraction and film as voyeurism. Even the entry of the camera cannot shatter the film's status as somehow consisting of the real object. However, it consequently underplays the paradoxes and tensions that exist in Vertov's work between the 'deceptive surface' and the truth.

Indeed, these conflicts around the assessment of Vertov can be accounted for by a tension in his own theorisation of his practice, one that indicates that while there may be no urge to penetrate the deceptive surface, this is because for Vertov film makes the truth below the surface immediately perceivable. For Vertov's position to work, the surface of the world has to be both deceptive and true at the same time. Whether it is one or the other depends not on it but on the act of perception and its levels of immediacy. The acme of the troubling of the division between the visible and the invisible, the deceptive and the true, the mediate and the immediate during the period was the telepathic. Despite his rejection of suggestion and magic, Vertov argues that kino-eye is necessary 'in order to show people without masks, without makeup, to catch them through the eye of the camera in a moment when they are not acting, to read their thoughts, laid bare by the camera' (Vertov 1984c: 41). Reflecting on the reception of *Three Songs of Lenin* on its release in 1934, Vertov asserts again that the aim of kino-eye is none other than the truth: 'Kinopravda . . . was made possible by means of kino-eye' (Vertov 1984f: 123). Vertov explains this link by recounting his debut in cinema when he was filmed jumping from the roof of a summer house. The resulting film shows, according to Vertov, not just what he did but what he thought as he did it:

> From the viewpoint of the ordinary eye you see untruth. From the viewpoint of the cinematic eye . . . you see the truth. If it's a question of reading someone's thoughts at a distance (and often what matters to us is not to hear a person's words but to read his thoughts), then you have that opportunity right here. It has been revealed by the kino-eye. (p. 124)

This insight founds kino-eye for Vertov. Kino-eye is a kind of telepathy. The thoughts of those represented in film are communicated to the viewer 'at a distance' using means other than the usual, that is, language. Vertov explains that in *Kinoglaz* (1924) he acted 'as I had that first time when I leaped from the roof' (p. 125). In the film, the camera penetrates 'into the intimate emotional experiences of people' (p. 125). The innovative, experimental nature of Vertov's practice is based on an idea of telepathy. *Three Songs of Lenin* too works 'through thoughts that fly from the screen to viewer without the viewer-listener having to translate thought into words' (Vertov 1984g: 118).

Thinking about Vertov's theory and practice in this way can account for the seeming contradiction in his dismissal of magic for its mystification in the epigraph and his use of the magical lexicon and figuration in the films themselves. The relation between film and the real event is at the heart of Vertov's work, and in both his writing and in the films themselves Vertov uses ideas of magic, and in particular telepathy, to work out this relation. However, his use of magic is paradoxical and contradictory. What it shows, though, is that magical practices were necessary, however problematic, in the creation of experimental film.

For Vertov, then, a telepathic relation between film and spectator enables a truth to be shown that is not otherwise visible. If the European avant-garde between the wars 'returned' to early cinema because of its construction around 'attractions' rather than diegesis, it was not because of a naïve belief that all truth could straightforwardly be shown, then, but was, rather, to repeat the relation between film and spectator it depended on. As Gunning suggests, the particular relation between spectator and film is just as constitutive of the cinema of attractions as the idea of showing rather than telling; indeed, the latter depends on the former:

> An aspect of early cinema which I have written about in other articles is emblematic of this different relationship the cinema of attractions constructs with its spectator: the recurring look at the camera by actors. This action, which is later perceived as spoiling the realistic illusion of cinema, is here undertaken with brio, establishing contact with the audience. From comedians smirking at the camera, to the constant bowing and gesturing of the conjurors in magic films, this is a cinema that displays its visibility, willing to rupture a self-enclosed fictional world for a chance to solicit the attention of the spectator. (Gunning 1990: 57)

What Gunning's examples here suggest, however, is the extent to which such contact with the spectator is necessary because what they need to see is not obvious. The immediacy of film needs to be mediated via the look which directs the spectator outside of the normal channels of communication. The look towards the audience in the cinema of attractions – both in early film and in later avant-garde film – does then, as Michael North argues, show that even 'direct inscriptions of real phenomena' must 'nonetheless be read'; but it also shows that telepathy is *immediate* reading. It is a form of reading, but reading which sees not surface but the invisible truth of the surface.

This question is crucial for Vertov. The revelation of the truth of the world founds kino-eye, but the truth he wishes to tell, while inherent in the material of things, resists a common-sense model of perception. This tension exists in any attempt to see inherent in the actual conditions of the world both the resistance to it being any other way and the conditions for the creation of a different world. While Marx saw his work as showing that the 'economic formation of society' is 'a process of natural history' (Marx 1990: 1.92), the extent to which truth is available to observation is a difficult question for him. Questions of vision and how things are seen are recurrent in Marx. In his preface to the first edition of *Capital*, empirical methods are set against magical obfuscation. The statistical reports of England are compared favourably by Marx to the lack of such reports in Germany and the consequent refusal to see conditions as they were: 'Perseus wore a magic cap so that the monsters he hunted down might not see him. We draw the magic cap down over our own eyes and ears so as to deny that there are any monsters' (p. 91). Here Marx suggests that straightforward sight would reveal the truth about capitalism that he is asserting. However, at the same time, the dialectic is not positivism. It is revolutionary precisely because it does not simply accept 'what exists':

> In its mystified form, the dialectic became the fashion in Germany, because it seemed to transfigure and glorify what exists. In its rational form it is a scandal and an abomination to the bourgeoisie and its doctrinaire spokesmen, because it included in its positive understanding of what exists a simultaneous recognition of its negation, its inevitable destruction. (p. 103)

While Vertov wishes to do away with the 'director-enchanter' and the conjuring the latter uses to overcome the consciousness of his audience, the question of how the truth of communism can be seen remains a difficult one. To show it, Vertov, in using kino-eye to achieve kino-pravda, constructs a telepathic relation between spectator and film and, at crucial moments, does this explicitly through the mechanics of magic. That telepathy should have this function for Vertov attests to a central element of the creation of the concept in the late nineteenth century which has so far been little commented on, that is, its relation to mimesis. In the following sections I will argue that debates around telepathy at the turn of the century show both that it was at heart perceived as a magical practice, and that questions around the status of mimesis are crucial to its existence as a concept. In doing this, I will begin to answer in more detail the question of why, despite his ostensible rejection of magic, Vertov saw in telepathy a model for the truth that film could show.

Telepathy and Magic

The word telepathy was coined by Frederic Myers – classicist and minor poet – not long after the founding, by him and a handful of others, of the Society for Psychical Research in 1882. Myers defined his neologism as 'the communication of impressions of any kind from one mind to another, independently of the recognised channels of sense' (Myers 1903: xxii). As Roger Luckhurst tells us in his *The Invention of Telepathy* (2002), the term appeared in the very first publication of the new Society, the *Proceedings for the Society of Psychical Research*, in December of that year (Luckhurst 2002: 60). Such communication across distance via an unaccounted for method was not without precedent in pseudoscientific and occult practices from the eighteenth century on. As Alison Winter has shown, mesmerism as a concept, a product of the late eighteenth century, was increasingly dispersed throughout the nineteenth century via a multiplicity of theories and practices. From the 1840s on, in particular through the developing idea of hypnotism, many 'consciousness-altering practices' flourished (Winter 1998: 184–5, 348). Both mesmerism and hypnotism share with telepathy an intensification, if not an outright usurpation, of ordinary perceptual powers. As the work of both Luckhurst and Winter shows, the struggle to own and define these three concepts was central in the construction of the boundaries of a number of scientific disciplines throughout the century. However, as I have argued in the Introduction, following the work of Randall Styers, such boundary-making could not help but raise the spectre of magic. The boundary-marking work around these concepts, and their inevitable consideration of perception in relation to the reproduction of images, thoughts and feelings, returned again and again to questions of immediacy, and therefore of magic.

As we know, since Roger Luckhurst's book, such unaccountable traversings of distance in the period abound, and the attempt to account for 'the enigmatic interspace' (Luckhurst 2002: 113) was made most centrally and most fruitfully by the concept of telepathy. Luckhurst convincingly identifies the concept of telepathy as functioning as a bridge that spanned territories whose relations could not be articulated by or produced much anxiety for contemporary hermeneutical discourses. Luckhurst's work examines, among other things, the work of the Society for Psychical Research, psychoanalysis, popular fiction and the work of Henry James to demonstrate how the idea of telepathy is a necessary by-product of modernity: 'Telepathy is the produce of ambivalent modernity: spooky experiences of distance and relation, of traumatic severances and equally disturbing intimacies, have only intensified in an increasingly globalized and technologically saturated world' (p. 276). The particular relations between subjects and objects, humans and nature, men and women, modern and 'non-modern', conscious and unconscious insisted on by the central forces of modernity deny the vitality and transformatory potential of the place of relation while at the same time wanting to instrumentalise it. The supposedly autonomous and inviolate subjects of modernity are forced to relate by capitalist necessity, but in doing so dangerously open up the space between. Luckhurst's analysis is one of the significance of distance, and as he suggests, it is of course no coincidence that telepathy as a concept is created at precisely the moment when the technologies of the second industrial revolution are producing numerous devices – the telephone, the gramophone, film – which appear to enact precisely 'impressions received at a distance' without using the usual channels of communication. Luckhurst's focus, then, is the space between; I want to shift this focus to what is happening at either end of the telepathic encounter. In both Sigmund Freud's use of telepathy and in the accounts of the Society for Psychical Research of their early experiments in telepathy, and in their focus on the relation between the original and the copy in the telepathic act, we can see how deeply telepathy is imbricated in questions of mimesis.

Between 1882 and 1892, the SPR's Committee on Thought-Transference was responsible for carrying out investigations into the reality of telepathy. In many ways the existence of telepathy was the bedrock for the Society's entire network of speculations on posthumous survival, its nature, and the possibility of communicating with the dead. While it was acknowledged that telepathy rather than the dead could account for the existence of some phenomena, still if telepathy were provable, its shattering of contemporary scientific assumptions would mean that survival and communication could no longer be dismissed as physically impossible. If telepathy were provable, it would suggest that human beings were more than the inert physical matter understood by scientific materialism. If telepathy were provable it would suggest there could be a residue left after the death of the physical body that could continue.

In the winter of 1882–3, the Society carried out two series of experiments on two young men, Douglas Blackburn and George Smith, who, following public performances of 'thought-transference' and 'muscle-reading' in Brighton, had attracted the Society's attention by their claims to produce 'genuine' telepathic phenomena. The two claimed that Blackburn could send telepathic messages to Smith, the recipient, whose sensitive abilities were also in evidence in his success as a hypnotist. The experiments were carried out in the Society's Dean's Yard headquarters in Westminster by Frederic Myers, William Barrett, Frank Podmore and Edmund Gurney, who until his death in 1888 led the investigations into telepathy by the SPR, and a number of leading scientists were in attendance as observers. Accounts of the experiments were published as 'Third Report on Thought-Transference' (Gurney et al. 1882–3). As Luckhurst says, these experiments 'secured, for the core workers of the SPR at least, the experimental proof of telepathy' (2002: 60). The bulk of the evidence in the Dean's Yard experiments was visual. A drawing was made by the investigators and shown to Douglas Blackburn, who then sent it 'telepathically' to George Smith, seated in another room. The majority of the 'Third Report' is made up of reproductions of these drawings, first the original and then Smith's telepathically produced copy. It is the nature of the relation between the original and the copy that is evidential for the SPR investigators. While the majority of the drawings reproduced are clearly proposed as evidential to the extent that Smith's drawings resemble the originals as faithfully as possible – they are straightforwardly mimetic – the exceptions to this are seen as 'decidedly striking' by the investigators. This seeming inconsistency is revealing of assumptions about the kinds of copies possible via a magical practice such as telepathy. Some way into the experiments, the authors of the report recount a change in their procedures:

> Down to Fig. 9 we had made rude geometrical drawings; at this point, one member of the committee, *without giving the least indication of his intentions*, now drew Fig. 10 outside the room as usual. The grotesque reproduction by Mr. Smith is decidedly striking; and so also is the reproduction of the next figure, when Mr. Smith again apparently imagined that a geometrical figure had been drawn. (Gurney et al. 1882–3: 163; emphasis in original)

That the investigators sensed that these reproductions in particular are evidential of telepathy – rather than suggestive of a code between Smith and Blackburn that was unable to communicate the change from the geometrical to the figurative – suggests that the 'degeneration' of the image, from the naturalistic to the schematic, the childlike or the 'primitive', makes it more likely that telepathy is involved. The relation between Smith's drawings and the originals recalls both the perplexing relation noted by Michael Taussig (and discussed earlier in the Introduction) among real turtles, magical turtle figures and those used as decoys by the Cuna (Taussig 1993: 11–13) and the attempts of modernist experiment to transfer attention from the inert, faithful copy, to the powerful copy of essential forms.

Frederic Myers was one of Freud's earliest disseminators in Britain, and Freud, famously, was an honorary member of the SPR. A paper by him – 'A Note on the Unconscious in Psycho-Analysis' – was published in the Society's *Proceedings* (Freud 1912). Luckhurst has given a detailed account of Freud's conflicted attitude to the occult in general and to telepathy in particular (2002: 272–3), but a reading of Freud's engagement with telepathy that pays attention to questions of mimesis indicates how necessary the magic of telepathy was to psychoanalysis as a theory and practice, but also that, while Freud cannot decide which kind of mimesis is magical, telepathy always is. Freud's work shows both the contemporary anxiety over mimesis – which sort is worryingly magical – and that telepathy is magic.

In an early essay on psychoanalysis the links to magic are made shamelessly clear by Freud. As Freud well knew, a confusion between wishes and desire and material reality was a central definition of magic from contemporary anthropology. Freud knew that the desire to combine the real object with human representations of it, and so control it, was precisely magic. Of course, such a

NO. 10. ORIGINAL DRAWING.

NO. 10. REPRODUCTION.

Mr. Smith had no idea that the original was not a geometrical diagram.

Figure 4.1 Drawings made during telepathic experiments
(Gurney et al. 1882–3: 191)

magical control of the world was also the barely concealed wish that critics detected behind psychoanalysis itself. In an article first published in 1905 in a family reference book for lay people, although probably written by him much earlier and not reprinted again in his lifetime, Freud too could admit that:

> words are the essential tool of mental treatment. A layman will no doubt find it hard to understand how pathological disorders of the body and mind can be eliminated by 'mere' words. He will feel that he is being asked to believe in magic. And he will not be so very wrong, for the words which we use in our everyday speech are nothing other than watered-down magic. (Freud 1952a: 283)

No. II. Original Drawing.

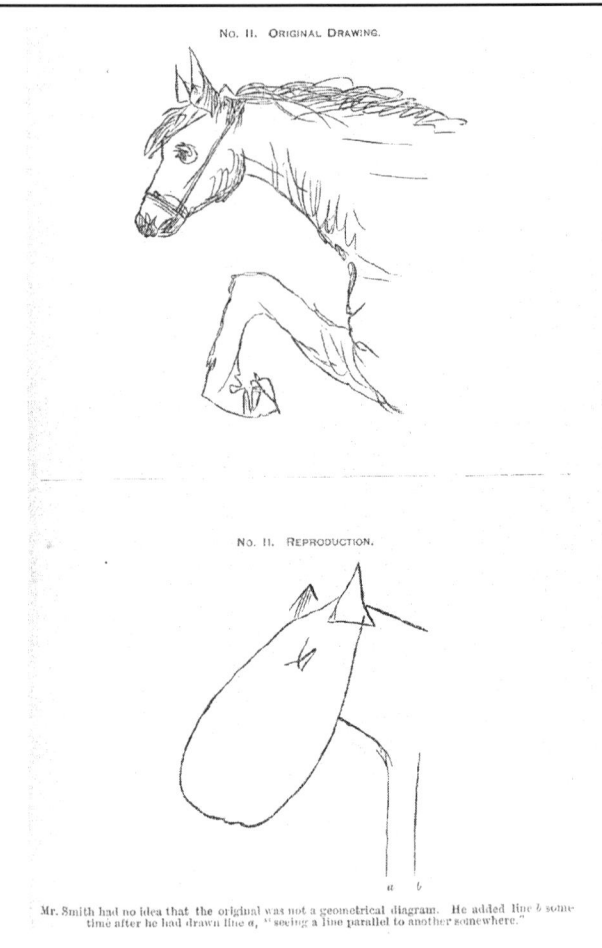

No. II. Reproduction.

Mr. Smith had no idea that the original was not a geometrical diagram. He added line *b* sometime after he had drawn line *a*, "seeing a line parallel to another somewhere."

Figure 4.2 Drawings made during telepathic experiments
(Gurney et al. 1882–3: 191)

In this paper, Freud is not interested in rescuing words from magic for the use of science; rather he shows how his science 'sets about restoring to words a part at least of their former magical power' (p. 283). Indeed, in justifying a model which sees the mind as capable of having effects on the body, and not just the other way round, Freud suggests that what he calls 'thought-reading' can be explained by his model, and thoughts can be communicated, not supernaturally, but via 'small, involuntary muscular movements' (p. 288). While Freud asserts that telepathic communication and 'miracle cures' are produced 'naturally' rather than 'supernaturally' (p. 290), the restoration of magic to words is achieved through science's (in the form of psychoanalysis) assertion of the power of mind. To do this Freud is not shy of linking psychoanalysis with magic:

> Psychical treatment was almost the only sort at the disposal of the peoples of antiquity, and they invariably reinforced the effects of therapeutic potions and other therapeutic measures by intensive mental treatment. Such familiar procedures as the use of magical formulas and purifactory baths, or the elicitation of oracular dreams by sleeping in the temple precincts, can only have had a curative effect by psychical means. (p. 292)

What is crucial for Freud here is that things produced by the mind are no less real than things produced materially. It is through hypnosis for him that finally '[w]ords have once more regained their magic' (p. 296). It is 'properly' mimetic words, words which are directly linked to or identified with the things they name, that could effect cure. If the distorted relations between wishes and symptoms that psychoanalysis reveals are the pathology, then health resides in such a straightforward mimesis. The cure of the hysteric, Freud had argued in 1895 in *Studies in Hysteria*, is effected when language and event are mimetically related:

> For we found, to our great surprise at first, that *each individual hysterical symptom immediately and permanently disappeared when we had succeeded in bringing clearly to light the memory of the event by which it was provoked and in arousing its accompanying affect, and when the patient had described that event in the greatest possible detail and had put the affect into words.* (Freud and Breuer 1974: 57; emphasis in original)

In later essays, Freud became much less happy to place his work on the side of magic. In his essays on telepathy from 1920 on, Freud attempts to wrestle it away from the occult and towards science. But throughout we can see at the centre a relation between the original and the copy, indeed the question of mimesis. However, in the later essays, telepathy is seen as a function of the symptom rather than the cure. The telepathically repeated thing is not the original which it appears to be; the thing it appears to be is a cover the purpose of which is to obscure that which it really is or means. The true original is something else, as in the claims made in *Studies in Hysteria*, and it is psychoanalytic interpretation which restores the link between the original and the 'proper' copy.

In 'Psychoanalysis and Telepathy' (1921) and 'Dreams and Telepathy' (1922), rather than seeing telepathy as a model for psychoanalytic practice, Freud explicitly sees it as a threat to the theories established so far by psychoanalysis. The former essay begins by suggesting that the threat from the occult emerges just as the psychoanalytic community has recovered from 'triumphantly repulsing two enemies' in the shape of Adler and Jung (Freud 1955: 177). The 'expedition' of the latter into the occult was in some part responsible for the split between Freud and Jung, so that the new threat from the occult is, unsurprisingly, a form of uncanny return. The threat of the occult has a number of facets, but at bottom, Freud argues, analysts are 'moved by an extreme distrust of the power of human wishes and of the temptations of the pleasure principle' and 'they embark on the investigation of occult phenomenon only because they expect in that way finally to exclude the wishes of mankind from material reality' (p. 179). At the end of his first paper, 'Psychoanalysis and Telepathy', Freud admits that thought-transference may seem trivial to the reader 'in comparison with the great magical world of the occult' (p. 193); in 'Dreams and Telepathy' he acknowledges that it is precisely this corner of that great world which again threatens psychoanalysis most forcefully. Telepathy is not a trivial element of the magical, but its acme to the extent to which it works, as Freud had claimed approvingly in the 1905 essay, along mimetic lines. It is this that makes telepathy, and telepathic dreams in particular, such a danger to the dream theory. Telepathic dreams would suggest, as anxiety dreams had also for Freud, that his theory that all dreams are wish fulfilments, enacted through a dreamwork which disguises the originating wish, was untrue. What Freud sets out to show in 'Dreams and Telepathy' is that the 'problem of telepathy concerns dreams as little as does the problem of anxiety' (Freud 1995: 179). Telepathy does not threaten Freud's theory of dreams – rather telepathy is subsumed in various ways by it. Freud's two examples in 'Psychoanalysis and Telepathy' are of patients who have had their fortunes told, and who, despite the fact that the fortune teller's predictions do not or could not come true, respond to the predictions in powerful ways. For Freud, these false predictions seem to have proved telepathy in that an unconscious wish has been passed from patient to the 'fortune teller' but in the transmission from percipient to recipient the work of the unconscious takes place, and the resulting fortune told by the teller is a *disguised* version of the original wish. Here telepathy works in the same way as dreams to disguise the fulfilment of a repressed wish rather than as an unmediated production of a direct copy. In 'Dreams and Telepathy', on the other hand, which deals with supposedly telepathic dreams rather than fortune tellers, Freud changes his model of mimesis and reveals that dreams are more mimetic than telepathy – because they tell us what is actually happening rather than just what seems to be happening on surface. In the central example of this paper, a man whose daughter is in the late stages of pregnancy dreams that his wife, the daughter's stepmother, has given birth to twins. Two days later he receives a telegram to tell him that, around the time of his dream, his daughter had unexpectedly and prematurely given birth to twins. The dream, like the fortune teller's prediction, is incorrect – it is the daughter not the wife who gives birth to twins. But Freud argues that the 'telepathic' dream actually tells us something more true – that is, unsurprisingly, of the father's repressed desire for his daughter to be his wife. In his later 'Dreams and Occultism' (1933), when Freud is no longer so defensive about his approach to the occult – he perhaps converted to a belief in telepathy in 1925 (see Luckhurst 2002: 273) – he explicitly details his change of attitude (Freud 1973: 85). In this paper he re-uses the same dream and claims that it is psychoanalysis that transforms it from a normal dream into a telepathic one: 'We must admit that it is only the *interpretation* of the dream that has shown us that it was a telepathic one: psychoanalysis has revealed a telepathic event which we should not otherwise have discovered' (p. 68; emphasis in original). It is only psychoanalysis that can tell us that the wife in the dream is in fact the daughter, so that the content of the dream is in fact, in this central detail, a direct copy of the real event. Freud goes on to recount another instance of a mistaken fortune told to one of his patients. Here again, it is psychoanalysis that produces telepathy: 'do not forget that it was only analysis that created the occult fact – uncovered it when it lay distorted to the point of being unrecognizable' (p. 72). The paper ends with Freud's claim that psychoanalysis may be of assistance in establishing the possibility of telepathy:

> The telepathic process is supposed to consist in a mental act in one person instigating the same mental act in another person. What lies between these two mental acts may easily be a physical process into which the mental one is transformed at one end and which is transformed back once more into the same mental one at the other end. The analogy with other transformations, such as occur in speaking and hearing by telephone, would then be unmistakable. And only think if one could get hold of this physical equivalent of the psychical act! It would seem to me that psychoanalysis, by inserting the unconscious between what is physical and what was previously called 'psychical', has paved the way for the assumption of such processes as telepathy. (pp. 85–6)

If telepathy transports an original to a truthful copy in an unmediated way, Freud's shifts in positions show him, among other things, changing his mind about what kind of mimesis is actually truthful and which kind can really effect the transformations of cure. While telepathy is always on the side of magic for Freud (whether that means for him that psychoanalysis can be near or must be distanced from it), the magic of mimesis shifts from repetition as the hysteric's cure to the distortion of the dreamwork. Tracking these issues in Freud is suggestive for a more detailed consideration now of the relations between magic, telepathy and mimesis.

Telepathy and Mimesis

The questions of distance and proximity, truth and illusion, inherent in the concept of telepathy have also been central in film theory and practice since their beginning. Tom Gunning's essay from 1986, 'The Cinema of Attractions: Early Film, its Spectator and the Avant-Garde', argues that both early and later avant-garde film constitute 'a cinema that displays its visibility, willing to rupture a self-enclosed fictional world for a chance to solicit the attention of the spectator' (Gunning 1990: 57). The explicit look of such films at the audience is in opposition to the voyeuristic pleasures of narrative cinema. The energy of the cinema of attractions, as Gunning argues, 'moves outward towards an acknowledged spectator rather than inward towards the character-based situations essential to classical narrative' (p. 59). Rather than the spectator being pulled into the closed off world of the narrative film, the cinema of attractions, by its look at the spectator, makes visible the distance between them. This distance is most apparent in those moments where the audience's status as spectator rather than participant is made most obvious, precisely moments of display, such as the famous gun directed at the audience at the end of *The Great Train Robbery* (dir. Edwin S. Porter, 1903), or the cannon directed at the audience at the beginning of Francis Picabia's and René Clair's Dada film, *Entr'acte* (1924). Here, the identification that Laura Mulvey has argued is at the centre of narrative cinema (Mulvey 1975) is impossible because the look is predicated on us being outside the action. The comic's wink shows that we are 'in' on the joke exactly to the extent that we are outside of the actual action 'on stage'; the violence turned on us as a gun points at the camera breaks the illusion of the reality of the action in the film by drawing attention to our presence as spectators beyond that action.

There is, though, another kind of distance implied in this conceptualisation of the two kinds of film; not just the distance between film and spectator, but between the film as representation and the world it purports to represent. Gunning argues that there is 'a fundamental conflict between this exhibitionist tendency of early film and the creation of a fictional diegesis' (1990: 57). Gunning's explanation here suggests that one element of the distinction between these two kinds of cinema is the opposition found in classical aesthetics between diegesis and mimesis, the opposition between telling and showing. While narrative cinema as it came to be understood seems to be more mimetic – in the sense that realist conventions claim to present the world as it is – what diegesis makes problematic is mimesis understood as the powerful connection between representation and the original object; that is, the understanding of mimesis that links it to magic. Diegesis is not mimetic in this way because it obscures its status as copy. The distance between film and spectator revealed in the cinema of attractions is precisely the distance necessary for the objects in the film to be a copy rather than the thing itself. Narrative cinema cannot admit that it is a copy of the world rather than the thing itself; but it is in the copy *as copy*, as I have argued, that magic exists. That magic consists of this paradoxical identity and non-identity (a copy yet the thing itself) can be seen in uses of telepathy in considerations of perception and representation.

Late nineteenth-century psychology and philosophy returned to the question of perception again and again. It worried about perception because it worried about the extent to which all perception was in fact a kind of representation, a copy of the thing perceived. It is this question that C. S. Peirce takes up in his essay 'Telepathy', from 1903, and his investigation of it uses telepathy to rethink the status of perception. His cautious attempt to allow the supposed phenomena of telepathy as valid subjects for scientific investigation makes it clear why telepathy proved such a resonant concept for those thinking through the nature and possibilities of film at the beginning of the twentieth century. Peirce had been involved in an intense debate in print with Edmund Gurney following the publication of *Phantasms of the Living* in 1886 by some of the central figures of the Society for Psychical Research – a huge work comprising a census of apparitions of those far away which were later verified as coinciding with a crisis for or death of those who appeared and theorisations of these as evidence of telepathy. Peirce published two essays deeply critical of the work's use of statistics, chance and probability (Peirce 1885–9). In these essays, Peirce is not trying to disprove telepathy, but to show that proof for it does not exist, and indeed that proof for 'the appearance of something that was not there' (p. 153) in general is far from the kinds of evidence that science, and physics in particular, as a rule concern themselves with. This too is his starting point in the 1903 essay, insisting that the claim that telepathic experiences are 'fundamentally different from those that everyday experience renders familiar' (Peirce 1998a: 361) itself precludes it from scientific interest, since science concerns itself with 'what always happens' (p. 362). However, the bulk of the essay moves to a consideration of the psychological rather than physical questions raised by the claims for telepathy. Here, rather than showing telepathy as an inappropriate subject for the hard sciences, Peirce argues that the phenomena of telepathy are no different from those investigated by psychology. In arguing this, Peirce examines, in effect, the relation between representation, perception and the external object. For Peirce, perception itself is a mimetic act, but rather than suggesting as a consequence that perception is an inert copy, he suggests instead that perception has the same status as telepathy.

Peirce posits three elements which make up the act of perception. First, the 'percept' is the object perceived, which stands for nothing, is 'absolutely dumb' (p. 370) but 'obtrudes itself upon [our] gaze' (p. 369) without the perceiver being 'conscious of any mental process by which the image has been constructed' (p. 371). However, as psychologists now, he argues, assume, 'notwithstanding its primitiveness, every percept is the product of mental processes' (p. 371), of representational acts, although the perceiver is not aware of them. The percept does contain elements of pure sensation or feeling, and these Peirce calls the elements of 'Firstness' (p. 371). The elements of 'Secondness' describes the way in which the self-sufficient elements of Firstness are connected and so bring with them the 'peculiar singleness of the percept' (p. 372). The second element of perception Peirce calls 'perceptual judgments', that is, what happens when we contemplate or analyse the percept: 'If one *sees*, one cannot avoid the percept; and if one *looks*, one cannot avoid the perceptual judgment' (p. 373; emphasis in original). Peirce goes on to ask, in what relation is the perceptual judgment to the percept? It does not represent it logically, it is not a copy of it. The only relation it can have is 'as an index, or true symptom' (p. 373). However, the index is something 'without rational necessitation, [it] is forced by blind fact to correspond to its object' (p. 373), so that the perceptual judgment is only minutely less forced upon us than is the percept:

> Thus, the forcefulness of the perceptual judgment falls short of the pure unreasonableness of the percept only to this extent, that is does profess to represent the percept, while the perfection of the percept's surdity consists in its not so much as professing anything. (p. 374)

That the perceptual judgment contains representation constitutes the element of 'Thirdness' (p. 374), that is, the 'idea of determining one thing to refer to another' (p. 374), that is, mediation. While the perceptual judgment in total is indexical in its relation to the percept, its subject (a chair in Peirce's example) is 'not a copy, icon, or diagram of the percept, however rough', but is a sign (p. 376). From this, Peirce goes on to argue that 'we cannot refuse the name of perception to much which we rightly reject as unreal; as indeed, dreams and hallucinations are quite commonly classed as perceptions' (p. 377).

Peirce argues that all perception, made up as it is of the percept and the perceptual judgment:

> forces itself upon your acknowledgment, without any why or wherefore, so that if anybody asks you why you should regard it as appearing so and so, all you can say is, 'I can't help it. That is how I see it.' (p. 379)

Here representation has the force of the real because the percept and perceptual judgment together constitute perception. Telepathy and perception per se are experienced as immediate even though mediated. To this extent, perception has inherent within it precisely the indexicality which in his categorisation of signs Peirce so influentially linked to the photographic (Peirce 1998b: 5–6).

Peirce finally concludes that all perception contains not just the perception of the thing, but also memory and conjecture about the future, and that this makes all perception a kind of telepathy: 'it is absolutely necessary to admit some original connection between human ideas, and the events that the future was destined to unfold ... But that is something very like telepathy' (1998a: 394). Not that because of this Peirce accepts the claims of the 'telepathists', as he calls them, and he asserts again at the end that 'science can make no use of a proposition so vague as that' (p. 395), but what Peirce's argument suggests is the extent to which contemporary debates about telepathy are rooted in the question of vision and its relation to the real objects of the world.

If the concept of telepathy expresses an unsettling account of what constitutes perception, then that anxiety is focused in part around the spatial relation of perceiver and object perceived. As has been noted by numerous historians of psychical research (Hall 1980; Cerullo 1982; Oppenheim 1985; Connor 2000; Chéroux et al. 2004), the nature of spiritualist phenomena shifted in the late nineteenth century, from the physical phenomena of its first phase to the mental phenomena of the turn of the century, and the establishing of the Society was in part an effect of this. While this 'evolution' is not entirely straightforward – the pre-eminence of ectoplasm in the early twentieth century in some ways seems to challenge this neat picture – it is certainly the case that, for the major psychical researchers, the move from the distastefully but necessarily proximate investigations of mediums, often working-class women, with their trumpets, moving furniture and draped full body materialisations to less corporeal pursuits was a welcome one. Telepathy was more than anything a name for a *lack* of material explanation for effects at a distance, and its investigation was possible without any of the examination of orifices and enforced handholding in darkened rooms made necessary in the previous phase. So, while, as Luckhurst argues, telepathy named the *problem* of distance – between material and non-material accounts of the world, between the sexes, between the coloniser and colonised (Luckhurst 2002) – it also established physical distance as a *solution*. The veridical nature of any supposed proofs of telepathy was for the SPR dependent on the establishing of distance between percipient and recipient in order to discount 'muscle-reading' as a cause: 'The primary aim in all cases must be to get the results *without physical contact or anything approaching it*' (Barrett et al. 1882–3: 30; emphasis in original). The many stories of telepathic experiences collected in the *Phantasms of the Living* were significant because, unlike the stage acts who claimed genuine telepathic powers, they were predicated on great physical distances between the two parties. So while telepathy as a concept allows Peirce to suggest all perception as both representation *and* at the same time as possessing the force of the immediate, in it too is a notion of distance which allows it to be magical in its operations. That it is both distance and immediacy means that, in an act of mimesis, the relation between the original and the copy is such that the copy both is and is not the same as the original.

The problems and nature of mimesis are of course at the heart of modernist experiment. In his history of telepathy, Roger Luckhurst only touches on the possible relations between telepathy and modernist literary experiment towards the end of his book. Here he argues that Frederic Myers' idea of the 'subliminal' self, the area of the self that the concept of telepathy depended on, provided numerous modernists, as different as D. H. Lawrence, May Sinclair and André Breton, with a model and a vocabulary for an expanded view of the human being that demanded changes in the techniques of narrative prose fiction: 'These kinds of conjecture, where telepathy, mystical communion, supernatural "possession", and sexual transference overlay each other, became nodal points for Modernist investigations of the limits of consciousness' (Luckhurst 2002: 262). Even the 'hard' modernists – such as T. E. Hulme – who rejected such psychologisation are linked to Myers, Luckhurst argues, through the elliptical, collage-like form of his supposed posthumous communications, the cross-correspondences (p. 264; see also Wilson 2012).

Luckhurst's brief account of Myers' afterlife among the modernists is suggestive, and one of the questions it raises is, of course, once again the precise nature of mimesis. If so many modernists saw in Myers' work, and in his 'invention' of telepathy in particular, a model for articulating something that they too believed to be true about human consciousness, why did they choose to represent this in their work using the formal innovations which alone have united them since within a critical category? As Luckhurst's book attests, many writers of the period – Rudyard Kipling, Arthur Machen, Bram Stoker – saw in telepathy a productive model, saw it as a truthful description of the world. While some of their work has been re-investigated as formally connected to later modernist experiment (Daly 1999), for none of them was mimetic innovation textually apparent in their fiction, nor was it an explicitly articulated concern in other writings. Interest in telepathy, and in Myers' wider views on the 'human personality', then, do not necessitate such clear challenges to conventional mimetic practices and assumptions. Again, as with Helen Sword's work, a gap exists between an account of the thematic uses of telepathy and its attendant subliminal selves and the formal techniques through which these accounts are expressed. The question remains, why should telepathy be imbricated in reimaginings of mimesis?

David Trotter's *Paranoid Modernism: Literary Experiment, Psychosis and the Professionalization of English Society* (2001) puts the question of mimesis at the heart of modernist innovation but in effect suggests that telepathy and its ways are inimical to such experiment. Trotter argues that literary experiment was the outcome of a will-to-abstraction propelled by the anxieties of professionalisation. Modernist writers were in the main part of a class whose capital was only symbolic, and as such it had to constantly assert its uniqueness: 'Brute force, laws, and imitation have always been identified as the enemy of expertise . . .' (Trotter 2001: 101). But in the second half of the nineteenth century, what the professional man or woman has to fear is only the last of those three enemies (p. 116). The mess and contingency of the world were disavowed and replaced by an anti-mimetic paranoid practice which 'puts meaning and value *in place of* the world' (p. 4). While, following Pierre Bourdieu, Trotter acknowledges that such symbolic capital is a magical power which 'exercises a sort of action from a distance, without physical contact' (Bourdieu quoted in Trotter 2001: 7), for him this magic is precisely a rejection of magical practices that are fundamentally mimetic; that is, the reproduction of similarity across a distance, as Bourdieu implies, is precisely what magic is. Trotter goes on to use Weber to argue that modernists, in defence against an expertise entirely subjected to bureaucratic efficiency and, in Weber's terms, the antithesis of charisma, through experiment construct a professionalism that need not necessarily exclude charisma (pp. 132, 137): 'What the advocacy of abstraction did for Hulme, and subsequently for Lewis, and indeed for Modernism in general, was to reunite charisma with expertise' (p. 233). However, while abstraction re-enchants for Trotter, it does so by eschewing precisely the ways of magic. In Trotter's argument, imitation is on the side of entanglement with the world, the very thing rejected by his paranoid modernists. Abstraction, on the other hand, resists such entanglement with the world. This is of course the argument that Wilhelm Worringer, in *Abstraktion und Einfühlung* (*Abstraction and Empathy*) (1907), so influential on Hulme, puts forward for abstraction. However, abstraction has more than one parent, and in Wassily Kandinsky, it is precisely telepathy that demands the formal innovations that lead to abstraction. In Kandinsky's *Über das Geistige in der Kunst* (*Concerning the Spiritual in Art*) (1912) – linked, through the publication of selections of it in the first issue of *Blast*, to the hard, masculine modernism about which Trotter is writing – the purpose of the work of art is to transfer emotion from the artist to the viewer, to enact action at a distance 'without physical contact'. For Kandinsky, art is more powerful when it is not directly linked with real material objects because then it is not an image of the material object that is reproduced in the head of the audience but rather a vibration which is set up in the heart (Kandinsky 2006: 31). This is not a rejection of entanglement with the world, rather it is through the 'non-material' sense of an object that 'the true harmony exercises a direct impression on the soul' (p. 32). In other words, it is through abstraction that a truer entanglement with the world can be effected. For Kandinsky, it is the forms of the various arts, not the objects they may reproduce, which have the most powerful psychic effects, but these psychic effects are about connection to the real of the world, not about withdrawal. Here art is a true copy of the world, but of a world other than the one conventionally supposed to exist. Central to this is the importance of the creation of objects rather than the mere reproduction of them (for a reading of abstraction as neither anti- nor hyper-mimesis see Cunningham 2005, 2009, forthcoming). Kandinsky was influenced by the theosophical works of Rudolf Steiner during his preparation of *Concerning the Spiritual in Art* (Ringbom 1986). In *Theosophy*, first published in German in 1910, Steiner insists that thought-forms speak more truly about the objects of the world because they are made of a truer part of those forms:

> Only because sense-perceptible things are nothing other than condensed spirit beings can we human beings . . . think about and understand them. Sense-perceptible things originate in the spirit world and are simply another manifestation of spirit beings; when we formulate thoughts about things, we are simply inwardly directed away from their sense-perceptible forms and towards their spiritual archetypes. (Steiner 1994: 149)

Thoughts, feelings and concepts are real, Steiner argues, even though invisible. He goes further, though, and suggests that, for the initiate, they are more real because they are visible:

> To such people, the soul phenomena of the soul environment and the spiritual phenomena of the spiritual region become supersensibly visible. They experience another being's feelings as raying out toward them like rays of light; when they turn their attention to others' thoughts, these thoughts radiate through spiritual space. For them, one person's thought about another person is not invisible, it is a perceptible process. (p. 160)

As Kandinsky moved towards abstraction, his use of theosophical writings led him not to an evacuation of content, but he answered his own question – 'what is to replace the missing object' (quoted in Ringbom 1986: 131) – by insisting that the non-figurative was not a rejection of the external world but a truer representation of it.

The significance of telepathy, with its model of perception, representation, and proximity and distance, in working through the relations between experiment, mimesis, the real and the created, is clear in works influenced by Kandinsky. In *The Foundations of Aesthetics*, by C. K. Ogden, I. A. Richards and James Woods, the work of art acts in a way analogous to telepathy:

> In the interpretation of works of art at an early stage, if we allow ourselves to take on the appropriate mood, we may . . . come into contact with the personality of the artist . . . This selection and arrangement [by the artist] is due to the direction and accentuation of his interest – in other words to the play of impulses which controls his activity at the moment; and it is often such that the same group of impulses are aroused in the spectator. We do not make the artist's selection because that is done for us. This seems to be the only way, unless by telepathy, of coming into contact with other minds than our own. (Ogden et al. 1922: 74–5)

For Worringer, then, abstraction is a mode of practice that distances itself from the world by insisting on its difference. It is anti-mimetic. For Kandinsky, abstraction is hyper-mimetic, a truer mimesis, because it uses a form of communication that bypasses the lesser truths of the world (material facts divorced from their full nature) in order to reveal a different kind of real.

Perception and Magic in Dziga Vertov

At almost the centre point of his *Kinoglaz (Kino-Eye)* (1924), Vertov places a longish scene which shows a Chinese magician on the street, entertaining a crowd of adults and children. This scene comes between the two famous sequences of reverse motion, the focus of much of the criticism of Vertov and his 'tricks'. In her seminal article on Vertov, Annette Michelson sees his movement as a filmmaker as being from magician to epistemologist. While the magician conceals his techniques and is invested in maintaining illusion, the epistemologist wants to show us how we see, and therefore show more truly what we see. As she asserts at the end of her argument, Vertov 'invited the camera to come of age, transforming with a grand cartesian gesture *The Man With the Movie Camera* from a Magician into an Epistemologist' (Michelson 1975: 111). At the centre of Michelson's argument is her reading of the insertion of the scene with the Chinese magician in *Kinoglaz* between two sequences constructed around reverse motion. This juxtaposition indicates for her that in his first long film, Vertov is demonstrating his assertion in the quotation used as an epigraph for this chapter; that the filmmaker, unlike the conjurer, brings things to the surface to counter 'magical suggestions'. For Michelson, Vertov's distinction between filmmaking and magic is at the heart of his ideological commitment:

> If the filmmaker is, like the magician, a manufacturer of illusions, he can, unlike the prestidigitator and in the interests of instruction of a heightening of consciousness, destroy illusion by that other transcendentally magical procedure, the reversal of time by the inversion of action. (p. 104)

However, the reverse motion of the sequences is not as straightforward as this suggests, and indicates a relation between Vertov and the magic of telepathy beyond the limits of sleight of hand. The first begins with a woman shopping in the market, considering whether to buy a piece of meat from a private seller. The woman rejects the meat, then reads a poster, one of many put up by her daughter and other Young Pioneers, which exhorts her, 'Don't buy from the private sector, buy from the cooperative'. A frame then shows her face from the front reading the poster superimposed over the longer shot of her, from behind, reading the poster. At the same time, slightly in the distance, we see the figure of the same woman as she walks toward the market. The reverse motion then begins, taking the woman to the cooperative, from where a piece of cooperatively produced meat, still through reverse motion, is transported to the cooperative and then back to slaughterhouse, where it is reconstituted with other pieces of meat to form a bull; 'The bull comes back to life', the intertitle tells us. The bull is then loaded onto a backwards moving train that returns it to the countryside, and to the field of its origin. Vertov argued that such filmic 'tricks' were not tricks at all, but part of the kino-eye struggle to show the truth: 'in returning food and objects to the workers and peasants who've made them, we are giving millions of laborers the opportunity to see the truth and to question the need to dress and feed a castle of parasites' (1984b: 34). While this is true for the meat, it is not for the mother of the Young Pioneer who is tempted by the privately produced meat. She does not 'return' to the cooperative, she has not come from there, and that is the problem Vertov wishes his viewers to 'see'. Here, both the shot where we see the woman three times, and her 'return' to the slaughterhouse are in fact a visual form of telepathy. The viewer sees something other than that perceivable in the world through the usual modes of perception. This telepathy is the magic of the film here – it is about changing what has happened, about renarrating the story. Here the cinema of attractions is a kind of re-narration. It is not just an observation, it is a transformation.

The second reverse motion sequence returns a loaf of bread to the bakery, and to the oven, from where it reappears as dough, and so on until the flour is returned to the mill, and then to its original existence as rye in the field. Here again Vertov uses a 'trick' of film to make visible the relation among a commodity, the labour which produced it, and its origins in nature. The reverse motion undoes the mystical character of the commodity by making visible the truth that commodities are physical things, which have a history, and are produced through people's labour. Indeed, for Marx, the problem of the commodity-form is in part the problem of the confusion over what is seen, and the status of the seen:

> The mysterious character of the commodity-form consists therefore simply in the fact that the commodity reflects the social characteristics of men's own labour as objective characteristics of the products of labour themselves, as the socio-natural properties of these things. Hence it also reflects the social relation of the producers to the sum total of labour as a social relation between objects, a relation which exists apart from and outside the producers. Through this substitution, the products of labour become commodities, sensuous things which are at the same time suprasensible or social. In the same way, the impression made by a thing on the optic nerve is perceived not as a subjective excitation of that nerve but as the objective form of a thing outside the eye. In the act of seeing,

of course, light is really transmitted from one thing, the external object, to another thing, the eye. It is a physical relation between physical things. As against this, the commodity-form, and the value-relation of the products of labour within which it appears, have absolutely no connection with the physical nature of the commodity and the material [*dinglich*] relations arising out of this. (Marx 1990: 1.165)

In this passage, Marx posits two possibilities about the truth of the act of seeing: either what is perceived is 'the objective form of a thing', unconnected with either the seer or the act of seeing, which therefore can take on a life of its own; or what is known is that sight is the effect of a physical relation between physical things. Telepathy complicates this opposition. What cannot be seen in the world by the recipient is 'seen' in their mind, but this mental image is experienced as something external to the mind, not as the product of it. Telepathy mediates the opposition between Marx's two possibilities, but in so doing creates a possibility for the movement from the seen (which may be a lie) to an unseen truth. As in his early 'jumping' film where what is untrue is naturally seen, and the truthful is seen via telepathy, Vertov's film uses that which it is impossible to see in the world – 'The bull comes back to life' – to restore to the commodity its physical form.

The two reverse motion sequences are in fact linked by two other sequences. First is a narrative on the relation between the Young Pioneers – the Soviet movement for young people founded in 1922 – and the village where their camp is located. In this sequence the relations between the symbolic activities of the Pioneers are linked to both their own work and the productive activities of the village. The next section is introduced by the intertitle 'Kino-Eye on the Chinese Magician'. The sequence foreshadows the succeeding reverse motion sequence showing the return of the loaf of bread to its origins through the intertitle, 'How the Chinese Magician Chan-gi-Wan earns his bread'. This intertitle suggests that what follows will be knit into the film's overriding concern with the dynamics and processes of work under communism – the value of cooperation and the eschewal of the private sector – and its concern to reveal the true workings of the world. However, what the viewer sees is the production of mystification, of the particular relation between causes and effects that the reverse motion sequences have aimed at destroying. The tricks the magician performs are not unmasked in the sequence. What propels the sequences is not a narrative of revelation, a demystification, but a shared delight between magician and audience in the production of magic. What is crucial here, though, is that what the spectator sees on the screen is an image of their own viewing experience.

The sequence is made up of around sixty shots, the vast majority of which alternate between a shot of the magician and a shot of the crowd which watches him. The establishing shots at the beginning, however, alternate between those of faces in the crowd and those of the magician from behind, so that we can see both him (from behind) and the crowd. In other words, the camera is outside the looks exchanged by magician and crowd, it is a mediating presence but an 'invisible' one in the tradition of realist cinema, not the explicit one of *Man With a Movie Camera*. After the first four shots, the next shot of the magician is from the front, seeing him from the point of view of the crowd. Two shots from this position are alternated with shots of the crowd. Once this new exchange of looks has been established, an intertitle tells us that 'Here is where the magic is'. The looks have become immediate rather than mediated by the camera. Here then the film shifts from being a film of diegesis to a film of 'attractions'. We move from looks mediated via the camera to an immediate look at us. The magician looks both at his audience in the world of the film and at us. The direct look here has the same effect as the inclusions of the shots of Mikhail Kaufman (the man with the movie camera) and his camera, or sequences of the editing of the film we are watching, or shots of audiences in a film theatre watching the film we are watching in *Man With a Movie Camera*.

For the rest of the sequence, shots alternate between shots of the crowd – some long, some medium, some close up – and shots of the magician (or his paraphernalia, or the carpet in front of him) from the crowd's point of view. Two-thirds of the way into the sequence this pattern of repetition is broken. A shot of a group of laughing children is followed by a wider view of the crowd. This break in the rhythm of shots is followed by an intertitle, 'There is nothing here – nothing here –.' It is the voice of the magician that is represented in this intertitle, commenting on the trick he is engaged in, placing balls under cups and making them disappear. Here the voice, rather than the look, of the magician is made analogous to the voice of kino-eye. What both the magician's words and the techniques of kino-eye show us is the visible made invisible and the invisible made visible. What both show us is that which it is impossible to see.

A similar scene is repeated in the second half of *Man With a Movie Camera*. The film here consists of images of people relaxing after work. Shots of sunbathers on the busy beach are intercut with a group of synchronised swimmers practising on land. Following this, we see a shot of a small carpet on the pavement, set out again with a magician's paraphernalia. As we look at this, the magician gradually fades up into vision, from invisibility to visibility. After more scenes of exercise and leisure, we are returned to the magician as he performs in front of a group of children. In this sequence, which lasts less than a minute, Vertov repeats the cutting between the magician and his tricks and the faces of the audience watching him. This time, though, there are no middle or long shots, just close-ups of children in the crowd, a girl with a bow, a boy in a hat, and two boys standing together. Here, again, there is nothing to suggest that it is the magician's magic that is being exposed, his invisible techniques made visible. The emotional focus of the sequence is the incredibly mobile faces of the children, each speaking without words the scepticism and amazement of anyone watching tricks. Indeed, it is the silent volubility of these faces that are magical here – they communicate beyond the usual channels. They do not speak, but the camera records each tiny movement, missed by the human eye, so that we can read their thoughts. The cutting between 'tricks' and spectator is repeated later in the film, in the final sequence, when Vertov's own 'tricks' are shown on a screen in a film theatre. We see the audience from behind, and on screen the film we too have been watching; but we also see the audience members in close-up, smiling, amazed, baffled. Both the sequence with the magician and the later cuts between the film and its own spectators make visible the tension between Vertov's commitment to the revelatory effects of film 'nonactors' in unscripted situations and the film viewers' own situation. In both these sequences the 'nonacted' responses of spectators are cut with shots of staged spectacles, with performance, even if it is the performance of the nonacted and nonstaged.

In his account of the foundational aims of kino-eye, Vertov, as I have suggested above, argues that the 'cinematic eye' enables a 'reading of someone's thoughts at a distance' (1984f: 124). He goes on to suggest that this is particularly the case in the filming of close-ups, where the camera reveals the truth that lies behind the face through an unflinching reproduction of the details of the face. As examples he cites a woman shockworker in *Three Songs of Lenin* (1934) – from whom Vertov got 'what I got from myself during the jump: the synchrony of words and thoughts' (p. 124) – and the wife of a dying man featured in *Kinoglaz*. While in these examples Vertov's use of the enlarged human face could be seen as analogous to Béla Balázs's claim that the close-up is 'able to photograph the subconscious' (Balázs cited in Koch 1987: 173), in the Chinese magician sequence magic is used not to reveal the underlying truth hidden behind the smiling faces of those on screen (which would, in the case of the magician, mean a revelation of how it is really done, and in the case of the audience an underlying knowledge that it is not really magic), but rather enacts the telepathic relation between spectacle and spectator. What the spectator 'reads' is neither the truth of the surface of the world nor a revelation of that surface as false; what they read is that which is visible but invisible except for the operations of telepathy.

GEORGE A. SMITH, EARLY FILM AND TELEPATHY

In *Kinoglaz*, Vertov reverses time in order to reveal the truth about the production of commodities. I will end with a return to early film, indeed the earliest, to show that such questions of the status of representation and its link to telepathy and magic more generally in many ways founds film as a mimetic act. In the experiment of the most important early British filmmaker, telepathy runs through all his work. This is not surprising. After George A. Smith, one of the two telepathists involved in the Dean's Yard experiments, severed his connection with the Society for Psychical Research in 1892 he returned to Brighton, although not to his role as a stage telepathist. Smith leased and ran the St Ann's Well Pleasure Gardens in Hove. However, the continuing relations between the occult investigations of the SPR and the wider visual culture of the pleasure garden were made clear when Smith advertised his new venture in the *Brighton and Hove Herald* by claiming that he would be known to many because of his 'highly successful hypnotic demonstrations' given in Brighton a few years ago and through his 'lengthy association with the Society for Psychical Research' (quoted in Hall 1980: 169). The Pleasure Gardens offered the usual array of late nineteenth-century popular attractions – a gypsy fortune teller, lectures and demonstrations, a monkey house – and between 1894 and 1897 Smith widened his repertoire first by becoming a photographer and then by making films. According to his own account, he began by making 'simple record films of the streets and beaches at Brighton' (quoted in Hall 1980: 171) in the style of the Lumière *actualités*, but Smith soon become a pioneer in early trick cinematography, developing the techniques of superimposition through double exposure and stop motion. He has been acknowledged as 'a major figure in early British cinema' (Gray 1996: 27) and indeed is thought by some to be the 'father of the British Film Industry' (quoted in Gray 1996: 30). By 1905, Smith had sold St Ann's Well and built a studio and workshop next to his house, experimenting with a two-colour process for film photography. In 1955 Smith was elected a Fellow of the British Film Academy, and in 1957 he was photographed at the opening of the National Film Theatre in London with René Clair, Akira Kurosawa, Laurence Olivier and Gina Lollobrigida (see Gray 1996: 31).

In a lecture on mesmerism in 1882, Smith had argued that most had the capacity for thought-reading. What was necessary was simply 'a strong power of concentration on the part of one person to enable him to form a vivid mental picture of the object to be thought of, and the maintenance of the other of a passive state of receptivity' (quoted in Gray 2000: 175). In their stage act and in the SPR experiments, Douglas Blackburn had been the person supposedly forming the 'vivid mental picture' and Smith the one in the 'passive state'. This model for telepathic communication is clearly repeated during the period in numerous understandings of the dynamics of the relation between film and its audiences. However, in Smith's later career as a filmmaker, the relation between film and spectator it is not passivity as such that is ascribed to the audience so much as the ability, via film, to see in a radically new way. More than the passivity of the audience, it is the mimetic implications of telepathy as seen in Smith's drawings of the bird and horse during the Dean's Yard experiments, the drawings which the investigators thought 'decidedly striking', which are reproduced in Smith's films.

Smith took his knowledge of the variety of contemporary manifestations of the occult gained from his work with the SPR into his filmmaking. A number of his films (now lost) from 1898 centre around the appearance of ghosts: *The Corsican Brothers* (about the telepathic abilities of twin brothers), *Photographing a Ghost, Faust and Mephistopheles* and *The Mesmerist, or Body and Soul* all show semi-transparent ghosts appearing and disappearing. As Frank Gray has argued, 'Smith's ghost films of 1898 represented the first manifestations of the ghost illusion in British film' (Gray 2000: 173–4). While many of Smith's early films were essentially one-shot, theatrically framed films, his interest in trick photography belied this 'simplicity' (see Gray 2004) and through his experiments 'Smith was instrumental in the development of continuity editing. He taught his contemporaries how to create a filmed sequence' (Gray 1996: 28).

Frank Gray has argued that the links between Smith's early career – as central to the SPR's experiments into telepathy in the 1880s and early 1890s – and his late were vital to the development of film in Britain in the 1890s and early twentieth century. He argues that the many elements of Smith's varied career all demonstrate 'his fascination with spectacle, visual pleasure and the different means of representing the uncanny' (Gray 2000: 170). Of Smith's 'supernatural' films from 1898 only one, *Santa Claus*, survives. As Frank Gray has argued, the film is based on the events in Clement Moore's poem of 1822, 'The Night Before Christmas' (Gray 2009). The film lasts for around one minute and ostensibly comprises one shot, of the children's bedroom on Christmas Eve, as they prepare for bed and then sleep. However, *Santa Claus* includes a superimposed scene of Santa Claus on the children's roof, preparing to climb down their chimney. At this point, the shot frames, on the left, the children's bed, with their stockings hanging on the end, ready to be filled with gifts, and on the upper right a circular inset delimiting the action taking place outside of the bedroom, on the roof. Frank Gray, in relation to Smith's films of 1898, has written of the importance of the 'vision scene' in all of them: 'The vision was not seen by any other character within the fiction, and therefore provided the audience with a privileged understanding of the central character's nature' (Gray 2000: 176). In *Santa Claus* the spectator sees that which should be invisible. The audience does not 'leave' the bedroom and move to the roof, as they would in a later realist film. The audience remains in the bedroom but 'sees' what is happening some distance away, as did Smith in the Dean's Yard experiments, as did those whose telepathic experiences were collected together in *Phantasms of the Living*. As Gray admits, in each case in Smith's films the vision is present through a supernatural agency – communication at a distance, a vision of the future, or a materialisation of desire. While the catalogue entry for the film misleadingly describes the children as having a 'dream vision', Gray argues that the fact that Santa Claus does then appear in the children's bedroom makes this 'an early form of crosscutting' (p. 177) whereby '[t]he main shot and the insert shot become objective point-of-view shots of two actions running in parallel. This is a literal depiction of two simultaneous events occurring in different locales, and both are presented within the same shot' (p. 177). In other words, for the spectator the vision scene is not dream but telepathy. That the status of Father Christmas is different for the spectator than it is for the children shows how the relation of the spectator to film in early cinema is constructed around the making visible of what is otherwise invisible, not as a dream, but as a magically produced reality.

5

'DISNEY AGAINST THE METAPHYSICALS': EISENSTEIN, POUND, ECTOPLASM AND THE POLITICS OF ANIMATION

'—"You sit stiller" said Kokka
"if whenever you move something jangles."'

Ezra Pound, Canto 74

As we have seen in Chapter 4, the work of both Dziga Vertov and Sergei Eisenstein shows a tension between realism as faithfulness to the truth of the world on one hand and realism as reproducing the myths of bourgeois capitalism on the other. For Vertov, facts were central in overcoming this problematic of representation, as expressed in his rejection of actors, filmscripts, created scenarios, and so on. For Eisenstein, however, the relation between the facts of world and their reproduction on the screen was in some ways more complex. He criticised Vertov and kino-eye in general for misunderstanding this relation. In 'The Problem of the Materialist Approach to Form' (1925), Eisenstein argues that kino-eye merely reproduces the world rather reconstructing it to a particular ideological end:

> Like the well-known Impressionist, *Cine-Eye*, sketchbook in hand (!), rushes after objects as they are *without rebelliously interrupting the inevitability of the statics of the causal connection between them, without overcoming this connection through a powerful social-organisation motive but yielding to its 'cosmic' pressure.* (Eisenstein 2010: 63; emphasis in original)

Eisenstein in his theoretical writing searched for a way to articulate this complexity of the relation between world and representation. His concern again and again is how to tell the truth about the world without reproducing the illusions of capitalism. A number of the central ways through which he explored and offered answers to these questions – the ideogram, the prelogical, the possibilities of the juxtaposition of ideas and images – are shared by an artist who, while a fellow self-conscious experimenter, was politically as far from Eisenstein as it is possible to be. As I have discussed in Chapter 2, Ezra Pound was also concerned with creating an artistic practice which was neither slavishly mimetic nor severed from referentiality. The link between him and Eisenstein, particularly in the use of the ideogram, was noted by Marshall McLuhan in a letter to Pound during his time in St Elizabeth's, perhaps unsurprisingly without mention of the political incompatibility of the two: 'You and Eisenstein have shown me how to make use of Chinese ideogram to elicit the natural modes of American sensibility' (McLuhan 1987: 217). What drew each to the ideogram was the sense that it solved the problem of the relation between the world and artistic representation and more particularly that it did so in a way that brought into representation the life – the movement and animation – most often associated with the natural.

This chapter argues that the occult phenomenon of ectoplasm plays a strange and suitably half-visible role in the theoretical and practical attempts of both Ezra Pound and Sergei Eisenstein to imagine the world other than as it exists via an art that is itself animated. It argues too, however, that the relation of each to the ectoplasmic was different, and that in this difference can be traced not only their own politics, but a relation between the occult and the political more broadly. A link between the occult and fascism has been argued for and explored by many critics – Marxist and otherwise – from the mid-twentieth century. Following Benjamin's much commented on formulation – that fascism aestheticises the political rather than politicising the aesthetic – it has been argued that one of the most powerful ways it does this is by co-opting the rituals, imagery and practices of a variety of occult discourses (Benjamin 1992: 234; Goodrick-Clarke 2005). Marxism, on the other hand, is the debunker of the metaphysical and numerous Marxist critics have nominated as magical the ideological work of capitalism, obscuring its real operations with sleight of hand in order to perpetuate them (for example Raymond Williams 1980). More particularly, animation has been seen, from Marx's claim in *The Communist Manifesto* that 'All that is solid melts into air', as the central property of capital, an animation in the face of which any stasis or fixity disappears. This chapter argues, not that this is untrue, but that it is not the whole story. As Paul Morrison has argued, Benjamin's formulation is anyway problematic for Pound, who, rather than aestheticising the political, 'is most frequently accused of contaminating his poetic with a great deal of economic nonsense'

(Morrison 1996: 9). I want to argue – via Eisenstein's engagement with the ectoplasmic and Pound's failure to do so – that it is possible to use the magical not as a subjection of politics to aesthetics but as a remaking of the aesthetic so that it fuses with and transforms the matter of world.

The relation of both Pound and Eisenstein to magical and occult practices has been well documented. For Pound, it has been argued, occult tradition was productive precisely as a tradition, but one free from what he saw as the betrayal and morbidity of mainstream European culture. As Leon Surette has forcefully argued, the tradition offered an intellectual framework from within which Pound could produce his own 'secret history', *The Cantos* (Surette 1993: 21). The tradition as read by Pound, according to Surette, provided a grounding in both a linguistic theory and a hermeneutics (p. 25). A sense of the magic of film, its ability to transform world and viewer, to create the world anew and in the viewer create the possibilities for a new world, underlies most of Eisenstein's theoretical writing (Moore 2000). This sense was for Eisenstein grounded in a rigorous exploration of actual magical practices. While in Paris during his travels in the late 1920s and early 1930s he searched for a copy of James Frazer's *The Golden Bough*. Unable to find one, he bought instead Lucien Lévy-Bruhl's *Les Fonctions mentales dans les sociétés inférieures* (1910) (*How Natives Think*) (Eisenstein 1983: 210). Reading this, Eisenstein began to make 'the most dizzying excursions into the secrets of what already takes on the more precise definition of "prelogic"' (p. 210). Eisenstein was in Paris on his way to the US and then on to Mexico, where he would come to believe that he had discovered 'sensual thinking' in practice. The footage shot for his proposed, although never completed, film, *Que Viva Mexico*, shows images of the country where nature and history, inanimate matter and the animated, the unchanging and the revolutionary, the past and the present are brought together to demonstrate their possible harmonies. What the book and the trip to Mexico incarnated for Eisenstein was a way of thinking about the relation between the conscious and the unconscious, 'the rationally-logical and the sensuous', in film, a relation which, as Naum Kleiman has argued, was for Eisenstein the central question of all art (Kleiman 1986: ix).

Links between Pound and Eisenstein and the occult or magical are then now central to the critical debate on them. Neither, however, expressed any interest in the beliefs, practices and phenomena of the contemporary occult. As I have shown in the Introduction, Surette's work, the most important linking of Pound and the occult, is insistent in denying any relation to magic, and to contemporary magic in particular (Surette 1993: 3–36). Eisenstein, while undoubtedly touched by Russian symbolism and its deep entwining with theosophy (see Yampolsky 1993: 185–6), critiques actual magical beliefs as backward-looking superstition in his films – for example in the gods sequence in *October* (1927) and in the religious procession in *Old and New/The General Line*

(1929) – in accordance with both Marxist and Soviet orthodoxies. Certainly the embarrassing phenomenon of ectoplasm – embarrassing in the incredible credulity evident in its apologists, embarrassing in its texture and *mise en scène*, so quotidian, so familiar and corporeal as to be positively abject – barely leaves a trace in the writings or work of either. Unlike telepathy, the vibrations of sound or ghostly creativity of words, ectoplasm is too shameful for anyone to even deign to critique, let alone take seriously. However, what links Pound and Eisenstein is a concern to reanimate art, and for both this is linked with movement. Movement, for Eisenstein, is film and for Pound, as we shall see, the problem of movement is often explicitly linked to film. This concern with movement and animation is most spectacularly seen in occult practices of the early twentieth century in the phenomena of ectoplasm, and the extent to which the dynamics of ectoplasm can be read in Pound and Eisenstein is a powerful indication of the nature of their struggles with, and failure or success in solving, the problem of animation.

For both Pound and Eisenstein, the relationship between aesthetic representation and the world is central, and it is central because for both of them art is deeply involved, or should be, in taking part in events that shape that world. Art depicts the contours of the world but more crucially it is a place where the world as it could be is present. Pound's rewriting of Baudelaire, 'Le paradise n'est pas artificiel', is repeated again and again in *The Cantos*, not because it is not created in artifice but because the creation of it in representation makes it real. And for this to happen in representation is essentially a magical act. However, what also links Pound and Eisenstein is a concern over movement and its relation to politics, albeit in very different ways and to very different effects. The question for them both is, how does the matter of the world change? That Eisenstein should focus so centrally on the relation between movement and politics makes his choice of film as medium obvious. For him, film's power is in its 'primal' basis in movement and action over fixed concepts and identities. For all art – and this is the reason for film being the most perfect art for Eisenstein – its 'nature is a conflict between natural existence and creative tendency. Between organic inertia and purposeful initiative' (Eisenstein 1977c: 46). Productive and expressive of such a tension is movement, *the* filmic element.

For Pound too both his aesthetics and his politics give a central place to movement and action. It is this 'life' in which Pound is attempting to school the reader in *Guide to Kulchur*: '"*Il sait vivre*," said Brancusi of Léger. This must also be said of the catechumens before they pass the third door' (Pound 1970: 145; emphasis in original). The 'life' to which Pound argues thought and art should be organically linked in any culture which approaches civilisation is expressed over and again in figures of movement. 'Paideuma', Pound's talismanic word, is defined early in *Guide to Kulchur* as meaning 'grisly roots of ideas that are in action' (p. 58). Ideas that are not 'in action' are static, moribund. Pound asserts this not just of aesthetic ideas, but abstractions per se. To live they have to be connected with life, and their connection with life is manifest in their movement. So Pound sets against various theories of money '[t]he actual achievements of the totalitarian states which won't stay still and will not be, at the date of publication six months or a year hence, what they are today' (p. 167). The fascist states of which Pound approves manifest the extent to which paideuma exists in movement and animation. In contrast, Pound suggests communism's correct premise is marred by its inability to stay properly animated:

> Communism as revolt against the hoggers of harvest was an admirable tendency. As revolutionary [sic] I refuse a pretended revolution that tries to stand still or move backward . . .
>
> A movement, against capital, that cannot distinguish between capital and property is a blind movement. (p. 191)

The presence of animation, of life, is the marker of value for Pound. Again, in *Guide to Kulchur*, he distinguishes between the anthropological work of James Frazer and Leo Frobenius according to the extent that the work of the former is retrospective, it recounts things that are dead and gone, and the work of the latter connects what is living in the past with what is alive now. Pound cites from Frobenius an account of the resistance of contemporary peasants to a railway cutting because 'a king had driven into the ground at that place' (p. 57). On digging into the ground, engineers 'unearthed a bronze car of Dis, two thousand years buried'. Not only this, but Frobenius states that large reserves of water were found at the site. For Pound this method of work represents a living connection between moments usually seen as temporally discrete: 'That kind of research goes not only into past and forgotten life, but points to tomorrow's water supply' (Pound 1970: 57).

That this value given to movement and the life evidenced by animation links Pound's work to cinema is acknowledged by that most careful reader of Pound, Marshall McLuhan. McLuhan's letters to Pound while he was in St Elizabeth's insist on Pound's method as essentially cinematic:

> Your Cantos, I now judge, to be the first and only serious use of the great technical possibilities of the cinematograph. Am I right in thinking of them as a montage of *personae* and sculptured images? Flash-backs providing perceptions of simultaneities? (McLuhan 1987: 193)

McLuhan's insight was provoked by Pound's remark during conversations between the two (and Hugh Kenner) in June 1948 that the first forty cantos are a detective story. In the same letter, McLuhan connects the idea of the reconstruction of a crime with the form of cinema:

> I've been pondering your remark that Cantos 1–40 are a detective story. Should be glad of further clues from you. But one thing about crime fiction that I have noted may or may not be apropos here. Poe in 1840 or so invented the cinema via Dupin. Dupin deals with a corpse as *still life*. That is, by cinematic montage he reconstructs the crime, as all sleuths have since done. Are Cantos 1–40 such a reconstruction of a crime? Crime against man and civilization? Are the entire Cantos such a reconstruction at once of a continuing crime and of the collateral life that might have been and might still be? (p. 194; emphasis in original)

The act of reconstruction is centrally figured in modernity by the detective's investigation of the crime and solution of whodunit. What makes this reconstruction cinematic is the need for the resurrection of the dead body, the object that is both evidence that a crime has been committed and the site of its solution. While the dead body remains literally dead, the work of the detective animates the past and the dead body itself in order to recreate the moment of the crime, this time with the identity of the criminal in full view. Like cinema, the detective brings back to life that which is dead and gone. Neither detection nor cinema are retrospective in the sense that Pound uses the word about James Frazer's work. What is crucial in Frobenius, in the detective, in cinema and in Pound's method in *The Cantos* is the idea of reanimation, the ability to see life and movement where others only see stasis and death.

The crime that the reader of *The Cantos* has to detect is of course usury (Ferrall 2001: 56). For Pound, the central crime of usury was the prohibition of movement and circulation. In Canto 45 that usury is 'contra naturam' is demonstrated by its cessation of movement, fecundity and production (Pound 1987: 229–30). It is movement in and of *The Cantos* (as the antidote to usury) that McLuhan links to cinema. The questions this provokes in a consideration of animation, movement, politics and representation are: why then does Pound not have cinema at centre of his thinking, and why is he a fascist? In short, what are the politics of animation?

Ectoplasm and the Politics of Animation

While the theory of animism as it related to the origins of religion was a much contested one in anthropology of the late nineteenth and early twentieth centuries, the belief that all things are animated and that the forces involved in this can be predicted and used was at the heart of most anthropology of early and 'savage' peoples. Indeed, at the centre of Andrew Lang's definition of 'savage' was the belief that 'all things, animate or inanimate, human, animal, vegetable, or inorganic, seem on the same level of life, passion and reason', that 'the savage is he who ... regards all natural objects as animated and intelligent beings' (Lang 1887: 47, 31). These definitions are of course based on the assumption that the 'modern' has gone beyond such beliefs; that the modern person separates the animate from the inanimate, and even within the class of the animated, distinguishes sharply between human beings and animals (p. 53). The continuation of such 'savage' beliefs into modernity was often, as we have seen in Chapter 1, a cause for scorn among anthropologists from Tylor to Malinowski, and even in an anthropologist more sympathetic to contemporary magical beliefs, such as Lang, belief in animation draws wry comment. Discussing the reverence among traditional peoples when a stone or tree is believed to actually have moved, despite an overarching theoretical belief in the animation of all things, Andrew Lang compares this to the attitude of the contemporary spiritualist.

> It thus appears that while the savage has a general kind of sense that inanimate things are animated, he is a good deal impressed by their conduct when he thinks that they actually display their animation. In the same way a devout modern spiritualist probably regards with more reverence a table which he has seen dancing and heard rapping than a table at which he has only dined. (pp. 54–5)

The banality of the actual objects animated in the magical phenomena of the nineteenth- and early twentieth-century occult is also the focus for Theodor Adorno, that most enraged of critics of the occult. While the focus of Marx's famous allusion to dancing tables – the table as commodity is 'far more wonderful than if it were to begin dancing of its own free will' (Marx 1990: 1.164) – has usually been seen to be the commodity as fetish, rather than a focus on animation per se, Adorno's ire is provoked by a belief in the beyond which finds its basis in the non-animistic world as it is, so confirming the status quo rather than challenging it:

> In order not to lose touch with the everyday dreariness in which, as irredeemable realists, they are at home, they adapt the meaning they revel in to the meaninglessness they flee. The worthless magic is nothing other than the worthless existence it lights up. This is what makes the prosaic so cosy. Facts which differ from what is the case only by not being facts are trumped up as a fourth dimension . . . (Adorno 1978: 242)

Here the problem with occult belief is not so much that its chairs and flower-vases are animated as that they are not, that spiritualist belief merely repeats the inertia of the world as it is according to bourgeois capitalism. The existence of a fourth dimension does not then transform the original three, but merely extends an identical space. Marx's footnote at the end of his reference to a table 'dancing of its own free will' complicates further the relation between the animation of objects and political change, however (on links made between animism and dialectics in the early twentieth century see Leslie 2002: 237–44).

'One may recall,' he tells us in the note, 'that China and the tables began to dance when the rest of the world appeared to be standing still – *pour encourager les autres*' (Marx 1990: 1.164). Here Marx refers to the craze for table-turning which coincided in Germany with the Taiping revolt in China, both taking place during the stasis following the defeat of the 1848 revolutions. Movement is linked to revolution; the inanimate to the status quo. This is suggestive in a way somewhat at odds with the more apparent thrust of Marx's argument here, and certainly at odds with the way Marx's link between the commodity and the fetish has been read ever since. The commodity as fetish claims life for itself, and those who have produced it are reduced to objects:

> To the producers, therefore, the social relations between their private labours appears as what they are, i.e. they do not appear as direct social relations between persons in their work, but rather as material [*dinglich*] relations between persons and social relations between things. (pp. 165–6)

Table-turning and the Taiping revolt are contrasted with political stasis, but what is notable about both is their unexpectedness in that both undermined and challenged consensual thought about 'what is there', that both were either literally or conceptually violent interruptions of the world as it was presumed to be. What the footnote suggests then is that it is not animation per se that is problematic for Marx, but animation in the wrong place. Animation, it would seem, is vital in changing the political status quo. The unexpected evidence of life and movement where none was thought to be here seems to be the very definition of political revolution.

Of course ostensibly for Adorno too it is animation in the wrong place that is problematic, but the right kind of animation is hard to find in Adorno, and certainly animation associated with the magical practices of his contemporaries draws unambiguous critique. But, as I have argued in Chapter 1, the unexpected place and the wrong place could be the same thing. It may be that, in the abjection and corporeality of ectoplasm, the wrong and the unexpected come together. Ectoplasm more than other magical phenomena resists transformation into the commodity; rather, ectoplasm is the transformation of the commodity (as muslin, cheesecloth or wool) into something else. While dancing tables are worth more than static ones, ectoplasmic matter reduces exchange value. Ectoplasm is rubbish. Its animation then is not that of the commodity; it is its status as animated *matter* beyond the commodity that is most suggestive for a rereading of art and political transformation.

Ectoplasm is unusual amid the phenomena of the occult in the late nineteenth and early twentieth centuries in that it has no parallel or precursor in what was believed to be 'primitive' magic. While telepathy and a belief in the power of words, written or spoken, to effect material change can be seen again and again in contemporary accounts of the magical beliefs and practices of 'primitive' people, ectoplasm seems, in a strange and paradoxical way, entirely modern. At the same time, while theories of animism dominate debates raging in contemporary anthropology, it really nowhere concerns the modern occult, which practises animation but not animism. That is, the belief that animate and inanimate objects have their own soul or lifeforce which animates them is replaced with the belief that an object can be moved by something supernatural external to itself. The moving tables of the spiritualist séance are moved by the spirits of the dead, not by the spirit of the table; the movement of objects in ritualistic magic are due to the will and power of the magician rather than their own animating force. However, the phenomena of ectoplasm blur this distinction. Ectoplasm was both matter and prime mover, both nature and animation, both what is and what could be, both reproducer and creator.

However, ectoplasm seems to confirm Adorno's horror at the occult, at its mere reproduction of the world that is, at its reproduction of stasis. As Karen Beckman has noted in her *Vanishing Women: Magic, Film and Feminism* (2003), when it came into contact with the technologies of visual reproduction, the magical matter that, when viewed with the naked eye, glowed, moved, created, reshaped and reformed itself, seemed to be the very matter of life, banishing once and for all any idea that matter is inert, turned, in the view of the camera, into precisely inert and banal matter. The German doctor, sexologist, and psychical researcher Albert von Schrenck-Notzing was one of the most notorious photographers of ectoplasm in the early twentieth century, and even he draws attention to the fact that:

> [w]hat is first noticed, during a superficial examination of the pictures, is their extraordinarily improbable appearance. Most of the products and objects photographed recall well-known objects familiar from our own observations. Thus the amorphous substance often resembles bunches and fibres of unravelled wool or cotton . . . (Schrenck-Notzing 1920: 261)

Seen through the super-eye of technology, the magical phenomena of ectoplasm do seem to be aligned with fascism. Both isolate the trouble with capitalist modernity, claim to transform it, but actually both merely throw over its continued existence a veil of distortion and delusion. What seems to be movement is actually stasis.

Beckman reads this non-animation of ectoplasm in front of the camera as significant beyond any attempt to establish it as 'real'. For her, ectoplasm and cinema exist in a mutually fraught relation, each revealing to each the other's failure to create and transform. Discussing G. A. Smith's *Photographing a Ghost* (1898), she suggests that the film is in part a 'quiet exposure of the inadequacies of the medium of photography in order to assert the supremacy of film in relation to insubstantial matters'. While the photographer in the film fails to capture an image of the ghost as it will not keep still, the film itself does, 'implicitly declaring itself the new master of the unsubstantial, ectoplasmic body' (Beckman 2003: 73). What is crucial here then is film's ability to capture and reproduce movement. Photography attempted to pin down the truth of ectoplasm, but failed: 'A frustration with photography's failure to capture properly the ectoplasm or moving image recurs throughout the literature of the period' (p. 87). As Beckman says, while eye-witness accounts always attribute to ectoplasm extraordinary vitality and animation, photographs of it reveal inert fabric (pp. 83–4). Beckman argues that this is about an inability to deal with temporality, with 'the sequence of events' (p. 87), but it is just as much about the problem of animation itself. Photography is linked to death, film to animation. Beckman cites a dictionary entry for ectoplasm which gives as a third definition: 'An image projected onto a movie screen' (p. 78). Many words associated with film are bodily in origin, especially connected with the idea of membrane or skin (p. 86), and Beckman argues that, in this sense at least, film is 'inseparable from ectoplasm' (p. 78), which makes it all the stranger that ectoplasm, while endlessly photographed, was rarely filmed. It was, however, by Schrenck-Notzing. He had become notorious just before the First World War on the publication of his *Materialisations-Phaenomene* in 1913 (published in English in 1920 as *Phenomena of Materialisation: A Contribution to the Investigation of Mediumistic Teleplastics*). The book detailed his investigation of a French medium, Martha Béraud, given the pseudonym Eva C., who claimed the ability to produce ectoplasm, sometimes manifested in the production of gauze-like strips of material from various orifices, sometimes manifested in the production of figures, limbs and faces. Schrenck-Notzing's book was the account of numerous sittings with Eva, and produced, as both illustration and evidence, many photographs of the medium and her emanations. Explaining Schrenck-Notzing's two later attempts to film ectoplasm (produced by the medium Stanislawa P.), Beckman asks why he only did this twice, why he never attempted to film Eva C., and why, in reproducing stills from the Stanislawa P. film in a book, he does not show them as a sequence, and so reproduce film's ability to capture movement, but as effectively photographs:

> As though wary of exposing cinema's failure to capture the elusive movement of life, Schrenck-Notzing turns the longed-for films back into photographs, perhaps in an attempt to perpetuate the possibility of cinema as he has imagined it. Ironically, cinema must vanish as a medium in order to persist as an idea, and in this sense it can only ever appear as a ghost of itself. (Beckman 2003: 91)

As a reason for this, Beckman suggests that ectoplasm was an *alternative* to film. Film's ability to animate the inanimate is aped by ectoplasmic phenomena: 'although film is largely repressed from the spiritualistic scene, the cinema returns to haunt the séances through the ectoplasm's meanderings' (p. 86). Beckman suggests that this birth of an alternative film was ultimately a 'stillbirth' (p. 78). Ectoplasm shows back to film its own capacity for death rather than vital transformation. But what her work makes clear at the same time is the extent to which ectoplasm and film are crucially linked. I want to argue that this link can be read in another way; that a tracing of ectoplasmic traces through the relations among experiment, movement through animation and political transformation can show an alternative relation between it and film. Beckman assumes that ectoplasm is linked only with spiritualism and its explanations for unexplained phenomena. However, Schrenck-Notzing denied that the spiritualist was the only possible explanation. As the English translator of *Materialisations-Phaenomene*, the physicist and psychical researcher E. E. Fournier d'Albe, explains in his preface to the 1920 English edition, after considering Schrenck-Notzing's evidence, he:

> does not venture an explanation, but agrees in the main with the author in regarding [the phenomena] as a new, or rather a hitherto unexplored, function of certain human organisms. He also takes the author's view that a spiritistic interpretation has not, so far, become unavoidable. (Fournier d'Albe 1920: ix–x)

Ectoplasm then was not necessarily about the use of matter by spirit, but about the possibilities of matter itself. I want to begin exploring the implications of this for form in film, and in art generally, by looking at the account by Thomas Mann of his visit to Schrenck-Notzing's laboratory in the early 1920s.

As if to draw attention to the links between ectoplasm and the materialities of artistic production, a strangely animated typewriter marks the climax of Mann's visit, recounted in his essay from 1923, 'Okkulte Erlebnisse' ('An Experience in the Occult'). As the medium, Willy, sits in a trance, 'the writing-machine begins to click, there on the floor ... Nobody is lying there on the carpet in the dark and playing on the machine, but it is being played on' (Mann 1929: 252). Mann acknowledges that on the publication of Schrenck-Notzing's *Materialisations-Phaenomene* the 'learned world' reacted with 'protests against such a combination of credulity, confused thinking and fraud' and the public 'held its sides with laughter' (p. 224). However, he argues, the publication of the second volume of the work after the First World War saw a different response, not necessarily less critical, but less self-assured in its criticism. The reason for this, says Mann, was a shift in the sense of what is possible in the world: 'People had borne so much they never dreamed of bearing, such outrageous experiences had been their lot, that even their honest indignation lacked the right ring' (p. 225). If the world could produce the horrors of the First World War, it could perhaps produce ectoplasm.

This change identified by Mann is part of a number of shifts in the explanation of ectoplasmic phenomena in the early twentieth century. Ectoplasm had been coined as a term by Charles Richet in 1894 as a result of his investigations of the physical medium Eusapia Palladino. Richet borrowed the term from biology, where it refers to the outer layer of cytoplasm, implying that the phenomenon was the outer manifestation of its inner animating force. In the early twentieth century, as Marina Warner notes, ectoplasm shifted away from being conceived as ethereal and towards the material; its affinities began to 'verge on the category of bodily wastes, palpable and tangible' (Warner 2006: 295). Even here, though, movement is fundamental to its conception. The alternative term, 'teleplasm', used in Schrenck-Notzing's title and preferred by later historians of occult phenomena (see Besterman 1930: 71), suggests that what characterises the production of such material is the inherent linking of form to movement. It crosses distance in a way not conventionally expected of inert matter; its existence as form is somehow imbricated in its achievement of movement. It is animated form. Indeed, the mechanical engineer and psychical researcher William Crawford, summing up his findings after his investigations into the occult claims of the Goligher Circle in Belfast between 1916 and 1920, finally suggested that ectoplasmic emanations were responsible for all otherwise unaccountable movement, that indeed ectoplasm was a making visible of the principle of movement that produced phenomena such as the levitation of bodies and furniture (Crawford 1921). This shift is linked also to the move from seeing ectoplasm as evidence of the beliefs of spiritualists – that it is evidence of an unseen, immaterial world of the spirit that can have communication with the material world of the living – to seeing it as evidence of previously unknown aspects of the material world itself. Ectoplasm, in other words, came to be seen first as a bridge between the material and the immaterial and then as evidence of an animating force inherent in the material world itself.

Mann, too, uses the alternative term for ectoplasm – teleplasm – and demonstrates its own animating effects on him as he moves from a response of shame and disgust to an acknowledgement that the production of teleplasm is linked to creation in the arts; to the ideoplastic. In trying to account for the phenomena he witnesses in Schrenck-Notzing's laboratory – the handkerchief which moves through the air, the bell which is rung by invisible hands, the typewriter tapped by unseen fingers – Mann argues that:

> the *idea* of the phenomenon, present in the subconsciousness of the somnambulist, mingled moreover with that of the other persons present, is by the aid of psychological energy 'ectoplastically' moved, by a biopsychical

projection, to a certain distance, and imprinted – that is to say, 'objectivated.' In other words, we call to aid an uninvestigated *ideoplastic* faculty possessed by the medial constitution. Ideoplastic – a word, and a conception, of Platonic power and charm, not without flattering unction to the artist's ear, who will be ready from now on to characterize, not only his own work, but universal reality as ideoplastic phenomena. (Mann 1929: 259)

The movement from shame and disgust is an interesting one when considering ectoplasm not as a marker of credulity or as a comment on early new technologies but in terms of politics. Mann opens his essay admitting that the subject of his interest is both a corrupt and a corrupting one, and certainly throughout the essay he tells the reader that its effect on him has been to produce nausea; he feels queasy, he feels seasickness, a '[p]rofound wonderment, with a tinge ... of disgust' (pp. 247, 248). Mann links the disgust to but also justifies the interest through an engagement with the world as it is and a sense that it could be different. An interest in the corrupting topic goes beyond charges of bad taste because 'here nature takes the field; and nature is an equivocal element: impure, obscene, spiteful, daemonic' (p. 223). At the same time, the *mise en scène* of the séance, the performance of the medium and the resulting phenomena challenge the limits of the known world and the language used to describe it: 'It was like nothing else in the world' (p. 239). The nauseating subject is justified because it is an experiment which has the potential to bring the new into the world, and those who concede this Mann describes as left-wing because they acknowledge that a movement is possible from the world as it seems to be to a new conception of it:

> In politics there is always a right and a left wing. So in the scientific world there is, with reference to the occult, a strongly conservative and a radical-revolutionist position, together with all sorts of shadings and groupings between, on the one hand, obstinate denial of all rationally unexplainable but persistently reported manifestations like telepathy, true-dreaming, and second sight, and, on the other, a fanatical and uncritical credulity, based, this last, less on solid reverence for the mystery than an inhuman prejudice against all reason and science. (pp. 225–6)

Mann's reading also links art and ectoplasm. Both are a making animate of the inanimate. In trying to think through the implications of this, Mann uses at first an organic trope. He explicitly figures the production of ectoplasmic effects as labour and birth – a 'masculine lying-in' (p. 239) – but what is clear from his attempts to describe the phenomena is that, despite his disavowals, what the spectacle most resembles is the production of film. After Willy has produced some of his phenomena, he sleeps. Mann, recalling his explanatory image of the phenomena as projected dreams, tries to probe that idea further:

> Certainly a man must stand in need of profound and dreamless sleep, after so intense a dream that the events of it are actually projected outside of him! Wait. Let me think. Let me withdraw within myself and try to divine where may be the point, when the magical moment, in which a dream-picture objectivates itself and becomes a spatial reality, before the eyes of other people. Nausea. Clearly this point does not lie within the plane of our consciousness, or of the laws of knowledge as we know them. (p. 249)

For Beckman, film wins out over ectoplasm, even though by doing so it acknowledges in itself what it disavows in its other, but here the ectoplasmic wins out over a certain conception of film. Mann's consciousness refuses to see that 'the magical moment' is in fact film because, as is evident in *The Magic Mountain* (1924), he can only see film as flickering images on a screen, and these are false movements that produce only stasis. In the novel, Hans Castorp goes to see a film with his cousin, Joachim, and a fellow consumptive, the dying Karen Karstedt. The cousins agree to visit the cinema only in order to please Karen. During the film, Hans Castorp imagines the robust criticism Settembrini, his intellectual mentor at the sanatorium, would have made of it, and in so doing shows that he too is sceptical of film's attractions. Near them, the 'ignorant red face' of a fellow inmate from the sanatorium shows huge enjoyment of the film, as do the faces of most of the rest of the audience. Despite this, however, what the moving pictures lead to is not movement in the world itself but to stasis. When the film ends, there is no applause, because there was nobody 'there to be applauded, to be called before the curtain and thanked for the rendition' (Mann 1983: 317). The 'phantoms' which appear on screen cannot return the look of the audience, and therefore ultimately the audience is paralysed: 'Their hands lay powerless in the face of the nothing that confronted them' (p. 317). In the end, even when present, those on screen cannot return the audience's look, and so their presence as well as their absence produces stasis. The face on screen, the 'charming apparition', 'seemed to see and saw not, it was not moved by the glances bent upon it, its smile and nod were not of the present but of the past, so that the impulse to respond was baffled, and lost in a feeling of impotence' (p. 318). The absence of the reciprocated look which produces stasis can be contrasted to the appearance, much later in the novel, of the ghost of Joachim to Hans during a séance at the sanatorium. In a darkened corner of the room, Joachim sits, looking as he had done in the few days before he died. As Hans looks at him, the 'quiet, friendly' eyes of the ectoplasmically reconstructed Joachim 'sought out Hans Castorp, and him alone' (p. 680). Joachim's returned look produces sudden action in Hans. Instead of following Dr Krokowski's instruction to speak to Joachim, Hans stands up, and leaves the room (p. 681). So while film produces stasis, other kinds of magical animation are acceptable if the viewer is acknowledged and so animation can be experienced by the viewer too. Willy's phenomena cannot be linked to film, however much everything about them suggests that connection, because the ectoplasmically produced being in Schrenck-Notzing's laboratory acknowledges Mann by throwing a luminous ring at him (p. 250).

If it is the screen that is the problem for Mann, its blank absence at the end of the film undoing the 'magical moment' of the film, giving a lie to the audience's connection to the movement they have just seen, then Robert Herring, in *Close Up* in 1929, suggests a solution. For him, film will become in the future a kind of ectoplasmic projection by *freeing* itself from the screen. Herring's article suggests an alternative aim for the avant-garde in film. He argues that the 'new cinema' will be new to the extent that it understands 'what is at the bottom of cinema' (Herring 1998: 50). At the heart of this is magic, and 'we can't get on unless we keep a firm hold on magic' (p. 50). Magic for Herring is the name for that which is most real: 'Anything that is real is magical; magic is the name for the thing that is larger than the thing itself, and this larger thing is what makes it real' (p. 50). Cinema then is truly magical, that is most itself, when it produces not a reproduction but the *thing* itself. Herring believes this is the future of cinema, and will mean that cinema in the end leaves the screen: 'why should not the visual image leave the screen, why should we not do without screens? We are giving stereoscopy to the images, giving them depth and solidity' (p. 56). Unlike Hans Castorp's experience of the cinema, where the final blank screen stands for the emptiness of the whole experience, Herring's 'new cinema' goes beyond the screen to produce the 'larger thing' that makes the thing real. His speculative description of this thing sounds like nothing so much as ectoplasm:

> First what he [man] did can survive, now what he is. First the work of his hands, work of brain, the effects of his hands and brain. But all still and mute. Then his voice could be kept, and his image could be kept. Moving. Now they will have to be detached, and instead of him contenting himself with making dolls and statues and music he could only hear as it was being played, he will have these images in which sound and sight meet, detached so to speak from their owners. Man making man, of a kind . . . There is logically . . . no reason why he [man] should not ultimately create himself in motion and speech, moving in the patterns of his creation, just as he made the best he could when he made dolls like himself . . . (p. 56)

Film here is most magical when it goes beyond the screen. The ectoplasmic, then, is entwined with film not through the idea of skin or surface, not because it is like an 'image projected onto a movie screen', but because both are animated matter.

Ezra Pound and Movement in the Wrong Place

This sense of the necessary link between ideas and the bringing of them to life in Mann's discussion of the ectoplasmic can be found with regard to poetry in Pound's quotation of a letter from the avant-garde Japanese poet Katue Kitasono in *Guide to Kulchur*. The letter sets out the problem of the relation between 'imagery and ideoplasty' in poetry (Pound 1970: 137). For Kitasono, poetry is made from a movement from language, to imagery, to ideoplasty. Without the latter, poetry cannot be created. For him, ideoplasty seems to refer to the extent to which the words on the page, creating images, then go beyond the page to have effects in the world through the creation of something new. This can be seen in his example of those who erroneously try to work backwards from ideoplasty to the image: 'it cannot be allowed as orthodox of poetry that imagery is performed by ideoplasty' (p. 138). Where this is attempted – 'by religionists, politicians, and satirists' – the writer begins with the world and works back to the poem (pp. 138–9). True poetry, on the other hand 'materializes intuitions perceptively and combines' rather than beginning with matter and turning it into poetry (p. 139). What is crucial is that it is a new form, a new plasticity, which is made beyond what already exists in the world. True poetry is then not an inert copy of the world but a way of using the world to bring the new into it.

Pound links the views expressed in Kitasono's letter to his own earlier articulations of the method of both Henri Gaudier-Brzeska and William Carlos Williams (p. 139). Finishing this chapter, Pound sets against the views of Kitasono 'the sickly and pasty-faced appearance of the lower deck men as seen some years ago' when the British fleet docked at Rapallo (p. 139). Pound details the terrible conditions, cramped and airless, below deck. He is not explicit about how this anecdote relates to Kitasono's ideas on true poetry, but rather shows the moribund state of British institutions – an often repeated claim in *Guide to Kulchur* – and the ghostly appearance of the crew, nearer death than life. Unlike the ideoplastic, which materialises and animates abstractions in order to bring something new into the world, the British fleet are literally and figuratively near the inertia of death.

This sense of the ability of constructed form to create the movement of life can be seen too in Pound's earlier essay on the Romanian sculptor Constantin Brancusi. Pound argues that Brancusi's work, like *The Divine Comedy*, works towards the formal perfection of 'Paradiso', and yet for Pound the most extraordinary element of the work is the promise of the movement of matter.

The achievement of Brancusi's ovoids, for Pound, is that 'from some angles at least the ovoid does come to life and appear ready to levitate' (Pound 1985b: 444). So, while Brancusi's forms are seen by many as abstract, what is crucial for Pound is not their rejection of the forms of the world but their ability to bring to the world new movement, to reveal the animation of that which had been thought inanimate. As Rebecca Beasley has shown, in the early 1920s Pound defended the sculptor for the utility of his work, for its connection to the world. In a letter to a left-wing journal whose reviewer had criticised Brancusi's work for its non-engagement, Pound argued that Brancusi's 'mystical residue', rather than separating him from the world, is in fact the marker of his engagement (quoted in Beasley 2007: 182). It is Brancusi's 'mysticism', his separation from the world of things, that paradoxically allows the most direct involvement with the world. His abstractions (almost) levitate. Like cinema, the sculpture Pound champions is that which animates the inanimate through new formal techniques, which is, in his words, a sculpture 'with something inside' (Pound 1985c: 153).

Given this, it is strange then that Pound's own attitude to cinema was so ambiguous. As Beasley points out, Pound's conclusion in a 'Paris Letter' from 1923 that Abel Gance's *La Roue* (1922) probably showed once and for all that 'the cinema is no use as art' coincides exactly with his collaboration with Fernand Léger, Dudley Murphy and George Antheil on *Ballet mécanique* (1924) (Beasley 2007: 188; see also Freeman 1996). Indeed, at times his attitude seems not so much ambiguous as straightforwardly hostile. From his essay 'Vorticism' (1914) to *Guide to Kulchur*, Pound uses the cinematic to demonstrate the opposite to his own sense of how form brings life. In 'Vorticism', he argues that the recent arts have shown two trajectories. In the first, impressionism leads to futurism; in the second, the initial opposition to the impressionists, the symbolists, have been followed by vorticism, in which Pound groups 'expressionism, neo-cubism, and imagism' (Pound 1916: 104). Both impressionism and futurism are associated by Pound with the cinema: 'The logical end of impressionist art is the cinematograph. The state of mind of the impressionist tends to become cinematographical. Or, to put it another way, the cinematograph does away with the need of a lot of impressionist art' (p. 103). If impressionism is made redundant by cinema, then futurism is even more so. It is 'a sort of accelerated impressionism' (p. 94), a merely sped up attempt to copy or imitate 'light on a haystack' (p. 107). What links the practices of which Pound disapproves to the cinema is the extent to which the viewer has an active part in the process:

> There are two opposed ways of thinking of a man: firstly, you may think of him as that toward which perception moves, as the toy of circumstance, as the plastic substance *receiving* impressions; secondly, you may

think of him as directing a certain fluid force against circumstance, as *conceiving* instead of merely reflecting and observing. (p. 103; emphasis in original)

In both cases the human being is plastic, a malleable form capable of being reshaped, but in the former this plasticity is moulded by external factors while in the latter the plasticity is projected outward into the world. The plastic, in other words, is itself animated from within. In Pound's infrequent references to cinema in *Guide to Kulchur* too the method of film is associated in general with passivity and set against an active creation of form in the world, and in particular with political passivity. Pound quotes George H. Tinkham, the 'Unkle George' of *The Pisan Cantos*: 'George H. Tinkham has aptly branded the techniques of some of the tyrants and bleeders as cinema technique: "gives 'em something new to think of before they have understood it" – "it" being the preceding wheeze' (1970: 170). Tinkham, a congressman from Massachusetts who, we are told in Canto 76, 'stood like a statue' (Pound 1987: 475), is used by Pound here to link political mendacity to the cinema. In both, impressions are launched in quick succession at the passive recipient in order to confuse and befuddle. The wrong kind of movement is linked elsewhere in Canto 76 to political and economic corruption and to the movement of the 'movies':

>   and if theft be the main principle in government
>   (every bank of discount J. Adams remarked)
>   there will be larceny on a minor pattern
>   a few camions, a stray packet of sugar
>   and the effect of the movies
>   (Pound 1987: 471)

Pound's essay on Brancusi, while not mentioning the cinema, is suggestive too with regards to the particular location of good as opposed to bad movement, and so with regards to Pound's sense of where animation comes from. What distinguishes Brancusi's ovoids is that they, unlike more conventional sculpture, are interesting and alive to the viewer from multiple angles. Great sculpture, says Pound, should allow the viewer to walk round the work of art and get something from it from all angles. This is in direct contrast to Pound's criticism of cinema, where viewer is made passive, can only be in one position in response to film, where movement is all in the film. It is precisely this ability of Brancusi's ovoid to be alive to the viewer from many different angles that promises to move it from inert form to animation: 'from some angles at least the ovoid does come to life and appear reader to levitate.' While Pound denies a supernatural origin of the readiness of the ovoid 'to levitate' – 'Crystal-gazing?? No.' (1985b: 444) – he does suggest that it is due to 'the possibility of self-hypnosis by means of highly polished brass surfaces'. The viewer is hypnotised (like the passive film viewer), but somehow it is self-hypnosis, and therefore productive of animation rather than 'accelerated impressionism'. Yet in the section from *Guide to Kulchur* where Kitasono's letter is quoted, the regulation of rhythm, the extent to which the impression made on the reader is due to self or the tyranny of the creator is ambiguous. After quoting the first section of Kitasono's letter, and before the second, Pound intervenes with a directive to the reader: *'This is where the present commentator suggests that his reader pause for reflection'* (Pound 1970: 138; emphasis in original).

The struggle over movement and its implications can be seen throughout *The Cantos*, but in particular from *The Pisan Cantos* onwards. The desire to bring animation to a deadened world dominates *The Cantos* from their confident séance-like beginning to their painful almost-end:

> I have tried to write Paradise
> Do not move
>   Let the wind speak
>   that is paradise.
> (Pound 1987: 816)

However, as this suggests, there is animation and animation for Pound; the wind moves but we are commanded to be still. While he may have been a keen cinema-goer, and fond of Disney films in particular (see Terrell 1993: 724, note 12), film is the wrong kind of movement for Pound. In Canto 116, Pound retains the idea of paradise but acknowledges its impossibility, because of his own errors and because the world as it is militates against it. While the poet 'cannot make it cohere', paradise still exists, 'it coheres alright' (Pound 1987: 810, 811). Here Pound maintains the existence of something that has not existed, and that possibly cannot exist. Amidst his painful detailing of failed attempts at paradise – 'Muss., wrecked for an error' (p. 809) – and his certainty that paradise still exists, he sets 'Disney against the metaphysicals' (p. 810). Which of these most properly enacts the animation which alone can lead to the 'great ball of crystal' (p. 809), which throughout *The Cantos* stands for the perfection of paradise, is not entirely clear.

In his essay 'The Metaphysical Poets' (1921), T. S. Eliot quotes the critical definition of Samuel Johnson; in the metaphysical poets 'the most heterogeneous ideas are yoked by violence together' (Eliot 1975: 60). While for Johnson this was a fault, Eliot argues that those poets called metaphysical wrote in the way they did because of a unified sensibility which could cohere the world of the senses with the world of the mind. For him, all great poetry should achieve the coherence of the disparate, should make the matter of the world meaningful and something beyond its inert and discrete existence:

> When a poet's mind is perfectly equipped for its work, it is constantly amalgamating disparate experience; the ordinary man's experience is chaotic, irregular, fragmentary. The latter falls in love, or reads Spinoza, and these two experiences have nothing to do with each other, or with the noise of the typewriter or the smell of cooking; in the mind of the poet these experiences are always forming new wholes. (p. 64)

What Eliot sees as the important element of the metaphysicals and all poetry that is for him real poetry is very close to Pound and Kitasono's 'ideoplasty'. Kitasono's letter quoted by Pound in *Guide to Kulchur* argues that 'a shell, a typewriter and grapes' (Pound 1970: 138) are given life as a unit through the ideoplastic work of poetry. The inert matter of the world comes to have meaning and life through the animating work of creation. Indeed, Pound's images for the creativity of living art in his early critical essays move towards exactly the image of animation that dominated occult practices during the period – ectoplasm. As we have seen, in 'Vorticism' Pound describes the active man as 'directing a certain fluid force against circumstance, as *conceiving* instead of merely reflecting and observing' (1916: 103). In the earlier essay, 'The Serious Artist' (1913), the crucial element in art is just such an animating force:

> We might come to believe that the thing that matters in art is a sort of energy, something more or less like electricity or radio-activity, a force transfusing, welding, and unifying. A force rather like water when it spurts up through very bright sand and sets it in swift motion. You may make what image you like. (Pound 1985a: 49)

However, beyond this Pound cannot go. While Pound is deeply concerned with the question of how to animate, his failure to engage more fully with the ecto- or teleplasmic is related to his aesthetic and political impasses. Mann's sense of ectoplasm as linked to artistic creation ends in nausea because he will not make the link to film; for Pound too his conception of film as a problem is suggestive of his inability to fully articulate the possibilities offered by the model of ectoplasm. His thinking around film focuses on the flickering images on the screen rather than on the other kinds of movement constitutive of film. The flickering images overwhelm the agency of the viewer, they are insubstantial, they lack the projection of force and energy into the world which Pound saw as necessary for a living art. In *The Pisan Cantos* this struggle is particularly visible. Kokka's aphorism in Canto 74 – 'You sit stiller . . . / if whenever you move something jangles' (Pound 1987: 447) – expresses the struggle between stasis and energy in a decadent society which elsewhere Pound attempts to resolve through the figures of the periplum as ordered movement and the crystal jet (p. 463) as halfway between the moving water of the early cantos and the fixed forms in crystal and jade of the later.

Pound cannot allow film to be ectoplasmic – substantial animated matter, moving in the world of things – and because of this his own ectoplasmically related theories of creation – the 'fluid force' directed against 'circumstance' – struggle to save him while he clings to an idea that the world could be other than it is amidst forced stagnation and inertia. Pound's economics underlie such an attempt – where the circulation of money is vital but so is a fixing of its value. Such a precarious unity between movement and fixity is expressed in Pound's gloss on Jefferson's economic theory: 'Jefferson's formula is SOLID. If the state emits ENOUGH money for valid and justifiable expenses and keeps it moving, circulating, going out the front door and coming in the tax window, the nation will not suffer stagnation' (Pound 1973b: 266; emphasis in original). In *The Pisan Cantos*, however, the simplicity of this figure for a perfect union of movement and stasis – out through the door and in through the window – is lost. The difficulty of distinguishing between clutter and fecundity, between entropy and movement, is central to Canto 74. Early on in the canto Pound gives the story of Ouan Jin – the writer whose words created the things they named – which leads to much moving and removing, but also to an impairment of the ability to move:

> Ouan Jin
> ... whose mouth was removed by his father
> because he made too many *things*
> whereby cluttered the bushman's baggage ...
> Ouan Jin spoke and thereby created the named
> thereby making clutter
> the bane of men moving
> and so his mouth was removed
> as you will find it removed in his pictures
> (Pound 1987: 440–1)

But clutter too is the unwanted effect of the wrong sort of economic movement.

> Never inside the country to raise the standard of living
> but always abroad to increase the profits of usurers,
> dixit Lenin,
> and gun sales lead to more gun sales
> they do not clutter the market for gunnery
> there is no saturation
> (p. 443)

Pound's aim in *The Cantos*, like Dante's in *The Divine Comedy*, was to create a world that had no empirical existence in the actual world and at the same time to demonstrate how human beings could move from one to the other. Dante of course has Virgil to guide him, as well as the considerable guide of

Catholic tradition. Dante's own movement, and the implied general movement from one thing to another, are controlled, taken for granted rather than the subject of anxiety and frustration. But in his essay on Cavalcanti, Pound asserts Cavalcanti's more modern mobility of mind over Dante's fixity: 'The tone of his mind is infinitely more "modern" than Dante's ... his position, here as on the rest of these cardinal points, shows him to be "very dangerous" to the peace of the medieval mind, if immobility may be considered "peace"' (Pound 1985c: 159). Pound's guides are more scattered, fragmented and diffuse; they figure movement, unlike Dante, but as such create a difficult to manage possibility of the wrong kind of movement. Kokka's aphorism is used ironically by Pound to demonstrate the rigidity associated with the search for paradise and the good society in the wrong places (see Pound 1970: 83). But in *The Cantos*, and particularly in *The Pisan Cantos*, Pound constantly moves towards and then retreats from any possibility of 'jangling'.

Eisenstein and the Plasmatic

If Pound retreats from the possibilities of both film and the ectoplasmic, in his theoretical writing on film Eisenstein embraces the animation of the plasmatic to make his politics and his aesthetics work together. Indeed, this reading, unlike many other readings of Eisenstein, makes it possible to consider both at once. That Eisenstein used anthropological ideas of magic in the creation of his filmic theory and method has been acknowledged and explored by numerous critics. However, Eisenstein's interest in magic has been mostly connected to his idea of inner speech, to an instinctive and emotional understanding. In what is the most comprehensive consideration of the importance of magic in Eisenstein's work, Rachel Moore acknowledges that: 'More than anyone, Eisenstein defines the effectiveness of magic in artistic production' (Moore 2000: 19). She acknowledges in her introduction that this effectiveness is linked to a particular idea of the medium of artistic production; she says that for Eisenstein, as for a number of the other film theorists she considers, 'the space between the word and its referent was a magical one' (p. 7). However, Moore's discussion of Eisenstein's use of magic is mostly connected to his idea of inner sense, to a psychologisation of it, and not to his politics. This is made clear in her linking of Eisenstein's concept of sensual thinking and its significance for art to Freud's theorisation of the unconscious. Freud argues in 'The Unconscious' (1915) that animism and the unconscious are linked, and Moore reads this link as follows:

> The unconscious, in Freud's argument, effectively rushes in to fill the vacancy created by rationality's dispersion of an animated universe. This history of inferences of a consciousness to things and people outside ourselves lays the foundation for the concept of the unconscious.

> Likewise, Eisenstein rests his case on inferences we at one point believed but that now resonate as artistic practices and poetic theory... (Moore 2000: 35)

However, in 'The Unconscious', Freud links animism as magical thinking not to the *creation* of the unconscious but to our capacity to acknowledge its existence. Magic does not create something but allows us to see it. Freud argues that psychoanalysis asks that we treat ourselves in the same way we treat other people, the same way that in the past people treated animals, rocks and trees:

> we must say: all the acts and manifestations which I notice in myself and do not know how to link up with the rest of my mental life must be judged as if they belonged to someone else: they are to be explained by a mental life ascribed to this other person. Furthermore, experience shows that we understand very well how to interpret in other people (that is, how to fit into their chain of mental events) the same acts which we refuse to acknowledge as being mental in ourselves. Here some special hindrance evidently deflects our investigations from our own self and prevents our obtaining a true knowledge of it. (Freud 1952b: 169–70)

This is about an act of perception, not about the unconscious as the locus of the 'primitive' in modernity. For Freud the act of perception that produced animism is the same as the act of perception that acknowledges the existence of the unconscious; for Eisenstein the act of perception which produces animism is the same as the act of perception which acknowledges the truths of Marxism. So where Freud and Eisenstein's ideas do overlap is neither in the idea of a survival or a 'return' to the primitive, nor in the transformation of primitive magic into psychology, but in the insistence that the perceived surface of reality and truth are not necessarily the same, and for Eisenstein this is due primarily not to psychical structures but to the obfuscations of capitalism. As her reading of Freud shows, the centrality of Eisenstein as a Marxist filmmaker and film theorist is almost lost in Moore's argument. She does acknowledge the eccentricity of Eisenstein's use of magic in the context of Marxist orthodoxy, but moves on quickly rather than trying to account for it:

> Leaders of the Revolution like Lenin and Trotsky grew up in landowner families on farms and had a lot of contact with peasants; nonetheless, Trotsky, for example, in *My Life*, rages against the peasants' stupidity when they failed to put his geometry lesson into practice to measure the land. Ironically, for Trotsky, what was wrong with primitive thinking – the 'dull empiricism of the peasant' – was peasants' inability to privilege theory over petty facts. Still, primitive speech and primitive customs became poetic theory for Eisenstein in 1935. (Moore 2000: 44)

This 'still', I would argue, is the marker of fact that Moore doesn't really consider how Eisenstein's idea of the prelogical fits with his Marxism, or rather does not consider its eccentricity, or what that eccentricity can tell us. In her discussion of the famous cream separator sequence in *Old and New/The General Line* (1929), Moore acknowledges that at the heart of the sequence is a process of magical transformation. The priestly procession which has proceeded the separator sequence has failed in its attempts to bring rain; the cream separator, newly bought by the collective farm, on the other hand, gushes liquid into the world. For Moore, it is the camera, not the priest, that has made it rain. But here, however, is the problem with this kind of analysis of Eisenstein, for whom, surely, it is communism that made it rain. The idea that it is the camera, the production of art, that makes it rain rather than communism sets Eisenstein's aesthetics against and over his politics. This can be seen too in Ian Christie's introduction to the volume *Eisenstein Rediscovered* (1993). While explicitly dealing with the relationship between Eisenstein and Soviet, and especially Stalinist, Russia, Christie does not really deal with Eisenstein and Marxism. He wants to rescue Eisenstein from charges of collusion with Stalin and defend him against charges that his work was built on 'a series of massive mistakes' (Christie and Taylor 1993: 2), but Christie does not do this by interrogating Eisenstein as a Marxist thinker or filmmaker, but rather by separating out his politics from his aesthetics: 'But although he initially identified cinema with the challenge of building communism . . . it was in fact cinema that led him to the philosophy and history of art' (p. 29).

In both these cases, the animation of cinema, that which produces movement, is linked finally to the aesthetic rather than the political. However, this separation clearly does not make sense in terms of Eisenstein. More recent work has acknowledged politics as absolutely central for Eisenstein. Richard Taylor has asserted that '[t]he ends justified the means and for Eisenstein the ends were always *ultimately* ideological, even if they were frequently expressed in aesthetic terms' (Taylor 2010: 3; emphasis in original). It is true, however, that a tension exists in Eisenstein's work between cinema's aesthetics and its politics, and I want to argue that Eisenstein attempts to work through this most clearly via a sense of the ectoplasmic.

Eisenstein the Marxist filmmaker was famously enchanted by three of the icons of the cinema of bourgeois capitalism – D. W. Griffith, Charlie Chaplin and Walt Disney. In her investigation of Eisenstein and magic, Moore writes about his fascination with the last, but does not really acknowledge the overwhelming tension in his writing on Disney between his sense of the power of Disney's works and its place in US capitalist society, between magic as consolation and magic as revolution. Moore notes the annotation Eisenstein wrote on one section of his manuscript notes on Disney – 'Between plasmation and fire'. She concentrates on fire over plasmation in her analysis, and indeed in this section of the manuscript Eisenstein does too. As Moore argues, Eisenstein uses the idea of fire to explore the attractions of animation, and the way it connects to sensuous, prelogical thinking:

> Persistent suggestion through fire, the appearance of fire, the play of fire, images of fire, is capable in certain cases of provoking 'unconscious' and 'impulsive' conditions – that is, of bringing 'sensuous thought' to the foreground, and forcing 'consciousness' into the background. (Eisenstein 1986: 32–3)

However, this image of fire throws all focus onto the object of perception, rather than a sense of its construction, which elsewhere in Eisenstein is so much to the fore. Indeed, Eisenstein links fire and plasmation through the idea that both are about the production of life, fire 'resembles the potentiality of primal plasma, from which everything can arise' (p. 45). Plasmation, on the other hand, and Eisenstein's use of it in his writings on Disney and elsewhere, suggest another way of thinking about the possibility of film to create life other than as it exists.

Eisenstein claims in his notes that the epos of Disney is 'Paradise Regained' (p. 2). In comparison to Chaplin's films, which have an epos of 'Paradise Lost', Disney films, because they are drawn, are able to produce such a paradise, such a 'complete return to a world of complete freedom' (p. 3). However, Eisenstein can only account for such powerful attractions in the context of US capitalism by constructing the films as at best an expression of all that the oppressed American worker has lost, at worst as escapism. Indeed, they are able to express such a critique *because* they are escapism:

> you can see how the drawn magic of a reconstructed world had to arise at the very summit of a society that had completely enslaved nature – namely, in America . . . for Disney's films are a revolt against partitioning and legislating, against spiritual stagnation and greyness. But the revolt is lyrical. The revolt is a daydream. Fruitless and lacking consequences. These aren't those daydreams which, accumulating, give birth to action and raise a hand to realize the dream. They are the 'golden dreams' you escape to. (pp. 3–4)

So far, Eisenstein's assessment of Disney in no way accounts for the astonished veneration for Disney that he expresses elsewhere. Indeed, he accounts for the pleasure and success of the films in terms similar to Pound's critique of film generally – they delude us by their speed: 'And if most of them did'nt [*sic*] flash by us so quickly in one or two short little reels, we would be made angry by the moral uselessness of their existence on the screen' (p. 8). Elsewhere, what Eisenstein isolates in Disney are those things which prove to be 'decisive features in any art form, but only in Disney, presented in their very purest form'

(p. 6). How this acme of art produces work which consoles but does not urge on to action is not really explored by Eisenstein, neither is the question of how something which exposes the horror of the situation of the worker should be experienced with such unanimous delight. In as much as he considers the effects on the viewer, Eisenstein's attempt to work through this again land at an impasse. Asking how it is that all ages, classes and nationalities are charmed by Mickey Mouse, Eisenstein answers his question as follows:

> First of all, one could say that Disney's work seems to contain all the faultlessly active features by which a work of art influences – seemingly in the greatest possible quantity and greatest possible purity.
>
> In terms of the faultlessness of its influence, Disney's work statistically scores the greatest possible number of points, considering the viewers won over by it. (p. 6)

Such a perfect influence sits strangely, however, with Eisenstein's assertion that the films of Disney produce no revolutionary effect in the world, unless such 'perfect' influence is entirely in collusion with capitalist shackles, that it influences perfectly to the extent that it constrains the viewer more deeply within the bonds of capitalism. If this is the case, then it is not clear how the films at the same time provide for the viewer a rush of energy beyond the utilitarian, a burst of unfettered jouissance, even if expressed only in laughter. It may be, of course, that the 'complete and total release' (p. 8) Eisenstein says that Disney films bestow on the viewer is the very means of such a tightening of the fetters of capitalism, but in this case their means of construction should be anathema to the Marxist filmmaker, not a model for the connection between film and the sensuous, the rational and the prelogical.

Elsewhere in Eisenstein's note on Disney – and in his 'Notes on Drawing' from 1932, predating the nascent essay on Disney – are suggestions of how this problem may be, if not solved, then productive. While Rachel Moore moves from Eisenstein's annotation – 'Between plasmation and fire' – toward a consideration of fire, I want to consider Eisenstein's concept of plasmation and argue that, if fire is a model for the viewer's fascination with the flickering images on the screen, the plasmatic is a model for an awareness of the revolutionary possibilities of the material movement of film. In his essay on Dada and film, Thomas Elsaesser has noted the contradictory organisation of the machine which produces the flickering images of film: 'the cinematic apparatus is devised to function so as to disguise the actual movement *of* the image (passing through the projector gate) in order to create a non-existent movement *in* the image' (Elsaesser 1996: 23). What Eisenstein sees in Disney, I want to argue, is a magic most obviously given body in the ectoplasmic, in that it draws attention to both the 'of' and the 'in'. The possibilities of drawing are alive for Eisenstein, and made clear in Disney's films, to the extent that they necessarily make visible and give body to the truth that the image is both a movement 'in' and a movement 'of'; and the name Eisenstein gives this is plasmation.

What is crucial about Disney for Eisenstein is that it makes visible the movement of the film through the projector as *the* crucial movement in film, rather than movement on screen. In his essay 'The Filmic Fourth Dimension' (1929), Eisenstein recounts his first discovery of the significance of this movement in editing the sequence of the religious procession in *Old and New/The General Line*. In looking at the stills from the sequence, 'deprived of motion, the reasons for their choice seem completely incomprehensible' (Eisenstein 1977b: 69). In explaining the discoveries he had made in the theory of montage editing in creating the film, Eisenstein draws a parallel between this and music. Around the dominant tone in music, he argues, are overtones and undertones, the relation between which has become 'one of the most significant means for affect by the experimental composers of our century, such as Debussy and Scriabin' (p. 66). It is visual overtones and undertones – 'All sorts of aberrations, distortions, and other defects' (p. 66) – which create the possible revolutionary effects of Eisenstein's form of montage: 'In combinations which exploit *these collateral vibrations* – which is nothing less than *the filmed material itself* – we can achieve, completely analogous with music, *the visual overtonal complex of the shot*' (p. 67; emphasis in original). In other words, this is a way of finding movement in the shot itself which is finally revealed through the moving processes of projection:

> And here is observed one further curious parallel between the visual and the musical overtone: It cannot be traced in the static frame, just as it cannot be traced in the musical score. Both emerge as genuine values only in the dynamics of the musical or cinematographic *process*.
>
> Overtonal conflicts, foreseen but unwritten in the score, cannot emerge without the dialectic process of the passage of the film through the projection apparatus, or that of the performance by a symphony orchestra. (p. 69; emphasis in original)

The idea that movement embedded *in* the shot is made visible by the movement *of* the projecting apparatus creates for Eisenstein a link between film and the fourth dimension, a concept already embedded in occult thinking and artistic practice by the late 1920s (see Henderson 1983; Clarke 2001; Clarke and Henderson 2002). The visual overtone is 'spatially inexpressible . . . only emerging and existing in the fourth dimension' (Eisenstein 1977b: 69). Eisenstein acknowledges the concept of the fourth dimension as spanning the occult and the discoveries of the new physics – 'Einstein? Or mysticism? Or a joke?' (p. 69) – but quotes Einstein to suggest that the fourth dimension is more everyday reality than occult mystery. However, elsewhere Eisenstein describes the relation between the shot and the montage which emerges in the movement through the projector in different terms. In his essay 'Through Theater to Cinema' (1934), the shot is figured as inert nature which needs to be brought into life through the animating properties of montage:

> The shot, considered as material for the purpose of composition, is more resistant than granite. This resistance is specific to it. The shot's tendency toward complete factual immutability is rooted in its nature. This resistance has largely determined the richness and variety of montage forms and styles – for montage becomes the mightiest means for a really important creative remolding of nature . . . The minimum 'distortable' fragment of nature is the shot; ingenuity in its combinations is montage. (Eisenstein 1977d: 5)

As François Albera has remarked, for Eisenstein 'the object, nature, is inert and passive (being-there) and . . . must be dynamised from the outside' and this fuels his aim of 'stripping bare' the process of the construction of movement in film (Albera 1993: 208), of making visible the fact that movement is created rather than recorded by film. If, for Eisenstein, the creation of movement in film is prioritised over the mere recording of movement in world, then this priority is due to the politically revolutionary possibilities of film. As Albera suggests, the sequence of the peasant boy leaping for joy into the Tsar's throne near the end of *October* is purely filmic in that it shows what could never occur in the real world: 'Here there is "movement" in the form of a violent displacement of the subject from one side of the frame to the other without any transition' (p. 202). This is an impossible movement at the moment of the political coming into being of another world, a world other than the one that previously existed. For Eisenstein, the recording of the 'real' can only reproduce the 'reality' of bourgeois capitalism, whereas the *creation* of movement can make visible the otherwise hidden possibilities that the world could be otherwise. This distinction in the end marks Eisenstein's fundamental criticism of D. W. Griffith, who 'at all times remains on a level of *representation and objectivity* and nowhere does he try through the *juxtaposition* of shots to shape *import and image*' (Eisenstein 1977g: 241).

This reading of Griffith is suggestive of the reason for Disney's importance for Eisenstein. In Disney animation, the movement on screen is impossible in nature; it is only possible in film. As Esther Leslie has noted, although without linking this to the contemporary occult, '[d]rawing was a form of magic for Eisenstein' (Leslie 2002: 223). For Eisenstein, the 'unforgettable symbol' of Disney's work is a family of octopuses whose 'legs' metamorphose into tails and trunks:

> How much (imaginary!) divine omnipotence there is in this! What magic of reconstructing the world according to one's fantasy and will! A ficti-

tious world. A world of lines and colours which subjugates and alters itself to your command. You tell a mountain: move, and it moves. You tell an octopus: be an elephant, and the octopus becomes an elephant. (Eisenstein 1986: 3)

This triumph over the 'fetters' of how things are is at the centre of Disney's power (p. 4). More than this, though, the shot – that is, each individual drawing – inherently contains movement in a way that the shot as recording of the world does not. With regard to this, Eisenstein revisits and redefines his idea of 'attraction' in relation to Disney. What all 'attractions' share is the 'rejection of once-and-forever allotted form, freedom from ossification, the ability to dynamically assume any form' (p. 21). But what makes drawing so important is that, unlike in the idea of the shot as nature discussed above, this potential already exists in the static drawing even before the animation of film. Eisenstein returns to the idea from 'The Filmic Fourth Dimension' that the shot itself contains movement. Attractions have:

> [a]n ability that I'd call 'plasticness', for here we have a being represented in drawing, a being of a definite form, a being which has attained a definite appearance, and which behaves like the primal protoplasm, not yet possessing a 'stable' form, but capable of assuming any form and which, skipping along the rungs of the evolutionary ladder, attaches itself to any and all forms of animal existence. (p. 21)

In animation, the shot, the drawing, is already more than just inert nature. It already constitutes movement – the movement of the hand and pencil or pen across the page. Eisenstein links the stroke drawing of a single contour to cave drawing and, as such, '[m]obility of contour is still a certain "link" with the past in the sense that then, drawing was *fundamentally* (and almost exclusively) *running*, a movement which was as if only accidentally erased' (p. 43; emphasis in original). Animation in Disney then is the movement of movement; it is the making visible through movement of an already existing movement inherent in the original material. However, this also constitutes the problem of Disney. Its effects of movement on screen, so fantastical, so beyond nature, their origin in drawing which already constitutes movement, are so powerful that they obliterate a sense that this is a production of the revolutionary possibilities of film. The awareness that the image is created through the movement of film through a projector is lost. So while Disney solves the problem for Eisenstein of whether the shot is inert or already contains movement, it produces a further problem in terms of the relation between the fact of projection and seeming autonomy of the images on screen.

In the first section, from 1932, of his 'Notes on Drawing', reproduced at the end of the 1986 edition of *Eisenstein on Disney*, Eisenstein attempts to resolve these tensions through the concept of ectoplasm. He asks why his drawings, mostly single enclosed contours, are so disturbing even though, like Disney cartoons, they are so clearly not imitative of real forms in the world. He answers that his drawings are 'protoplasmic', they 'capture the process between the primal protoplasm and formed man' (1986: 69). Their imitativeness is not of fixed appearances, but of a more fundamental movement and change. Eisenstein uses the word ectoplasm at the end of his notes of 1946 in its biological sense in order to describe the way that, in certain kinds of drawing, the original plasmatic form is shown in the process of reforming: 'And again, an *Ebenbild* [similarity] to pseudopods, forced out by an impulse from within and pushed back into a ball-sphere by the pressure of the ectoplasm (an external pressure, as opposed to the endoplasm)' (p. 89). In his earlier notes, however, his summation of the effects of his drawing implicitly acknowledges the ectoplasmic as the place where different forms of movement attain for a moment some kind of politically liberatory dynamic in a sense that is much closer to the occult phenomenon: 'In my drawings, the truly appealing theme is *the coming into being* of the human form from plasma' (p. 69; emphasis in original). The three kinds of plasmatics identified by Eisenstein – the penetration of objects by other objects, the flowing of objects, and the levitation of objects (p. 70) – conform nicely to the characteristics of occult ectoplasm, which always emerges from and disappears into the body of the medium, which changes shape as a fluid, and which is able to propel itself into space. In the later notes (from 1946), the underlying animation of closed, single contour drawings, which Eisenstein had a habit of drawing on the blackboard while he was lecturing (p. 83), he attributes to the fact that they are in the process of being shaped by a movement outwards from and a movement inwards towards the original plasmatic blob. The dual action of these movements form 'pseudopods' which enact an animated coming into being (p. 84): 'It's as if the ellipse pushes in and out, settling on the object according to its contour' (p. 89) (see Figure 5.1). This is, he argues, 'like a large, deliberate rebuff' to the tendency 'of a drop towards a circle' (p. 84).

In Eisenstein, then, taking things back into their most fundamental state of reality – an animated protoplasm – is what both drawing and film are about. His argument in his essay 'Film Form: New Problems', from 1935, that the prelogical is linked to art via form rather than content is stated explicitly in his notes on drawing from 1944 (Eisenstein 1977e). In answering his question as to how composition can be both generalisation (and therefore abstraction) and the sensuous and prelogical, Eisenstein reiterates his argument that 'the prelogical and the sensuous component must comprise composition – and this *par excellence*, for it is the limit of maximal emphasis on *form* (even the *conception* of form)' (Eisenstein 1986: 82; emphasis in original). Here we can see a challenge to the distinction in conventional aesthetics between form

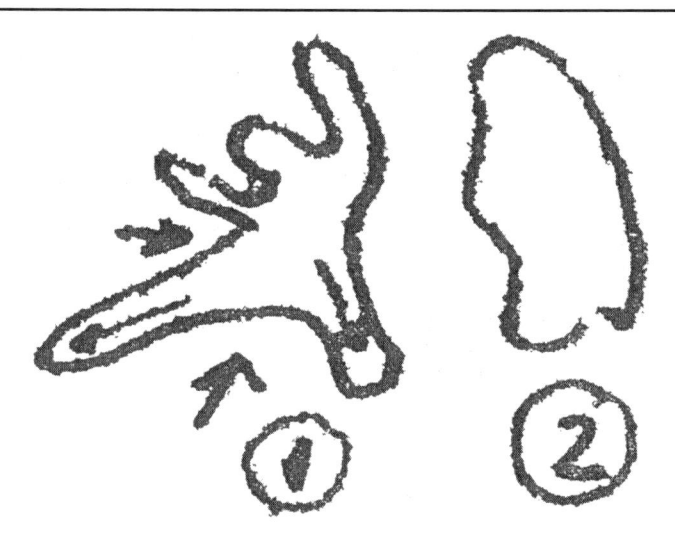

Figure 5.1 From Sergei Eisenstein, 'Notes on Drawing' (Eisenstein 1986: 84)

and matter, where art takes matter and transfigures it into form. Instead, for Eisenstein, what art should strive for is to return to matter and in this way to engage the viewer via a primary, sensory interaction with the world. However, the model of ectoplasm is significant here for the way that it makes this relation more complex than a straightforward banishing of mediation. As a Marxist artist, Eisenstein is very aware of the question of whether nature, matter can be experienced, 'returned' to beyond the remakings of capitalism, or whether it is always already implicated within it. In other words, at the centre of his theory is the question of how matter can be recovered from capitalism without falling into the naïve belief that it is beyond or outside it. His early distinction between the shot and montage in 'Through Theater to Cinema' – the first as nature and the latter as creation – is an attempt to address this. The ectoplasmic model goes beyond this separation. Plasmation, or ectoplasm, is matter in its most basic state, but it is more than inert matter unresistant to forces around it, utterly shaped by them, because it is matter *animated*. What is crucial is that matter and agency or force come together in it. Still drawings of the kind explored by Eisenstein are important because they already have within them movement and animation.

The importance of this can be seen in an animated cartoon particularly commented on by Eisenstein in his writings on Disney, a Mickey Mouse film from 1937, *Lonesome Ghosts* (dir. Burt Gillett). Eisenstein's comments on this film occur in the 'Between plasmation and fire' section of his notes. Rachel Moore does not mention the film, and it is definitely about plasmation rather than fire. Indeed, Eisenstein cites the film as a moment where the movement inherent in plasmation which he has been considering as formal becomes part of the content. In the cartoon, Mickey, Goofy and Donald Duck are working as ghost exterminators, and business is slack. Some mischievous ghosts, living in a generic haunted house, see their advertisement in a newspaper and decide to have some fun. They ring the trio and book them to come and rid the house of ghosts. The three turn up at the house, and the ghosts bemuse and befuddle them through their ability to appear and disappear, and to reshape the material world in unexpected ways. Doors and walls become elastic, furniture moves, and a mirror no longer shows the correct reflection. At the climax of the film, the three exterminators are propelled into the corner of a cellar, where flour and molasses have been stored. The force of their fall upsets the barrels and splits the stacks, and when they stand up again they are coated in a white sticky mess that unites their three bodies. The 'real' ghosts spot the new creature, all wild movement and protruding pseudopods, and flee. Eisenstein locates the significance of the cartoon in the way that the forces of logic – the ghost exterminators – only achieve their aim of banishing the 'real' ghosts from the house after they have themselves moved over into the 'fantastical, alogical and sensuous order' (1986: 22), that is, after they have become ghosts themselves. This is of course correct, but significant too is what distinguishes the two sets of ghosts. The 'real' ghosts are translucent, only just present. In the film they are the principle of movement. They move between visibility and invisibility, and they move the objects and furniture in the house so that it looks, to the trio of ghost hunters and sometimes to the viewer, as though the objects were propelling themselves. When Mickey, Goofy and Donald are covered in dough at the end, they look much more substantial than the see-through ghosts, much more like a conventional ghost, much more like the enclosed single contour drawings so important to Eisenstein, and much more like ectoplasm. When the three are covered in dough at the end, matter and form come together, and this constitutes the real triumph. Mickey and his friends are ghosts in the same way that film moves through a projector; their creation remains fused with the possibilities of matter. The 'real' ghosts, on the other hand, are the flickering images of movement on screen.

Ectoplasm's relation to film entwines image and process. This is the reason for its almost articulated importance in Eisenstein's work. Beckman argues that ectoplasm is linked to film via the image on screen, but I have argued that it is linked to the process of the production of those images because of its insistence on itself as matter animated. Ezra Pound's struggle with stillness and movement as it expresses itself in his attitude to film focuses on the movement on screen, not on the material creation of that movement. The link often made between fascism and occult practice and thinking has therefore conceptualised the problem in reverse – it has argued that fascism as a political ideology is made possible in part through too much magical thinking. However, my reading has suggested that the problem with Pound is not that he is too magical, but not magical enough. Pound refuses to see the possibilities of the ectoplasmic as Eisenstein does. In other words Pound splits matter from movement, whereas for Eisenstein in the end animation must be inherent in matter.

That ectoplasm only hovers around the struggles of both Pound and Eisenstein with questions of movement, animation, art and politics is no surprise. The error of magic is everywhere present in the work of experimental artists – in Joyce's parodies, in Mann's disgust, in Pound's amusement, in Vertov's disavowal. However, the error of magic is everywhere present too in their work in their attempts to 'make it new'; it is used to remake representational practices, to make the word and the visual arts forces in the world, so that through magical mimesis the copy is no longer inert but has the power to transform the original.

BIBLIOGRAPHY

Adorno, Theodor W. (1978), *Minima Moralia: Reflections from Damaged Life* (1951), London: Verso.

Adorno, Theodor W. (1981), *Prisms*, translated by Samuel and Shierry Weber, Cambridge, MA: MIT Press.

Adorno, Theodor W. and Max Horkheimer (1997), *Dialectic of Enlightenment* (1944), translated by John Cumming, London: Verso.

Adorno, Theodor, Walter Benjamin, Ernst Bloch, Bertolt Brecht and Georg Lukács (1980), *Aesthetics and Politics: The Key Texts of the Classic Debate Within German Marxism*, with an afterword by Fredric Jameson, London: Verso.

Albera, François (1993), 'Eisenstein's Theory of the Photogram', in Ian Christie and Richard Taylor (eds), *Eisenstein Rediscovered*, New York and London: Routledge.

Anderson, Margaret (1991), *The Unknowable Gurdjieff* (1962), London: Arkana.

Armstrong, Tim (1998), *Modernism, Technology and the Body*, Cambridge: Cambridge University Press.

Barkan, Elazar and Ronald Bush (eds) (1995), *Prehistories of the Future: The Primitivist Project and the Culture of Modernism*, Stanford: Stanford University Press.

Barrett, W. F., Edmund Gurney and F. W. H. Myers (1882–3), 'First Report on Thought-Transference', *Proceedings of the Society for Psychical Research*, I, pp. 13–34.

Bazin, André (1967), 'The Evolution of the Language of Cinema', in *What is Cinema?*, edited and translated by Hugh Gray, vol. 1, Berkeley: University of California Press.

Beach, Sylvia (1960), *Shakespeare and Company*, London: Faber and Faber.

Beasley, Rebecca (2007), *Ezra Pound and the Visual Culture of Modernism*, Cambridge: Cambridge University Press.

Beckett, Samuel (1983), 'Dante ... Bruno. Vico ... Joyce' (1929), *Disjecta: Miscellaneous Writings and a Dramatic Fragment*, London: John Calder.

Beckman, Karen (2003), *Vanishing Women: Magic, Film and Feminism*, Durham, NC: Duke University Press.
Benjamin, Walter (1979), 'On Language as Such and on the Language of Man' (1916), in *One-Way Street and Other Writings*, translated by Edmund Jephcott and Kingsley Shorter, London: New Left Books.
Benjamin, Walter (1992), 'The Work of Art in the Age of Mechanical Reproduction' (1936), in *Illuminations*, edited and with an introduction by Hannah Arendt, translated by Harry Zohn, London: Fontana.
Benjamin, Walter (2005a), 'On Astrology' (1932), in *Selected Writings, volume 2, part 2, 1931–1934*, edited by Michael W. Jennings, Howard Eiland and Gary Smith, translated by Rodney Livingstone and others, Cambridge, MA, and London: Belknap Press of Harvard University Press.
Benjamin, Walter (2005b), 'Doctrine of the Similar' (1933), in *Selected Writings, volume 2, part 2, 1931–1934*, edited by Michael W. Jennings, Howard Eiland and Gary Smith, translated by Rodney Livingstone and others, Cambridge, MA, and London: Belknap Press of Harvard University Press.
Bennett, Arnold (1923), 'Is the Novel Decaying?', *Cassell's Weekly*, 28 March, p. 47.
Bennett, Arnold (1971), *The Journals*, selected and edited by Frank Swinnerton, London: Penguin.
Bennett, Arnold (2003), *Riceyman Steps and Elsie and the Child*, Cornwall: House of Stratus.
Bergson, Henri (1977), *The Two Sources of Morality and Religion* (1932/5), translated by R. Ashley Audro and Cloudesley Brereton with the assistance of W. Horsfall Carter, Notre Dame, IN: University of Notre Dame Press.
Bergson, Henri (2007), '"Phantasms of the Living" and "Psychical Research": Presidential Address to the Society for Psychical Research, London, May 28, 1913', in *Mind-Energy*, translated by H. Wildon Carr, edited by Keith Ansell Pearson and Michael Kolkman, introduction by Keith Ansell Pearson, Basingstoke: Palgrave.
Berry, R. M. (2006), 'Language', in David Bradshaw and Kevin J. H. Dettmar (eds), *A Companion to Modernist Literature and Culture*, Oxford: Blackwell.
Besant, Annie and C. W. Leadbeater (1905), *Thought-Forms*, London and Benares: Theosophical Publishing Society, Chicago: Theosophical Book Concern, New York: John Lane.
Besterman, Theodore (1930), *Some Modern Mediums*, London: Methuen.
Bewes, Timothy (2002), *Reification, or the Anxiety of Late Capitalism*, London: Verso.

Blavatsky, H. P. (1877), *Isis Unveiled: A Master-Key to the Mysteries of Ancient and Modern Science and Theology*, 2nd edn, New York: Bouton.
Blavatsky, H. P. (1888), *The Secret Doctrine: The Synthesis of Science, Religion and Philosophy*, London: Theosophical Publishing Company.
Blavatsky, H. P. (1893), *The Key to Theosophy*, 3rd edn, London, New York, Madras: Theosophical Publishing Society.
Bowers, Brian (2001), *Sir Charles Wheatstone FPS 1802–1875*, London: Institution of Electrical Engineers/Science Museum.
Bracken, Christopher (2007), *Magical Criticism: The Recourse of Savage Philosophy*, Chicago and London: University of Chicago Press.
Bucknell, Brad (2001), *Literary Modernism and Musical Aesthetics: Pater, Pound, Joyce and Stein*, Cambridge: Cambridge University Press.
Cassirer, Ernst (1955), *The Philosophy of Symbolic Forms* (1925), volume 2, *Mythical Thought*, translated by Ralph Mannheim, New Haven, CT: Yale University Press.
Cerullo, John J. (1982), *The Secularization of the Soul: Psychical Research in Modern Britain*, Philadelphia: Institute for the Study of Human Issues.
Chéroux, Clément, Andreas Fischer, Pierre Apraxine, Denis Canguilhem and Sophie Schmit (2004), *The Perfect Medium: Photography and the Occult*, New Haven, CT, and London: Yale University Press.
Christie, Ian and Richard Taylor (eds) (1993), *Eisenstein Rediscovered*, New York and London: Routledge.
Clark, Brian R. (1999), *Wittgenstein, Frazer and Religion*, Basingstoke: Macmillan.
Clarke, Bruce (2001), *Energy Forms: Allegory and Science in the Era of Classical Thermodynamics*, Ann Arbor: University of Michigan Press.
Clarke, Bruce and Linda Dalrymple Henderson (eds) (2002), *From Energy to Information: Representation in Science and Technology, Art and Literature*, Stanford: Stanford University Press.
Connor, Steven (1999), 'The Machine in the Ghost: Spiritualism, Technology, and the "Direct Voice"', in Peter Buse and Andrew Stott (eds), *Ghosts: Deconstruction, Psychoanalysis, History*, Basingstoke: Macmillan.
Connor, Steven (2000), *Dumbstruck: A Cultural History of Ventriloquism*, Oxford: Oxford University Press.
Crawford, W. J. (1921), *The Psychic Structures of the Goligher Circle*, London: John M. Watkins.
Cunningham, David (2005), 'Asceticism Against Colour, or Modernism, Abstraction and the Lateness of Becket', *New Formations*, 55, Spring, pp. 104–19.
Cunningham, David (2009), '"Very Abstract and Terribly Concrete":

Capitalism and *The Theory of the Novel*', *Novel: A Forum on Fiction*, 42/2, pp. 311–17.
Cunningham, David (forthcoming) 'The Visible and the Invisible: Abstraction, Money and the Visual Culture of the Metropolis', *Journal of Visual Culture*.
Daly, Nicholas (1999), *Modernism, Romance and the Fin de Siècle: Popular Fiction and British Culture, 1880–1914*, Cambridge: Cambridge University Press.
Dann, Kevin T. (1998), *Bright Colours Falsely Seen: Synaesthesia and the Search for Transcendental Knowledge*, New Haven, CT, and London: Yale University Press.
Docherty, Thomas (2003), '"sound sense"; or "tralala"/"moocow": Joyce and the anathema of writing', in Laurent Milesi (ed.), *James Joyce and the Difference of Language*, Cambridge: Cambridge University Press.
During, Simon (2002), *Modern Enchantments; The Cultural Power of Secular Magic*, Cambridge, MA, and London: Harvard University Press.
Eaglefield Hull, A. (1920), *A Great Russian Tone-Poet: Scriabin*, 2nd edn, London: Kegan Paul, Trench, Trubner.
Eisenstein, Sergei (1977a), 'The Cinematograhic Principle and the Ideogram' (1929), in *Film Form: Essays in Film Theory*, edited and translated by Jay Leyda, New York and London: Harcourt.
Eisenstein, Sergei (1977b), 'The Filmic Fourth Dimension' (1929), in *Film Form: Essays in Film Theory*, edited and translated by Jay Leyda, New York and London: Harcourt.
Eisenstein, Sergei (1977c), 'A Dialectic Approach to Film Form' (1929), in *Film Form: Essays in Film Theory*, edited and translated by Jay Leyda, New York and London: Harcourt.
Eisenstein, Sergei (1977d), 'Through Theater to Cinema' (1934), in *Film Form: Essays in Film Theory*, edited and translated by Jay Leyda, New York and London: Harcourt.
Eisenstein, Sergei (1977e), 'Film Form: New Problems' (1935), in *Film Form: Essays in Film Theory*, edited and translated by Jay Leyda, New York and London: Harcourt.
Eisenstein, Sergei (1977f), 'Achievement' (1939), in *Film Form: Essays in Film Theory*, edited and translated by Jay Leyda, New York and London: Harcourt.
Eisenstein, Sergei (1977g), 'Dickens, Griffith, and the Film Today' (1944), in *Film Form: Essays in Film Theory*, edited and translated by Jay Leyda, New York and London: Harcourt.
Eisenstein, Sergei M. (1983), *Immoral Memories: An Autobiography*, translated by Herbert Marshall, London: Peter Owen.

Eisenstein, Sergei M. (1986), *Eisenstein on Disney*, edited by Jay Leyda, translated by Alan Upchurch, introduced by Naum Kleiman, Calcutta: Seagull Books.
Eisenstein, Sergei (1993), 'Imitation as Mastery', translated by Naum Kleiman, in Ian Christie and Richard Taylor (eds), *Eisenstein Rediscovered*, New York and London: Routledge.
Eisenstein, Sergei (2010), 'The Problem of the Materialist Approach to Form' (1925), in *Selected Works, volume 1, Writings, 1922–1934*, edited and translated by Richard Taylor, London and New York: IB Tauris.
Eliot, T. S. (1975), 'The Metaphysical Poets' (1921), in *Selected Prose of T. S. Eliot*, edited and with an introduction by Frank Kermode, London: Faber.
Eliot, T. S. (1978), 'American Literature and Language', in *To Criticize the Critic and Other Writings*, London: Faber.
Eliot, T. S. (1985), *Collected Poems, 1909–1962*, London: Faber.
Elsaesser, Thomas (1996), 'Dada/Cinema?', in Rudolf E. Kuenzli (ed.), *Dada and Surrealist Film*, Cambridge, MA: MIT Press.
Emden, Christian J. (2005), *Nietzsche on Language, Consciousness and the Body*, Urbana and Chicago: University of Illinois Press.
Fenollosa, Ernest and Ezra Pound (2008), *The Chinese Written Character as a Medium for Poetry: A Critical Edition*, edited by Haun Saussy, Jonathan Stalling and Lucas Klein, New York: Fordham University Press.
Ferrall, Charles (2001), *Modernist Writing and Reactionary Politics*, Cambridge: Cambridge University Press.
Fournier d'Albe, E. E. (1920), 'Translator's Preface', in Baron von Schrenck-Notzing, *Phenomena of Materialisation: A Contribution to the Investigation of Mediumistic Teleplastics*, translated by E. E. Fournier d'Albe, London: Kegan Paul, Trench, Trubner.
Fournier d'Albe, E. E. (1922), *The Goligher Circle, May to August 1921*, with appendix containing extracts from the correspondence of the late W. J. Crawford, London: John M. Watkins.
Fournier d'Albe, E. E. (1923), *The Life of Sir William Crookes*, London: T. F. Unwin.
Fournier d'Albe, E. E. (1925), *Hephaestus, or The Soul of the Machine*, London: Kegan Paul, Trench, Trubner.
Frazer, James (1996), *The Golden Bough: A Study in Magic and Religion* (1922), abridged edition, London: Penguin.
Freeman, Judi (1996), 'Léger's *Ballet mécanique*', in Rudolf Kuenzli (ed.), *Dada and Surrealist Film*, Cambridge, MA: MIT Press.
Freud, Sigmund (1912), 'A Note on the Unconscious in Psycho-Analysis', *Proceedings of the Society for Psychical Research*, 26/66, pp. 312–18.
Freud, Sigmund (1952a), 'Psychical (or Mental) Treatment' (1905), *Standard Edition*, VII, London: Hogarth Press.

Freud, Sigmund (1952b), 'The Unconscious' (1915), *Standard Edition*, XIV, London: Hogarth Press.
Freud, Sigmund (1955), 'Psychoanalysis and Telepathy' (1921), *Standard Edition*, XVIII, London: Hogarth Press.
Freud, Sigmund (1973), 'Dreams and Occultism' (1933), in *New Introductory Lectures on Psychoanalysis*, Pelican Freud Library, vol. 2, London: Penguin.
Freud, Sigmund (1995), 'Dreams and Telepathy' (1922), in *Psychological Writings and Letters*, edited by Sander L. Gilman, New York: Continuum.
Freud, Sigmund and Josef Breuer (1974), *Studies in Hysteria* (1895), Pelican Freud Library, vol. 3, London: Penguin.
Gilbert, Stuart (1952), *James Joyce's* Ulysses*: A Study* (1930), New York: Vintage.
Goodrick-Clarke, Nicholas (2005), *The Occult Roots of Nazism: Secret Aryan Cults and their Influence on Nazi Ideology*, 2nd edn, London: Tauris Parke.
Gray, Frank (1996), 'From Mesmerism to Moving Pictures in Natural Colours – The Life of G. Albert Smith', in Frank Gray (ed.), *Hove Pioneers and the Arrival of Cinema*, Brighton: University of Brighton.
Gray, Frank (2000), 'George Albert Smith's Visions and Transformations: The Films of 1898', in Simon Popple and Vanessa Toulmin (eds), *Visual Delights: Essays on the Popular and Projected Image in the Nineteenth Century*, Trowbridge: Flick Books.
Gray, Frank (2004), '*The Kiss in the Tunnel* (1899), G. A. Smith and the Emergence of the Edited Film in England', in Lee Grieveson and Peter Krämer (eds), *The Silent Cinema Reader*, London and New York: Routledge.
Gray, Frank (2009), Lecture on G. A. Smith, Magic Lantern Society, University of Westminster, 10 December.
Grayling, A. C. (1988), *Wittgenstein*, Oxford: Oxford University Press.
Gunning, Tom (1990), 'The Cinema of Attractions: Early Film, its Spectator and the Avant-Garde' (1986), in Thomas Elsaesser (ed.), *Early Cinema: Space, Frame, Narrative*, London: British Film Institute.
Gunning, Tom (1995), 'Phantom Images and Modern Manifestations: Spirit Photographs, Magic Theater, Trick Films, and Photography's Uncanny', in Patrice Petro (ed.), *Fugitive Images: From Photography to Video*, Bloomington and Indianapolis: Indiana University Press.
Gurney, Edmund, F. W. H. Myers, Frank Podmore and W. F. Barrett (1882–3), 'Third Report on Thought-Transference', *Proceedings of the Society for Psychical Research*, I, pp. 161–215.
Gurney, Edmund, F. W. H. Myers, Frank Podmore, Henry Sidgwick, J. H. Stack, Eleanor Sidgwick, Richard Hodgson (1885), 'Report of

Committee Appointed to Investigate Phenomena in connection with the Theosophical Society', *Proceedings of the Society for Psychical Research*, III, pp. 201–400.
Hacker, P. M. S. (1988), 'Wittgenstein's *Tractatus Logico-Philosophicus*', in Roy Harris (ed.), *Linguistic Thought in England 1914–1945*, London: Duckworth.
Hall, Trevor (1980), *The Strange Case of Edmund Gurney*, 2nd edn, London: Duckworth.
Henderson, Linda Dalrymple (1983), *The Fourth Dimension and Non-Euclidean Geometry in Modern Art*, Princeton: Princeton University Press.
Herring, Robert (1998), 'A New Cinema, Magic and the Avant Garde' (1929), reproduced in James Donald, Anne Friedberg and Laura Marcus (eds), *Close Up 1927–1933: Cinema and Modernism*, London: Cassell.
Hulme, T. E. (1924), 'Romanticism and Classicism', in *Speculations*, edited by Herbert Read, London: Kegan Paul, Trench, Trubner.
Hulme, T. E. (1972), 'Autumn', in Peter Jones (ed.), *Imagist Poetry*, London: Penguin.
Hulme, T. E. (1994), *The Collected Writings of T. E. Hulme*, edited by Karen Csengeri, Oxford: Clarendon Press.
Huxley, Aldous (2004), *Crome Yellow* (1921), London: Vintage.
Jolas, Eugene (1927a), 'Introduction', *transition* 1, April, pp. 137–8.
Jolas, Eugene (1927b), 'Suggestions for a New Magic', *transition* 3, June, pp. 178–9.
Jolas, Eugene (1927c), 'Enter the Imagination', *transition* 7, October, pp. 157–60.
Jolas, Eugene (1927d), 'On the Quest', *transition* 9, December, pp. 191–6.
Jolas, Eugene (1928), 'Notes', *transition* 14, Fall, pp. 180–5.
Jolas, Eugene (1929a), 'Super-Occident', *transition* 15, February, pp. 11–16.
Jolas, Eugene et al. (1929b), 'Proclamation', *transition* 16/17, June, p. 13.
Jolas, Eugene (1929c), 'Logos', *transition* 16/17, June, pp. 25–30.
Jolas, Eugene (1929d), 'Reality', *transition* 18, November, pp. 15–20.
Jolas, Eugene (1930), 'Literature and the New Man', *transition* 19–20, Spring–Summer, pp. 13–19.
Jolas, Eugene (1998), *Man From Babel*, edited, annotated and introduced by Andreas Kramer and Rainer Rumold, New Haven, CT, and London: Yale University Press.
Joyce, James (1991), *A Portrait of the Artist as a Young Man* (1916), London: Everyman.
Joyce, James (2000a), *Ulysses* (1922), London: Penguin.
Joyce, James (2000b), *Finnegans Wake* (1939), London: Penguin.
Kahn, Douglas (1992), 'Introduction', in Douglas Kahn and Gregory

Whitehead (eds) *Wireless Imagination: Sound, Radio and the Avant-Garde*, Cambridge, MA, and London: MIT Press.
Kandinsky, Wassily (2006), *Concerning the Spiritual In Art* (1912), translated by Michael T. H. Sadler, London: Tate.
Kiberd, Declan (2009), *Ulysses and Us: The Art of Everyday Living*, London: Faber and Faber.
Kittler, Friedrich A. (1999), *Gramophone, Film, Typewriter* (1986), translated by and with an introduction by Geoffrey Winthrop-Young and Michael Wutz, Stanford: Stanford University Press.
Kleiman, Naum (1986), 'Introduction', in S. M. Eisenstein, *Eisenstein on Disney*, edited by Jay Leyda, translated by Alan Upchurch, Calcutta: Seagull Books.
Koch, Gertrude (1987), 'Béla Balázs: The Physiognomy of Things', *New German Critique*, no. 40, Winter, pp. 167–77.
Landy, Joshua (2009), 'Modern Magic: Jean-Eugène Robert-Houdin and Stéphane Mallarmé', in Joshua Landy and Michael Saler (eds), *The Re-Enchantment of the World*, Stanford: Stanford University Press.
Lang, Andrew (1887), *Myth, Ritual and Religion*, vol. 1, London: Longmans, Green.
Latour, Bruno (1993), *We Have Never Been Modern*, translated by Catherine Porter, Cambridge, MA: Harvard University Press.
Leadbeater, C. W. (1913), *The Hidden Side of Things*, vol. 1, Adyar, Madras and Benares, India: Theosophical Publishing House.
Lehnert, Herbert and Peter C. Pfeiffer (eds) (1991), *Thomas Mann's Doctor Faustus: A Novel at the Margins of Modernism*, Columbia, NC: Camden House.
Leslie, Esther (2002), *Hollywood Flatlands: Animation, Critical Theory and the Avant-Garde*, London: Verso.
Lewis, Pericles (2010), *Religious Experience and the Modernist Novel*, Cambridge: Cambridge University Press.
Lewty, Jane (2002), 'Broadcasting Modernity: Eloquent Listening in the Early Twentieth Century', unpublished PhD thesis, University of Glasgow.
Liebregts, P. Th. M. G. (2004), *Ezra Pound and Neoplatonism*, Madison, NJ: Fairleigh Dickinson University Press.
Longenbach, James (1991), *Stone Cottage: Pound, Yeats and Modernism*, New York: Oxford University Press.
Luckhurst, Roger (2002), *The Invention of Telepathy*, Oxford: Oxford University Press.
McCorristine, Shane (2011), 'William Fletcher Barrett, Spiritualism and Psychical Research in Edwardian Dublin', *Estudios Irlandeses*, 6, pp. 39–53.
McLuhan, Marshall (1987), *Letters of Marshall McLuhan*, selected and edited

by Matie Molinaro, Corinne McLuhan, William Toye, Oxford, New York, Toronto: Oxford University Press.
McMahon, April (2003), 'Language: "History is a nightmare from which I am trying to awake"', in David Bradshaw (ed.), *A Concise Companion to Modernism*, Oxford: Blackwell.
Mahon, Peter (2007), *Imagining Joyce and Derrida: Between* Finnegans Wake *and* Glas, Toronto, Buffalo, London: University of Toronto Press.
Malinowski, Bronislaw (1978a), 'Balaam, The Spirits of the Dead in the Trobriand Islands' (1916), in *Magic, Science and Religion and Other Essays*, with an introduction by Robert Redfield, London: Souvenir Press.
Malinowski, Bronislaw (1978b), 'Magic, Science and Religion' (1925), in *Magic, Science and Religion and Other Essays*, with an introduction by Robert Redfield, London: Souvenir Press.
Mann, Thomas (1929), 'An Experience in the Occult' (1923), in *Three Essays*, New York: Knopf.
Mann, Thomas (1983), *The Magic Mountain* (1924), translated by H. T. Lowe-Porter, London: Penguin.
Mann, Thomas (1985), *Doctor Faustus: The Life of the German Composer Adrian Leverkühn As Told by a Friend* (1947), translated by H. T. Lowe-Porter, London: Penguin.
Marcus, Laura (1998), 'Introduction' to part 3, in James Donald, Anne Friedberg and Laura Marcus (eds), *Close Up: Cinema and Modernism, 1927–1933*, London: Cassell.
Marx, Karl (1990), *Capital*, 3 vols, introduced by Ernest Mandel, translated by Ben Fowkes (vol. 1), David Fernbach (vols 2 and 3), London: Penguin Books in association with New Left Review.
Materer, Timothy (1979), *Vortex: Pound, Eliot and Lewis*, Ithaca, NY: Cornell University Press.
Materer, Timothy (1995), *Modernist Alchemy: Poetry and the Occult*, Ithaca, NY, and London: Cornell University Press.
Mendelson, Edward (1991), 'Introduction', in Arnold Bennett, *Riceyman Steps*, London: Penguin.
Michelson, Annette (1975), 'From Magician to Epistemologist: Vertov's *The Man With a Movie Camera*', in P. Adams Sitney (ed.), *The Essential Cinema: Essays on the Films in the Collection of Anthology Film Archives*, vol. 1, New York: Anthology Film Archives and New York University Press.
Michelson, Annette (1984), 'Introduction', in Dziga Vertov, *Kino-Eye: The Writings of Dziga Vertov*, edited and with introduction by Annette Michelson, translated by Kevin O'Brien, London and Sydney: Pluto Press.

Moore, F. C. T. (1999), 'Magic', in John Mullarkey (ed.), *The New Bergson*, Manchester: Manchester University Press.

Moore, Rachel (2000), *Savage Theory: Cinema as Modern Magic*, Durham, NC, and London: Duke University Press.

Morrison, Paul (1996), *The Poetics of Fascism: Ezra Pound, T. S. Eliot, Paul de Man*, Oxford: Oxford University Press.

Mulvey, Laura (1975), 'Visual Pleasure and Narrative Cinema', *Screen*, 16.3, Autumn, pp. 6–18.

Myers, F. W. H. (1883), 'Greek Oracles', *Essays – Classical*, London: Macmillan.

Myers, F. W. H. (1903), *Human Personality and its Survival of Bodily Death*, vol. 1, London: Longmans, Green.

Nagai, Kaori (2011), '"Tis optophone which ontophanes": Race, the Modern and Irish Revivalism', in Len Platt (ed.), *Modernism and Race*, Cambridge: Cambridge University Press.

New York Times (1912), 'Makes Light Audible', 27 June, p. 5.

Nietzsche, Friedrich (1974), *The Gay Science*, translated by Walter Kaufman, New York: Vintage.

Nietzsche, Friedrich (1999), 'On Truth and Lying in a Non-Moral Sense', in *The Birth of Tragedy and Other Writings*, edited by Raymond Geuss and Ronald Speirs, Cambridge: Cambridge University Press.

North, Michael (1999), *Reading 1922: A Return to the Scene of the Modern*, Oxford: Oxford University Press.

North, Michael (2005), *Camera Works: Photography and the Twentieth-Century Word*, Oxford: Oxford University Press.

Ogden, C. K. (1929), 'Preface', in James Joyce, *Tales Told of Shem and Shaun: Three Fragments from Work In Progress*, Paris: Black Sun Press.

Ogden, C. K. (1994), *From Bentham to Basic English*, edited and introduced by W. Terrence Gordon, London: Routledge/Thoemmes Press.

Ogden, C. K. and I. A. Richards (1994), *The Meaning of Meaning: A Study of the Influence of Language Upon Thought and of the Science of Symbolism* (1923), edited and introduced by W. Terrence Gordon, London: Routledge/Thoemmes Press.

Ogden, C. K., I. A. Richards and James Woods (1922), *The Foundations of Aesthetics*, London: George Allen and Unwin.

Oppenheim, Janet (1985), *The Other World: Spiritualism and Psychical Research 1850–1914*, Cambridge: Cambridge University Press.

Owen, Alex (1989), *The Darkened Rook: Women, Power and Spiritualism in Late Victorian England*, London: Virago.

Owen, Alex (2004), *The Place of Enchantment: British Occultism and the Culture of the Modern*, Chicago and London: University of Chicago Press.

Peirce, C. S. (1885–9), 'Criticism on "Phantasms of the Living": An Examination of an Argument of Messrs. Gurney, Myers, and Podmore' and 'Mr Peirce's Rejoinder', *Proceedings of the American Society for Psychical Research*, 1/1–4, pp. 150–215.

Peirce, C. S. (1998a), 'Telepathy' (1903), in *Collected Papers of Charles Sanders Peirce, volume 7, Science and Philosophy*, edited by Arthur W. Bucks, London: Thoemmes Press.

Peirce, C. S. (1998b), 'What is a Sign?', in *Selected Philosophical Writings, volume 2 (1893–1913)*, Bloomington: Indiana University Press.

Pennethorne Hughes, C. J. (1998) 'Dreams and Films' (1930), reprinted in James Donald, Anne Friedberg and Laura Marcus (eds), *Close Up: Cinema and Modernism, 1927–1933*, London: Cassell.

Platt, Len (2007), *Joyce, Race, and Finnegans Wake*, Cambridge: Cambridge University Press.

Postgate, J. P. (1994), 'Introduction', in C. K. Ogden and I. A. Richards, *The Meaning of Meaning: A Study of the Influence of Language Upon Thought and of the Science of Symbolism* (1923), edited and introduced by W. Terrence Gordon, London: Routledge/Thoemmes Press.

Pound, Ezra (1916), 'Vorticism' (1914) in *Gaudier-Brzeska: A Memoir*, London: John Lane.

Pound, Ezra (1970), *Guide to Kulchur* (1938), New York: New Directions.

Pound, Ezra (1972), 'In a Station of the Metro', in Peter Jones (ed.), *Imagist Poetry*, London: Penguin.

Pound, Ezra (1973a), 'I Gather the Limbs of Osiris' (1911–12), in *Selected Prose 1909–1965*, edited and with an introduction by William Cookson, London: Faber.

Pound, Ezra (1973b), 'What is Money For?' (1939), in *Selected Prose 1909–1965*, edited and with an introduction by William Cookson, London: Faber.

Pound, Ezra (1984), *Ezra Pound/John Theobold, Letters*, edited by Donald Pearce and Herbert Schneidau, Redding Ridge, CT: Black Swan Books.

Pound, Ezra (1985a), 'The Serious Artist' (1913), in *Literary Essays of Ezra Pound*, edited and with an introduction by T. S. Eliot, London: Faber.

Pound, Ezra (1985b), 'Brancusi' (1921), in *Literary Essays of Ezra Pound*, edited and with an introduction by T. S. Eliot, London: Faber.

Pound, Ezra (1985c), 'Cavalcanti' (1934), in *Literary Essays of Ezra Pound*, edited and with an introduction by T. S. Eliot, London: Faber.

Pound, Ezra (1987), *The Cantos*, London: Faber.

Pound, Ezra (2001), 'The Jewel Stairs' Grievance' (1926), in *Personae: Collected Shorter Poems*, London: Faber.

Proust, Marcel (1989), *Remembrance of Things Past*, 3 vols, translated by C. K. Scott Moncrieff and Terence Kilmartin, London: Penguin.

Rabaté, Jean-Michel (2007), 'The Fourfold Root of Yawn's Unreason', in Luca Crispi and Sam Slote (eds), *How Joyce Wrote Finnegans Wake: A Chapter-by-Chapter Genetic Guide*, Madison: University of Wisconsin Press.

Ricoeur, Paul (2003), *The Rule of Metaphor*, London: Routledge.

Ringbom, Sixten (1986), 'Transcending the Visible: The Generation of the Abstract Pioneers', in *The Spiritual in Art: Abstract Painting, 1890–1985*, New York and Los Angeles: Abbeville Press and Los Angeles County Museum of Art.

Ross, Stephen (2009), 'Uncanny Modernism, or Analysis Interminable', in Pamela L. Caughie (ed.), *Disciplining Modernism*, Basingstoke: Palgrave.

Russell, Bertrand (1919), *Introduction to Mathematical Philosophy*, London: George Allen and Unwin.

Russell, Bertrand (1974), 'Introduction' (1922), in Lugwig Wittgenstein, *Tractatus Logico-Philosophicus*, London: Routledge.

Russell, Bertrand (1979), *A History of Western Philosophy* (1946), London: Unwin.

Salisbury, Laura (2011), 'Linguistic Trepanation: Brain Damage, Penetrative Seeing, and the Revolution of the Word', in Deirdre Coleman and Hilary Fraser (eds), *Minds, Bodies, Machines, 1770–1930*, Basingstoke: Palgrave.

von Rohr Scaff, Susan (2002), '*Doctor Faustus*', in Ritchie Robertson (ed.), *The Cambridge Companion to Thomas Mann*, Cambridge: Cambridge University Press.

Schrenck-Notzing, Baron von (1920), *Phenomena of Materialisation: A Contribution to the Investigation of Mediumistic Teleplastics*, translated by E. E. Fournier d'Albe, London: Kegan Paul, Trench, Trubner.

Sheppard, Richard (2000), *Dada-Modernism-Postmodernism*, Evanston, IL: Northwestern University Press.

Shiach, Morag (2007), '"To Purify the Dialect of the Tribe": Modernism and Language Reform', *Modernism/Modernity*, 14/1, January, pp. 21–34.

Sinclair, May (1915), 'Two Notes: I. On H. D. II. On Imagism', *The Egoist*, II/6, 1 June, pp. 88–9.

Steiner, Rudolf (1994), *Theosophy: An Introduction to the Spiritual Processes in Human Life and in the Cosmos* (1910), translated by Catherine E. Creeger, New York: Anthroposophic Press.

Steiner, Rudolf (1995), *The Genius of Language*, translated by Gertrude Teutsche and Ruth Pusch, New York: Anthroposophic Press.

Sterne, Jonathan (2003), *The Audible Past: Cultural Origins of Sound Reproduction*, Durham, NC, and London: Duke University Press.

Styers, Randall (2004), *Making Magic: Religion, Magic and Science in the Modern World*, Oxford: Oxford University Press.

Surette, Leon (1993), *The Birth of Modernism: Ezra Pound, T. S. Eliot, W. B. Yeats and the Occult*, Montreal and Kingston, London, Buffalo: McGill-Queen's University Press.

Sword, Helen (2002), *Ghostwriting Modernism*, Ithaca, NY: Cornell University Press.

Tadié, Benoit (2003), '"Cyberjugglers going the highroads": Joyce and Contemporary Linguistic Theories', in Laurent Milesi (ed.), *James Joyce and the Difference of Language*, Cambridge: Cambridge University Press.

Taussig, Michael (1993), *Mimesis and Alterity: A Particular History of the Senses*, New York and London: Routledge.

Taylor, Richard (2010), 'Introduction', in *Sergei Eisenstein, Selected Works, volume 1, Writings, 1922–1934*, edited and translated by Richard Taylor, London and New York: IB Tauris.

Terrell, Carroll F. (1993), *A Companion to The Cantos of Ezra Pound*, Berkeley and Los Angeles: University of California Press.

Terrence Gordon, W. (1994a), 'Editorial Note', in C. K. Ogden and I. A. Richards, *The Meaning of Meaning: A Study of the Influence of Language Upon Thought and of the Science of Symbolism*, edited and with an introduction by W. Terrence Gordon, London: Routledge/Thoemmes Press.

Terrence Gordon, W. (1994b), 'Introduction', in C. K. Ogden, *From Bentham to Basic English*, edited and with an introduction by W. Terrence Gordon, London: Routledge/Thoemmes Press.

Thacker, Andrew (1990), 'Language and Reification in Imagist Poetics 1909–1930', unpublished PhD thesis, University of Southampton.

Thacker, Andrew (2006), 'A Language of Concrete Things: Hulme, Imagism and Modernist Theories of Language', in Edward P. Comentale and Andrzej Gasiorek (eds), *T. E. Hulme and the Question of Modernism*, Aldershot: Ashgate.

Thurschwell, Pamela (2001), *Literature, Technology and Magical Thinking, 1880–1920*, Cambridge: Cambridge University Press.

Trotter, David (2001), *Paranoid Modernism: Literary Experiment, Psychosis and the Professionalization of English Society*, Oxford: Oxford University Press.

Trotter, David (2007), *Cinema and Modernism*, Oxford: Blackwell.

Truzzi, Marcello (1974), 'Definition and Dimensions of the Occult: Towards a Sociological Perspective', in Edward A. Tirykian (ed.), *On the Margin of the Visible: Sociology, the Esoteric, and the Occult*, New York: John Wiley.

Tylor, E. B. (1883), 'Magic', in *Encyclopaedia Britannica*, London: Encyclopaedia Britannica.

Tylor, E. B. (1920), *Primitive Culture: Researches into the Development of*

Mythology, Philosophy, Religion, Language, Art, and Custom (1871), 6th edn, vol. 1, London: John Murray.
Vaget, Hans Rudolf (1991), 'Mann, Joyce, Wagner: The Question of Modernism in Doctor Faustus', in Herbert Lehnert and Peter C. Pfeiffer (eds), *Thomas Mann's Doctor Faustus: A Novel at the Margins of Modernism*, Columbia, NC: Camden House.
Vertov, Dziga (1984a), 'The Council of Three' (1923), in *Kino-Eye: The Writings of Dziga Vertov*, edited and with introduction by Annette Michelson, translated by Kevin O'Brien, London and Sydney: Pluto Press.
Vertov, Dziga (1984b), 'On the Film Known as *Kinoglaz*' (1923), in *Kino-Eye: The Writings of Dziga Vertov*, edited and with introduction by Annette Michelson, translated by Kevin O'Brien, London and Sydney: Pluto Press.
Vertov, Dziga (1984c), 'The Birth of Kino-Eye' (1924), in *Kino-Eye: The Writings of Dziga Vertov*, edited and with introduction by Annette Michelson, translated by Kevin O'Brien, London and Sydney: Pluto Press.
Vertov, Dziga (1984d), 'To the Kinoks of the South' (1925), in *Kino-Eye: The Writings of Dziga Vertov*, edited and with introduction by Annette Michelson, translated by Kevin O'Brien, London and Sydney: Pluto Press.
Vertov, Dziga (1984e), 'Kino-Eye' (1926), in *Kino-Eye: The Writings of Dziga Vertov*, edited and with introduction by Annette Michelson, translated by Kevin O'Brien, London and Sydney: Pluto Press.
Vertov, Dziga (1984f), '*Three Songs of Lenin* and Kino-Eye' (1934), in *Kino-Eye: The Writings of Dziga Vertov*, edited and with introduction by Annette Michelson, translated by Kevin O'Brien, London and Sydney: Pluto Press.
Vertov, Dziga (1984g), 'Without Words' (1934), in *Kino-Eye: The Writings of Dziga Vertov*, edited and with introduction by Annette Michelson, translated by Kevin O'Brien, London and Sydney: Pluto Press.
Vertov, Dziga (1998), 'From a Kino-Eye Discussion' (1924), in Vassiliki Kolocotroni, Jane Goldman and Olga Taxidou (eds), *Modernism: An Anthology of Sources and Documents*, Edinburgh: Edinburgh University Press.
Viswanathan, Gauri (1998), *Outside the Fold: Conversion, Modernity and Belief*, Princeton: Princeton University Press.
Viswanathan, Gauri (2000), 'The Ordinary Business of Occultism', *Critical Inquiry*, 27/1, Autumn, pp. 1–20.
Warner, Marina (2006), *Phantasmagoria: Spirit Visions, Metaphors, and Media into the Twenty-First Century*, Oxford: Oxford University Press.

Washington, Peter (1995), *Madame Blavatsky's Baboon: A History of the Mystics, Mediums, and Misfits Who Brought Spiritualism to America*, New York: Schocken.

Williams, Raymond (1980), 'Advertising: The Magic System' (1961), in *Problems in Materialism and Culture: Selected Essays*, London: Verso.

Williams, William Carlos (1927), 'A Note on the Recent Work of James Joyce', *transition* 8, November, pp. 149–54.

Williams, William Carlos (1970), *Spring and All*, in *Imaginations*, edited and with an introduction by Webster Schott, New York: New Directions.

Wilson, Leigh (2012), 'The Cross-Correspondences, the Nature of Evidence and the Matter of Writing', in Tatiana Kontou and Sarah Willburn (eds), *Ashgate Research Companion to Victorian Spiritualism and the Occult*, Aldershot: Ashgate.

Wilson, Leigh (2013), '"Miraculous constellations in real material": Spiritualist Phenomena, Dada Photomontage and Magic', in Sas Mays and Neil Matheson (eds), *The Machine and the Ghost: Technology and Spiritualism in Nineteenth to Twenty-First Century Art and Culture*, Manchester: Manchester University Press.

Winter, Alison (1998), *Mesmerized: Powers of Mind in Victorian Britain*, Chicago: University of Chicago Press.

Wittgenstein, Ludwig (1974), *Tractatus Logico-Philosophicus* (1921/2), translated by D. F. Pears and B. F. McGuiness, with an introduction by Bertrand Russell, London: Routledge.

Wittgenstein, Ludwig (1979), *Remarks on Frazer's Golden Bough*, edited by Rush Rhees, translated by A. C. Miles, revised by Rush Rhees, Reford: Brynill Press.

Woolf, Virginia (1966), 'Mr Bennett and Mrs Brown' (1924), in *Collected Essays*, vol. 1, edited by Leonard Woolf, London: Hogarth Press.

Woolf, Virginia (1977), *To the Lighthouse* (1927), London: Panther.

Woolf, Virginia (1979), *The Diary of Virginia Woolf, volume 1, 1915–19*, edited by Anne Olivier Bell, London: Penguin.

Woolf, Virginia (1988), *The Diary of Virginia Woolf, volume 2, 1920–24*, edited by Anne Olivier Bell, assisted by Andrew McNeillie, London: Penguin.

Yampolsky, Mikhail (1993), 'The Essential Bone Structure: Mimesis in Eisenstein', in Ian Christie and Richard Taylor (eds), *Eisenstein Rediscovered*, New York and London: Routledge.

Žižek, Slavoj (2010), *Living in the End Times*, London: Verso.

FILMS

Ballet mécanique (dir. Fernand Léger and Dudley Murphy, 1924, France)
The Corsican Brothers (dir. G. A. Smith, 1898, UK)
Entr'acte (dir. René Clair and Francis Picabia, 1924, France)
Faust and Mephistopheles (dir. G. A. Smith, 1898, UK)
The Great Train Robbery (dir. Edwin S. Porter, 1903, USA)
Kinoglaz (dir. Dziga Vertov, 1924, USSR)
La Roue (dir. Abel Gance, 1922, France)
Lonesome Ghosts (dir. Burt Gillett, 1937, USA)
Man With a Movie Camera (dir. Dziga Vertov, 1929, USSR)
The Mesmerist, or Body and Soul (dir. G. A. Smith, 1898, UK)
October (dir. S. M. Eisenstein, 1927, USSR)
Old and New/The General Line (dir. S. M. Eisenstein, 1929, USSR)
Photographing a Ghost (dir. G. A. Smith, 1898, UK)
Santa Claus (dir. G. A. Smith, 1898, UK)
Three Songs of Lenin (dir. Dziga Vertov, 1934, USSR)

INDEX

Adorno, Theodor, 23, 37, 141, 142, 143
  Dialectic of Enlightenment, 67
  on Walter Benjamin, 28–32
Albera, François, 162
Anderson, Margaret, 85–6
Artaud, Antonin, 106

Ballet mécanique, 151, 152
Basic English, 52
Beach, Sylvia, 52, 73
Beasley, Rebecca, 151
Beckett, Samuel, 73–4, 75
Beckman, Karen, 143–5, 148, 166
Benjamin, Walter, 23, 29–33, 136
  'Doctrine of the Similar', 32–3
  'On Astrology', 32
  'On Language as Such and On the Language of Man', 33
Bennett, Arnold, 23, 33–7
  'Is the Novel Decaying?', 33
  on James Joyce, 34
  Riceyman Steps, 33–7
Bentham, Jeremy, 54–5
Bergson, Henri, 38
  on experiment, 26–8
Berry, R. M., 56–7
Besant, Annie, 85
Bewes, Timothy, 31–2
Blackman, Douglas, 113–14, 132
Blavatsky, Helena, 5, 20, 66, 80, 81, 84, 91, 100
  on sound, 81–3
Bracken, Christopher, 14
Brancusi, Constantin, 151, 152–3
Bucknell, Brad, 77–8
Butts, Mary, 2

Cassirer, Ernst, 45
Chladni's plates, 84–5, 93, 97, 101
Christie, Ian, 158
Close Up, 105, 107, 149
Connor, Steven, 76
Crawford, William, 146
Crowley, Aleister, 3

Disney, 153, 158–67
Docherty, Thomas, 69
Doolittle, Hilda (H.D.), 2, 13, 106
During, Simon, 38

ectoplasm, 21, 136, 138, 140, 142–50, 154, 164–7
Eisenstein, Sergei M., 17, 20, 21, 135–6
  on *Finnegans Wake*, 75–6
  and magic, 137–8
  and Marxism, 157–8, 165
  October, 137, 162
  Old and New/The General Line, 137, 158, 161
  and the plasmatic, 156, 160–7
  Que Viva Mexico, 137
  on Dziga Vertov, 107, 135
Eliot, T. S., 57, 71, 153–4
Elsaesser, Thomas, 160
experiment, 23–8
  Henri Bergson on, 26–8
  and *transition*, 39–42

fascism, and the occult, 20, 136–7, 167
Fenollosa, Ernest, 60–1, 69
film, 20, 21
  and distance, 120–1

and ectoplasm, 143–5, 148–50
and language, 104–6
Fournier d'Albe, E. E., 97–8, 145; *see also* optophone
Frazer, James, 7, 15, 23–4, 25, 44, 55, 62, 137, 139
   Wittgenstein on, 49–51
Freud, Sigmund, 156–7
   and telepathy, 113, 114–19

ghosts, 44, 52, 54–5, 62
Gunning, Tom, 105, 110, 120
Gurdjieff, G. I., 85–6
Gurney, Edmund, 113, 121

Herring, Robert, 149–50
Horkheimer, Max, *Dialectic of Enlightenment*, 67
Hulme, T. E., 58–60, 62, 76–7, 104, 124
Huxley, Aldous, 47

imagism, 57–62

James, William, 27
Jolas, Eugene, 23, 39–42, 56, 72, 80, 81, 104
Joyce, James, 19–20, 21, 34, 66–74, 167
   Finnegans Wake, 21, 39, 66, 73–4, 75–6, 80, 83–4, 89, 95–102
   Portrait of the Artist as a Young Man, 96
   and theosophy, 66, 76, 97
   Ulysses, 21, 22, 34, 67–73, 89, 95, 98

Kahn, Douglas, 79, 82
Kandinsky, Wassily, 5, 125–6, 127
Kittler, Friedrich, 37–8

Landy, Joshua, 38–9
Lang, Andrew, 140, 141
Latour, Bruno, 40, 45
Leadbeater, C. W., 85
Leslie, Esther, 162
Lévy-Bruhl, Lucien, 137
Lewis, Pericles, 9, 63
Lewty, Jane, 73

Lonesome Ghosts, 165–7
Luckhurst, Roger, 112–13, 123, 124

McAlmon, Robert, 105, 107
McLuhan, Marshall, 136, 139–40
magic
   as error, 8, 24, 28, 31, 44–5, 50–1
   and experiment, 25–6, 27, 38–9
   as language, 44–55
   and mimesis, 15–19
   and science, 7–8, 24
   and sound, 81–8
Malinowski, Bronislaw, 25, 52, 141
Mallarmé, Stéphane, 37–9, 56
Mann, Thomas, 145–9, 167
   Doctor Faustus, 76, 88–95
   and James Joyce, 89
   The Magic Mountain, 65–6, 100, 148–9
Marx, Karl, 111, 128–9, 136, 141, 142
Marxism, 136
   and representation, 20, 28–33
Materer, Timothy, 2, 58
Michelson, Annette, 104, 127
mimesis
   in Arnold Bennett, 35–7
   experiment and, 12
   and magic, 15–19
   and telepathy, 120–7
Moore, F. C. T., 26–7
Moore, Rachel, 104–5, 108, 156–8, 159, 160, 165–6
Mulvey, Laura, 120
Myers, Frederic, 111, 113, 114, 124

Nagai, Kaori, 98
Nietzsche, Friedrich, 45–6
North, Michael, 19, 49, 105, 106, 110

Ogden, C. K., 51–5, 59, 104, 126
   and James Joyce, 83–4
   The Meaning of Meaning, 51–5, 81, 83, 84
optophone, 97, 98, 99, 100

Palladino, Eusapia, 5, 146
Peirce, C. S., on telepathy, 121–3

Platt, Len, 66, 95
post-structuralism, 13–14, 56–7, 69–70
  and James Joyce, 69
Pound, Ezra, 2, 20, 21, 71, 81, 135, 136, 150, 167
  The Cantos, 20, 21, 137, 138, 140, 152, 153, 154, 155–6
  and Ernest Fenollosa, 60–1
  and film, 151–5, 159, 166
  and imagism, 59, 62
  and magic, 137–40
  and sound, 77–8
primitivism, 4
Proust, Marcel, *À La recherche du temps perdu*, 63–5

Rabaté, Jean-Michel, 73
reification, 31–2
Richards, I. A., 51–3, 126
Ricoeur, Paul, 61–2
Ross, Stephen, 10–11, 23
Russell, Bertrand, 46–7, 59, 60

Saussure, Ferdinand de, 45, 53, 56, 69
Scaff, Susan von Rohr, 91, 94
Schrenck-Notzing, Albert von, 26, 98, 143, 144–5, 146
Scriabin, Alexander, 5, 99–100
séance
  as magic, 8–9
  and literary experiment, 62–74
Sheppard, Richard, 48–9
Sinclair, May, 57–8
Smith, George (G.A.), 113–14, 131–4
  Photographing a Ghost, 144
  Santa Claus, 133–4
Society for Psychical Research (SPR), 4, 9, 26, 111, 112, 113, 121, 123, 132
sound
  and artistic experiment, 76–81
  in *Doctor Faustus*, 88–95
  in *Finnegans Wake*, 95–102
  and magic, 76, 81–8
spiritualism
  and magic, 3
  and science, 5–6
  see also séance

Stein, Gertrude, 81
Steiner, Rudolf, 5, 91, 126
  on language and sound, 86–8, 95–6, 97
Sterne, Jonathan, 78, 84
Styers, Randall, 7, 44–5, 78
Surette, Leon, 2, 3, 20, 137
Sword, Helen, 13–14, 16, 18, 56, 69–70, 95, 124

Taussig, Michael, 15–19, 114
Taylor, Richard, 158
telepathy, 9, 21
  and Sigmund Freud, 114–19
  history of, 111–12
  and kino-eye, 109–10
  and mimesis, 114–19, 120–7
  and George Smith, 113–14, 131–4
  and the SPR, 111–12, 113–14
teleplasm *see* ectoplasm
Thacker, Andrew, 60
theosophy
  and *Finnegans Wake*, 66, 76, 97
  history of, 5
  and magic, 3, 6–7
  and science, 5–6
  and sound, 81–8
transition, 23, 39–42, 105, 106
Trotter, David, 124–5
Tylor, E. B., 7, 15, 23, 24, 25, 30, 60, 141

Vaget, Hans Rudolf, 89
Vertov, Dziga, 20, 21, 135, 167
  Kinoglaz, 109, 127–31
  Man With A Movie Camera, 106, 108, 127, 130–1
  and telepathy, 106–11, 129, 131
  Three Songs of Lenin, 109, 131

Warner, Marina, 146
Weaver, Harriet, 73
Wheatstone, Charles, 101–2
Williams, William Carlos, 56–7, 80, 150
Winter, Alison, 112
Wittgenstein, Ludwig, 59, 60
  Philosophical Investigations, 49, 51

Remarks on Frazer's Golden Bough, 49–51, 55
Tractatus Logico–Philosophicus, 47–51
Woolf, Virginia
  'Mr Bennett and Mrs Brown', 33

and the occult, 12, 171
To The Lighthouse, 12
Worringer, Wilhelm, 125, 127

Yeats, W. B., 2, 3, 13, 71, 98
  and theosophy, 5